FOUR SEASONS
in a DAY

Travel, Transitions and Letting Go
of the Place We Call Home

DEBORAH L. JACOBS

PREFACE

L IKE SO MANY OTHER PEOPLE who have left jobs sooner than expected, I was terrified at the prospect of losing a steady paycheck. But finding myself at a career crossroads, I saw an opportunity. My husband, Ken, and I had always wanted to live overseas together. Free from obligations, we could finally follow this dream.

Our plan was to rent our Brooklyn, New York townhouse for three months and downsize to smaller quarters in rural France. We would explore new vistas and eat better but manage with fewer belongings and give up various creature comforts. Our most important goal was to experience French life through the eyes of the locals rather than as the tourists we had previously been. We would shop in open-air markets, cook with seasonal ingredients and communicate with people in their own language.

To prepare, Ken enrolled in an elementary French class at Baruch College, and I worked my way through lessons 1 through 80 of the "Coffee Break French" podcasts.

After searching homesharing websites, we rented a former winemaker's cottage in the Loire Valley that sounded idyllic. A high-speed internet connection there would make it possible to continue my work as a writer.

We spent several months making various repairs and improvements to stage our Brooklyn house for a family from the Midwest who would live there while we were away. Their departure would coincide with our return.

Our French adventure was an education in language and culture, and the more foreign and unpredictable world of the newly emerged sharing economy. This term is broadly used to describe online transactions in which peers swap or sell access to goods and services.

We would be operating on both sides of the sharing economy. By listing our home on sites like those operated by Airbnb, HomeAway and SabbaticalHomes, we could reach a broad audience of potential renters. As travelers, we could use the same sites to rent housing anywhere in the world.

These companies charge homeowners, renters, or both, for use of the technology they have developed – known as the platform. Price structures vary and are subject to change, but they were nominal relative to what we stood to earn.

The sharing economy seemed like the perfect tool for what might either be a self-funded sabbatical or a new stage of life. But after a series of misadventures we realized that each deal involves elements of risk and trust. No matter how carefully both parties vet each other, you're either lucky or not.

Almost from the moment we left home, nothing went according to plan. And when that happened, I took another risk: I wrote this book, without a publishing contract in hand.

It is a story not only about travel and the sharing economy but also about our most important transition yet. We are among the many baby boomers who have left traditional work arrangements, by choice or circumstance, prematurely – a function of technology, a prolonged economic downturn, physical decline or demographics. For longtime employees or others who expected to be rewarded for good work, losing one's corporate "home" is a game-changer. So much of our identity and financial security has been linked to employment. With little or no leverage in the job market, we must rethink priorities and what we want to do with the rest of our lives. That might be 20 or 30 more years but not necessarily healthy ones. Suddenly there's an urgency to cram as much in while we can.

We were a youth-oriented generation. And though many of us continue to feel young, now we are surrounded by external reminders that we're not. At business meetings, if we are still going to them, we notice that we are by far the oldest person in the room. There, and in public places with a younger crowd, we don't always feel welcome or even wanted. When doing FaceTime on our smartphones or posing for selfies, those screens are brutally honest about the force of gravity. Images of our younger selves exist only in old photos or in our minds.

And yet there's a significant bright spot: Just as boomers have had more life choices at earlier stages – about whether to marry or whether to have children, for example – they do at this one, too. While some of us are able to retire, others aren't ready psychologically or financially. More of us will choose an un-retirement, continuing to work in some capacity but most likely with a decline in earned income.

By renting our house, we turned it into an additional source of revenue. Between career disruptions and this financial strategy, we let go of home in every sense of the word.

You'll read here about the practical steps we took to do that and the emotional strain of letting strangers occupy our intimate space. Then, as *locataires* (the French word for tenants), we struck out into the vast unknown. We weren't always comfortable with that, either.

Our journey, filled with history, art, new tastes and local color, enriched us in surprising ways. It took us through the Loire Valley, to

Basque Country and finally to Paris. Along that route we had a glimpse of a slower, more gracious lifestyle; witnessed a kinder, gentler approach to aging; and found that our efforts to speak the language opened many doors. Despite frequent power outages in the remote villages where we lived, Wi-Fi in all our lodgings enabled us to manage our finances, my business as well as communication with our family, from a distance.

Everything you will read here happened in the manner and sequence that I have told it. All the people mentioned, no matter how brief our encounter with them, are real. We met a lot of characters. None of those I have written about is a composite, though some are identified by fictitious names, pseudonyms or only by their first or last names. Our tenants and, with one exception, our sharing economy hosts, remain anonymous. So do all the individuals who have inquired about renting our house.

If you opened this book because you are thinking of using your home to subsidize foreign travel, you'll find several chapters with specifics about how to do that. Many more will whet your appetite to explore the places we visited, with insights one doesn't normally get from guidebooks. Avid travelers and armchair adventurers can choose which elements of our experience they might want to replicate. Francophiles will compare notes. Anyone who has ever fantasized about taking a break from the rat race will want to follow the thread of how our escapades became a book.

Though mine is a baby boomer's perspective, I write for readers of all ages. I hope that Gen Xers and millennials will be persuaded that each life experience builds on the previous one, whether it was positive or negative. Others, who are already retired, on the verge of retiring or think they never will, can relate to the broader themes that motivated our journey and were a continuing subtext.

The road to reinvention, no matter what our age, is not easily charted. In her pioneering book, *Lean In: Women, Work, And the Will to Lead*, Sheryl Sandberg, the chief operating officer of Facebook, describes her career as "a jungle gym scramble" – a metaphor she attributes to *Fortune* magazine editor Pattie Sellers. "I could never have connected the dots from where I started to where I am today," she writes. Going forward, that is likely to be true for many more of us. Not knowing what's ahead can make us feel uneasy – or extremely anxious.

One thing we can be sure of, though, is that nothing will happen while we are standing still. When we move away from the familiar, whether it is the workplace or a house that we have occupied for many years, possibilities that we might never have even imagined start to emerge. If you think change is hard – or never considered that your strong suit – make a list of at least three things you would still like to do. Then think expansively about how you can achieve at least one of those goals.

Life transitions, like foreign travel, are a curious mix of fantasy, experience and interpretation. I would do you a disservice, dear reader, by over-romanticizing our life in France. What you will find here is an honest assessment, including all the bumps in the road.

As travelers who enjoy going off the beaten path, we have learned to embrace the unexpected. Our three-month sojourn led to a new way of life and persuaded us, once again, that anything is possible. Whether you choose to take bigger risks or smaller ones, I hope that our story will lead you to the same conclusion.

PART ONE

CHARTING
a COURSE

1

EXIT PLAN

"Hold fast to dreams
For if dreams die
Life is a broken-winged bird
That cannot fly."
– Langston Hughes, *Dreams*

I CAN'T PINPOINT THE JOURNEY when my husband, Ken, and I turned into a couple of tenderfoots. It might have been a gradual process as we stacked up birthdays. Bit by bit it dawned on us that we were spending less time eating street food in Third World countries and more time dining at European restaurants with white tablecloths.

We had tried to frontload physically demanding travel into our early years together. Back in those days I had written, with what now seems like traveler's machismo, about our close encounters with what were euphemistically known as "Sipadan squirrels." Named for the tiny island 35 miles off the coast of Malaysia that they inhabited, and which we visited, these nocturnal and omnivorous rat-like creatures had an annoying habit of scampering up and down the walls of our little cottage while we tried to sleep. Upon reading about our experience, in *The New York Times* travel section, a friend told me, "I enjoyed your article. And I won't be going there."

Sipadan has since been turned into a fancy resort, and I have no idea what happened to the rats. If we didn't have pictures (and a newspaper clipping) to prove that we were there in 1993, I wouldn't believe it. While a bed and perhaps an en suite bathroom used to be enough (in Sipadan we used an outhouse and showers shared with ten other cottages), we got to a point when we wouldn't consider a home rental that didn't have Wi-Fi and a washing machine.

That was the stage we had reached when we began planning to live in France for three months. During the year leading up to our impending status as empty nesters, we hoped to compensate for one regret: that we had never lived overseas together. In 25 years we had gone all over the world as independent travelers, but we were always tourists. This time we wanted to set up house in one place and try to experience it like locals. As our son, Jack, was applying to college, we saw a unique opportunity to follow our dream.

We came up with a strategy that we called living on the sharing economy. The concept was to rent our historic townhouse in Brooklyn, New York and live on the proceeds. They could cover all of our expenses, including the rent for 90 days (the maximum time in a six-month period that we could stay in the European Union without a visa); a car; and food, assuming we prepared most of our own meals and stayed away from too many of those restaurants with white tablecloths.

This was not an impulsive move. The summer before taking the big step, we did a trial run, using the sharing economy to arrange two French rentals. As our base for visiting the D-Day beaches of Normandy, we spent a week in an adorable first-floor apartment in the fishing village of Port-en-Bessin-Huppain, which had been a fueling station during World War II. The following week we rented a slightly larger apartment in the old city of Quimper, in Brittany. In both places we shopped at outdoor markets and cooked with whatever equipment was in the apartment.

The vacation confirmed that we enjoyed what's sometimes called "slow travel" and helped us fine-tune our plans to live abroad. Both our vacation rentals had been studios, which we decided would be inappropriate for a longer stay – in such a small space, we would get on each other's nerves. And neither apartment had a sofa, something that was essential if we were living somewhere for more than about a week.

After researching parts of France that are attractive in the fall, even when the weather gets chilly, we chose the Loire Valley as our home base. Known as the Garden of France, it includes a 170-mile stretch of river, about two hours southwest of Paris by car, along which for centuries royalty and aristocrats built châteaux and manor houses.

Many were proximate to the city of Tours, which also has a university. And though we wanted a rural living experience, I thought briefly about the possibility of teaching there and residing in a nearby town. Meanwhile, I began to explore housing, using the same sharing economy websites that had worked so well for us in Normandy and Brittany.

In the course of this, a listing for an old winemaker's cottage in Amboise, about 20 minutes by car from Tours, caught my eye. It had two bedrooms; a living room with a sofa and leather easy chairs; and

a beautiful kitchen with granite countertops. The lush gardens, photographed when the roses and wisteria were in bloom, would give us
outdoor space. With high-speed internet access and a phone line from
which it was possible to make free calls to the U.S., I could work re-
motely. And it was just a five-minute drive to the center of the village,
famous for its château and for being the place where Leonardo da Vinci
spent the last three years of his life.

The owners of the winemaker's cottage had an intriguing background. Oliver and Lisa Douglas, as I will call them, were retired
American professors and indicated on the HomeAway website that
they had directed a university's program abroad in Tours for decades.
Half hoping that they could provide career guidance, I sent a note
introducing myself and asking for suggestions about how to apply for
a visiting professorship. Lisa replied that both getting a job and the
required work permit would be extremely challenging. But "If you are
interested in a quote about our cottage, please write back," she said.
Within a week we had a deal.

For the next nine months, visions of our ethereal autumn in Amboise, fueled by follow-up e-mails and a long phone interview with
Lisa, danced in my head. Based on the website photos, which I had
looked at so many times that I could see them in my mind's eye, I
composed a fantasy of our life in France. We would eat croissants for
breakfast in the garden, harvest fresh figs from our own tree, shop at
the Friday and Saturday markets on the banks of the Loire and go
for leisurely strolls along the river. I would take my laptop outside
and work in the little gazebo, under the roses. On chilly evenings I
would make soup for dinner. Afterward, we would curl up in front of
a roaring fire in the living room and read.

Such thoughts sustained me as I made a wrenching decision. What I didn't tell Lisa during our initial correspondence was that I was on the verge of resigning from an oppressive staff job. I knew that if I later changed my mind, I could not put the genie back in the bottle. Because of my age and seismic changes in my industry, if I left that editorial job, I wasn't likely to ever find another one.

A 2012 report by the Tow Center for Digital Journalism, which I had carefully read, described the economic pressures on news organizations to produce more with less. Increasingly, they were filling their insatiable need for what had become known as "content" by publishing articles submitted by people who were not writers. Sometimes this material was written by ghostwriters. More often, it was the work of amateurs who were looking to "build their brand" with online visibility. This trend had drastically reduced pay rates for freelance journalists. Meantime, many stellar writers had been fired or given buyout packages to cut high salaries from the budget.

Just ten years earlier all this would have been unthinkable. At the time I was happily self-employed, busily juggling writing assignments with the joys of motherhood, while earning more than many colleagues on the corporate payroll. Then, as our industry began to implode and my income declined precipitously, I was suddenly offered a position as an editor at a prestigious publication. Thrilled to become part of this company, I was also enormously relieved to have a steady paycheck.

I loved being a writer and expected to stay in my new journalistic home until I was in my mid-60s, or older. But on many days, my role, covering personal finance for baby boomers, reminded me of the *I Love Lucy* episode in which Lucy gets a job in a chocolate factory. In one hilarious scene, Lucy and her friend Ethel stuff chocolates into their mouths, under their hats and down their dresses, when they can't keep up the pace of wrapping candy as it comes off the conveyor belt.

At what I privately referred to as The Content Mill, I worked in a much more high-tech sweatshop. Data on my blog traffic was updated every 15 minutes. Management used metrics to express monthly performance goals. Although I far exceeded them, nothing was ever enough. The stress took a heavy toll on me, both physically and emotionally.

In other industries, too, the tyranny of metrics was radically altering the standards by which organizations measure productivity. Workers of every generation who wanted to secure their financial future needed to be nimble – and mobile.

After three years at The Content Mill, I yearned to escape the company's slave-driving management and reclaim my independence as a writer. Life was just too short to spend any more of it being judged by the number of daily, weekly and monthly online "clicks" that my articles generated. And so I quit the job from hell to live in France on the sharing economy.

As a parent, I wanted to model this major life decision to Jack. In his senior year of high school, he seemed terrified of the unknown. I thought he needed me around. And since he would be going away to college soon, we had precious little time left to spend together as a family. So at least for a couple of months, I wanted to convey the impression that I was ditching it all, dialing back and transforming myself into a calm (rather than frenetic) presence at home. I wanted him to believe that we can get comfortable with uncertainty and embark on adventures that are not clearly charted for us. It took me decades to develop that perspective. I hope someday Jack will come to believe it for himself. The sooner, the better.

That said, the circumstances surrounding my latest transition were so completely different from anything that had come before it, that I didn't feel quite so firm-footed, especially not financially. I examined our bank statements and checked Internal Revenue Service life expectancy tables – the ones I had written about numerous times in articles explaining how to calculate minimum required withdrawals from a traditional or inherited IRA. Again and again, I ran the numbers to see whether our family could afford for me to quit my job. There was no clear answer to that question. It depended on factors we couldn't control: how long we lived; interest rates and stock market performance; and whether we had catastrophic medical expenses as we aged.

Ken, who is four years older than I, had been sidelined several years earlier by back problems and a profound hearing loss. Without a steady paycheck, my earning power would be seriously diminished. According to those IRS life expectancy tables, as a 62-year-old, Ken could expect to live 23.5 more years, and, at 58, I had another 27 ahead of me. That meant we had a lot of living expenses (and potential health care costs) to cover. Work had always given me a sense of purpose, and I couldn't imagine a life without it. But now, more than ever, I would need to define what that work would be. Meanwhile, our unconventional downsizing plan would help pay the bills. If our experiment of living on the sharing economy was successful, this could be a new way of life.

In planning our strategy, we recognized that many – perhaps most – Americans are not in a position to give up a "perfectly good job." We felt extremely fortunate to own a home in one of the world's most expensive cities. Still, our property deed didn't tell the whole story.

We had always lived frugally, especially since we were self-employed for most of our careers. Uncomfortable with debt because our yearly income fluctuated, we made as big a down payment as we could possibly afford, and took a mortgage for about 40 percent of the purchase price. When business profits exceeded what we needed to live on, we put every dime of it toward our mortgage. By the time we celebrated the fifth anniversary of home ownership, the property had doubled in value and we owned it free and clear. But it was also our largest asset.

Just as we could not have anticipated the disruption in the journalism industry or the health issues that derailed Ken's career, we never could have imagined that the roof over our heads would someday provide us with a source of income. We envied friends who had other safety nets – government pensions, company stock options or tenured jobs, for example. We had our house, and this was a blessing. And our ability to monetize it was greatly enhanced by another unexpected development: the emergence of sharing economy websites.

The weekend before I submitted my resignation, Ken and I signed a lease with the Douglases, for a rental that would begin 11 months later, and sent them a deposit of $2,250, representing 25 percent of the three-month rent. The balance wasn't due until a month before our arrival in France.

During the time leading up to our departure, I helped Jack with college applications; wrote a series of freelance articles; and published a fourth edition of my book *Estate Planning Smarts*. With very mixed emotions, I also prepared to rent out the house that had been the backdrop of our lives for the previous 17 years.

2

LEAVING HOME

⁓

WHEN I TOLD friends and family that we planned to rent our house, furnished, many of them had the same reaction. "Good for you. I could never do that," they would say. No doubt they were thinking, "How creepy to think of a stranger sleeping in my bed. And what would I do with all my stuff?"

To be clear: We felt the same way. This wasn't something we wanted to do. Nor did I want to keep working at a place that had become completely unbearable. Letting go of my home seemed better than hanging on to a job that was destroying me. Neither alternative was attractive, but we needed a plan.

As Michael Klein, head of U.S. sales and marketing at Onefinestay, a high-end vacation-rental company, would tell me many months later, in an interview, "Everyone who does this does it for the money." And we all have our price.

16

Onefinestay, a start-up, handles every aspect of the rental process and takes a lot of the hassle out of home rentals. After hearing Klein speak, at a Cardozo Law School program on the sharing economy, I contacted him to explore the possibility of listing our house with Onefinestay. We would probably earn less that way than renting through other sharing economy companies. But they would help prepare the house for our guests (even sending someone to empty closets and drawers), handle the upkeep while we were away and reassemble our home when we returned.

The stumbling block was that we wanted a long-term fall rental, preferably for the full three months that we would be in France, and the team at Onefinestay wasn't confident they could deliver. They wanted to book shorter stays of a week or so, and we were dead set against that idea. Such transience would expose our house to extreme wear and tear. In mid-April we went live with our own listing on three websites: Airbnb, HomeAway and SabbaticalHomes.

The first inquiries we received were from several real estate agents, whom we initially turned away. When one of them persisted and contacted us a second time, after we had gone a month with no action from our own listings, we decided to meet. Terry Baum, a broker with Warren Lewis Sotheby's International Realty, in Brooklyn, New York, was smart, experienced and about my age. The first time we met, we clicked.

Terry lived in the neighborhood and knew other baby boomers pursuing a strategy similar to ours. One client, who was downsizing to a Brooklyn co-op she bought in 2015, planned to rent her house nearby instead of selling it. A retired couple divided their time between a home in Santa Cruz, California and a Brooklyn condo that they bought with Terry's help. As they shuttled between the two places, they rented whichever home they weren't using. People were out there making sound choices, and we were in very good company.

One of the things that sold us on Terry was her genuine appreciation of our house. We had bought it after looking at nearly 100 homes over the course of five years. At the time, Jack was one year old, and we had outgrown the one-bedroom apartment we owned in Brooklyn Heights; we were renting a separate one-bedroom, four flights up, that we used as offices. Our goal was to put everything under one roof.

I answered an ad in *The New York Times* placed by the owner, who described the house to me over the telephone. When I hung up, I told Ken, "I think I found our new home." And the minute I walked in, several days later, I was sure of it. One look at the mahogany wall panels, and oak parquet floors with a different ornament in each room, and I was sold.

It was one of 39 houses, lining opposite sides of the street, that were built over a two-year period in the early 1900s as part of a housing boom that began in 1883 after the opening of the Brooklyn Bridge. Designed by the architect Arthur R. Koch and constructed by the eminent builder Otto Singer, their exteriors incorporated details inspired by Classical, Romanesque and French Renaissance traditions.

Prior owners of our house – we would become the fourth – had removed some of the Victorian, and Arts and Crafts, interior detail, like the built-in dining room cabinets and mantel. But in a series of renovations, we found 21st-century craftsmen to fill the void.

Most notable was William B. Streett, who was our neighbor for slightly less than two years. The former dean of the Cornell School of Engineering, Bill was retired and in his early 70s when he moved into the house next door to ours in 2002. His wife, Mary Sansalone – a former student whom he married after his first wife died – had a new job, in New York, and Bill was the trailing spouse.

Bill, whose many achievements included inventing concrete-testing equipment, had a hobby of building reproduction Stickley furniture. Their house was filled with beautiful pieces he had built, and in time ours would be, too. More than anything else, I cherish the furnishings that he made for my office – cherry bookcases, with a desk, computer table and file cabinets to match. Bill created a comfortable and elegant place for me to work. I have been very productive in that space. During tough times that office has been my refuge.

Our house is also filled with folk art collected during our travels. We have a tortilla basket from Mexico and a Thai rice pot displayed in our kitchen; a framed Balinese shadow puppet and lacquer tiffin from Burma in our dining room; and hand-carved masks, also from Bali, in our living room. We bought the two Oriental rugs on our staircase landings in India; they were custom made to fit the space. Above the stairs hangs a Tibetan tangka – a painting of a religious subject on fabric. This one depicts the longevity Buddha. It's a daily reminder to make the most of life.

In preparation for renting the house, we began to shed other belongings. "Operation Declutter," as we called it, was a sometimes painful and, at other times, amusing process. We found things I didn't even know I had, like six pairs of white kid gloves that came from either my grandmother or from Ken's mother (we can't recall). Separation would assume many guises.

For advice about deeper disposal, I read the bestselling 2014 book *The Life-Changing Magic of Tidying Up: The Japanese Art of Decluttering and Organizing*, by anti-clutter guru Marie Kondo. I found it hard to take much of her advice seriously. Say good-bye to my socks and thank them for their good service as I threw them out? She had to be kidding.

The most poignant part of Operation Declutter was letting go of various papers and objects that triggered memories, and it made us realize how much time had slipped away. In a big blue Tiffany box that 23 years earlier held a dozen Champagne glasses we received as a wedding gift, I had stored all the greeting cards that Ken and I ever gave to each other. We agreed to toss them. As Yi-Fu Tuan notes in his 1977 book *Space and Place: The Perspective of Experience*, a person's "comfortable mementos threaten to stand in the way of his present and future projects."

We had become the victims of our own good recordkeeping, too. As self-employed people, we extensively documented everything in case of a tax audit. During Operation Declutter, we threw away things like receipts for bottled water at our hotel in Cochin, India in 2001. (I wrote a story about the trip.) We scanned important documents, shredded others and for many weeks hauled out dozens of bags of the resulting confetti, for recycling. Starting on January 1, we went paperless with all of our bills and financial statements.

Together, our notes to each other and financial records reminded us of many nights spent apart while Ken traveled all over the country and the world, working as a focus-group moderator. I found a valentine I sent in 2004, addressed to him at the Hilton Hotel in Shanghai, China; and numerous undated notes he left under Jack's pillow before leaving on business trips. Enclosed in a letter he sent me in May 1999, on notepaper from a Dallas hotel, was a clipping from a travel brochure about the Pangkor Laut resort in Malaysia, where we planned to celebrate the millennium. His handwritten note read, "Just a reminder of the payoff for all our hard work!"

We were still traveling on frequent-flyer miles earned from those business trips but had paid dearly for them in lost family time. Those were the years when Jack was a baby, a toddler, a preschooler and then a big boy in elementary school, whose father got up early to catch a plane and called at bedtime to say "good night." Jack was three years old the evening I tried to hand the phone to him and he pushed it away, saying, "Don't want to talk to Daddy – want to see Daddy."

More recently, we had done practically no maintenance on our house, and it was suddenly in need of repairs. I contacted various tradesmen whom I had dealt with in the past. On one week during the winter, we had visits from the tile guy, the plumber and the roofer, along with someone from Home Depot to discuss window replacements in our kitchen.

Some of our nesting was finished by the time we met with Terry, and we were optimistic about the exposure her listing would bring. She would enter the ad in a system that both Realtors and individuals could access. It would feed to many other sites in the U.S. and overseas. Terry would vet potential tenants and coordinate all showings. The service would be free to us; the tenant would pay Terry's commission.

We were excited to quickly get two nibbles, but with each of them, there was a catch. The first was reminiscent of the nursery rhyme, "There was an old woman who lived in a shoe. She had so many children, she didn't know what to do." This potential tenant had five children between the ages of 3 and 14; a full-time nanny; a full-time daily house cleaner; and a Labradoodle. She was looking for a place to put all these people, plus the Labradoodle, while she renovated her house.

Our ad clearly said we didn't allow pets, but apparently the woman-in-the-shoe thought this was negotiable – or she was desperate. She offered to pay a surcharge for the dog, plus a separate pet deposit for any damage the Labradoodle caused. This unleashed my imagination about what that damage might be. I could just see that Labradoodle chewing the legs of my cherry office furniture; barfing and urinating on our Oriental rugs; and leaving scratches on the parquet floors as it followed five children all over the house. By the time this family's house was in move-in condition, ours would surely be completely trashed. We confirmed Terry's suspicion that this was a non-starter.

During the next several weeks, there was considerable back-and-forth about another family in transition. We named this prospect "The Devil Wears Prada" – a reference to the movie by the same name starring Meryl Streep as a prima donna magazine editor and Anne Hathaway as her assistant. After the first walk-through, this couple presented us with a wish list. The first order of business would be to move Ken's enormous granite desk and his ergonomic chair out of his office on the second floor, down two narrow flights of stairs, to the basement. Why? Because the nanny would use the sleep sofa in Ken's office, on the occasions when she stayed overnight, and the office furniture would get in her way.

Next on the list was the master bedroom. The enormous, double-hung walk-in closet in that room was not enough space for the clothing of these two adults. In addition to two large dressers and all the drawers in the walk-in closet, which we offered to clear for their use, they insisted that they *also* needed the second, smaller, closet in the master bedroom. This was where we were planning to stash all our own clothes. But that just would not do. Our belongings, they said, needed to be moved down *three* flights of stairs, to the basement, where they could keep Ken's office furniture company.

While they were at work, their three children under the age of five would be cared for in our house by round-the-clock nannies. Oh, yes, and since the darlings were accustomed to riding their tricycles indoors, they assumed there would be no problem with a little tricycle traffic on our 100-year-old oak parquet floors. Wrong!

After having nightmares about the daily phone calls, texts and e-mails we might receive in France, complaining about one thing or another, Ken and I agreed that no amount of money would have compensated us for the aggravation these potential tenants were capable of causing. We were about to give up on the idea of renting the house and declare our new lifestyle a failure before it even started, when we had another inquiry. This one, via the VRBO website (affiliated with HomeAway), came from a midwestern couple. The wife was a homemaker, the husband would be in New York on temporary assignment, and his company would be footing the bill. They stopped by to see our house a week later.

Without being asked, they left their shoes in the vestibule and went barefoot as we showed them around. (This happened to be our protocol to protect the floors.) They admired all the old detail and described themselves as "neat freaks." Another good sign. When we offered that we could arrange to have someone remove the air conditioners when the weather got chilly, the husband volunteered that he was "handy" and could do it himself. At that point they were earning extra-credit Brownie points.

By the end of the day, we had a signed contract with June and Ward Cleaver, as we called them (after the wholesome parents on *Leave It to Beaver* – a TV sitcom of our youth), and they had given us a $10,000 non-refundable deposit. After they sent the balance of the rent (plus a $1,500 security deposit), the following week, they brought their two preschoolers to show them the house. They were on their way to nearby Prospect Park when they visited, and could not have been more considerate about arranging a time that would be convenient for us.

Again, without any prompting, everyone took off their shoes as they came in. They kept their visit brief. I had put on the living room hearth a few wooden toys that had belonged to Jack, and a couple of his stuffed animals, still in good condition, that I had also saved. While the younger child picked up the string on one of the pull toys, the older one played with a crocodile puppet. I told him that I would leave it for him when we went away.

"But where are you going?" he asked.

"Far away," I replied. "And you are going to live here with Mommy and Daddy while we are gone."

"But I want you to stay here with us," remarked this four-year-old. Adorable!

I was less charmed when I showed him Jack's room, where he would be sleeping, and he immediately started jumping on the bed. "Don't do that – it's not our house yet," his father said.

My back arched. In Hollywood that scene would have been the foreshadowing that moviegoers come back to at the end of the film. But this was not Hollywood. This was Brooklyn, we were headed to Amboise, France, and we had finally snagged a tenant. So when the child stopped jumping, I let the whole thing slide, but not without wondering what would await us when we returned.

Two weeks later Ken had surgery for spinal stenosis – a narrowing of the spinal column. This condition, which in his case was congenital, causes intense pain and loss of mobility as nerves are compressed. It was Ken's fourth such operation. Though we knew the drill, it was still an ordeal. His surgeon promised that he would be able to travel to France in late August and could finish recuperating there.

Much of my time during the next seven weeks was spent supervising a parade of workmen. Knowing that we had a tenant in place (and with the rent in hand), we embarked on many additional home repairs and improvements to increase the street appeal of our house, improve the quality of living there and decrease the likelihood that anything would go wrong.

The only way I could get past the creepiness of strangers sleeping in our bed was to provide them with separate linens, pillows and mattress pads. That made our bed seem like just a surface – not something intimate that we would be sharing with God knows whom. Sure, I had slept in plenty of hotel beds without any idea who had occupied them, but, for some reason, this felt different. So I took advantage of summer sales to stock up on bedding. Our linen closet, situated in my office, began to look like a hotel supply room.

Ken's surgery had gone well, and he was recovering slowly, but at times I felt overwhelmed by our huge transition. Just one of those moments was on a steamy day in early July when FedEx arrived with a new toilet for our basement. Had I not heard the truck and gone out to meet the deliveryman, he would have left it on our stoop.

What did he expect me to do with the toilet, in all of its porcelain heaviness, packed in a box that was large enough to be a playhouse for three toddlers? I told him that my husband was recovering from back surgery, and at the risk of stating the obvious, pointed out that I am not exactly Wonder Woman. Then I shamelessly pleaded with him to bring the toilet into the house rather than leaving it on my front stoop.

He explained that he was not allowed to carry it more than three feet into the house. Under that interpretation, I said, a prerequisite was to carry the toilet down the basement stairs. And that is how I got the toilet, in the box, down the stairs and three feet into the basement. It stayed there for two weeks, with all the workmen squeezing by it, until the plumber came to do the installation.

Soon after, during heavy rainstorms, the sewer backed up twice from that newly installed toilet. Fortunately, there was no damage to our basement, but we couldn't leave our tenant vulnerable to future, similar incidents. Our longtime trusty plumber blamed it on the antiquated and overloaded infrastructure in our neighborhood. Meaning there was nothing we could do?

"We just rented our house for three months for a lot of money, and I can't have this happen to our tenants!" I screamed out of sheer frustration. He suggested we have the house snaked, and in the process his team could send a camera down the pipes to see what was going on. We acquiesced.

The plumber's camera diagnosed a problem that we couldn't blame on the city. There was a serious blockage in our plumbing, like a clogged artery. The plumber cleared the obstruction. Adding to the total bill, for nearly $2,000, was the need to remove the toilet that we had just paid to install, and then put it back.

It seemed like every time I thought I was done cleaning up, something else would suddenly go wrong with the house. I just hoped that every possible foul-up was occurring in *advance* of our departure, and therefore things would go completely smoothly for our tenants.

The choreography of events around our house would have been comical if they were happening to someone else. One day, in mid-August, the roofer was right outside my office window fixing an issue with the kitchen skylight, while inside I was researching the Minnesota laws of intestate succession (what happens if you die without a will), to prepare for a one-hour radio interview the following day.

Ken, meantime, was outside trying to pry the license plates off our 18-year-old Honda. To reduce our living expenses, we had decided to go carless and had sold the car, for $350, to Sonja, the woman who cut my hair. She was arriving momentarily to pick it up.

Jack was in a foul humor. Having expressed a desire to "kick back" for the six weeks between the end of high school and his departure for college, he generally slept until at least noon. By the time he stumbled downstairs and asked what there was for breakfast, I felt like I had put in a full day.

Outside of Jack's earshot (easy, because he slept for most of our waking hours), we began to joke that our hermit crab had grown too big for his house. It was a reference to Eric Carle's charming 1987 picture book *A House for Hermit Crab* – the story of the lovable crab who twice outgrows his shell and needs to find a new place to live.

The afternoon before our hermit crab's assigned move-in day, at the University of Colorado, we all flew to Denver together. Without any sarcasm or sappy sentimentalism, we actually enjoyed one another's company that evening, sharing plates of comfort food – chicken wings, coconut shrimp and French fries – at an Outback Steakhouse before bedding down at a Residence Inn in Louisville, Colorado. Jack was the child on the sleep sofa for one last night before we delivered him to his dorm the next morning.

He stands tall in a photo taken minutes before we said good-bye – a cool guy in dark sunglasses. Beside him, I am smiling broadly but look pale and haggard. After this parting shot, he turned and walked in the direction of the mountains. Only then did I start to cry.

Friends and family who heard that we would be leaving for three months in France, the week after taking Jack to college, had mixed reactions. Some applauded our plans to start a new chapter of our own lives. Others speculated that since we, too, would be going away, we wouldn't notice the vacancy in our home.

A third group offered to help out if Jack needed anything while we were in Europe. Certainly they meant well, but they seemed to think that we were abandoning him, while our goal was to help launch him as a young adult. Of course, we wanted to know any details of his new adventure that he was inclined to share. But we didn't see a purpose – or benefit to him – of being on standby alert "just in case." (And "just in case" what, for example?) The transition was hard enough without all of the second-guessing.

The greatest gifts a parent can give a child are confidence and independence. But for children to reach that point, we need to give them permission to separate. If we do our job well, we become obsolete.

Back in New York, after the Boulder drop-off, we felt the void. I had dusted off Jack's classic old wood toys, building blocks and play table, and arranged them in our living room for our tenants' children. Any family photos not attached to the walls were packed away in boxes. It didn't seem like our house anymore. Ken said it felt as if someone had died.

For most of our marriage and Jack's life, our home had been a bedrock. Though I felt grateful that it could now provide us with an income source, waves of sadness and nostalgia came over me as I prepared it for other people to inhabit.

PART TWO

THE ALLURE
of the LOIRE

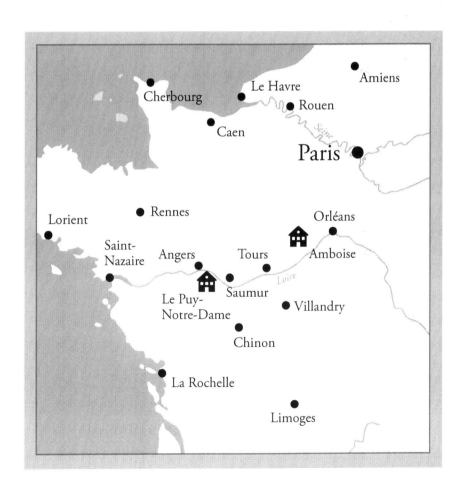

3

THE WINEMAKER'S COTTAGE

AFTER BIDDING ADIEU to our house for three months and
wondering what we were forgetting, Ken and I flew overnight
across the Atlantic. Without even stopping for coffee, we picked up
our rental car and drove two hours from Paris to the Loire Valley. We
couldn't wait to begin our life in France.

Our first view of Amboise was from the bridge connecting the north
side of the river to the south. The château, set high on top of a rock
spur, loomed directly in front of us like a gigantic chess piece. A medieval fortress that had reached its heyday as a royal residence during
the Renaissance, it had a dreamlike quality. In fact, we *were* practically
dreaming, since we had been too excited to sleep on the plane.

"Can you believe we're going to be living here for three months!" I
said to Ken, gaping at the garrets and towers.

The more humble winemaker's cottage that we had rented, also centuries old, was only about five miles from there, but it took us another half hour to reach it. First there was heavy traffic to contend with. We were arriving in late August, at the tail end of the French *vacances* (vacation season). Quai du Général de Gaulle, the main thoroughfare, was choked with cars and tour buses. Although we knew that Amboise was a popular tourist destination, we didn't expect to have nearly this much company in our sleepy little French village.

Following the hand-drawn map that our landlords had sent, we left the center of town. From there, a twisting road climbed into a hamlet, and the route to the cottage became less clear. After several wrong turns we found a bank of mailboxes, including one for the Douglases. Assuming it couldn't be far from there, we asked directions from a man who was walking by. He pointed to a green, wooden double gate that he helped us open.

Behind it was a driveway littered with hundreds of rotten apples. The Douglases had told me there were apple trees and that we should feel free to pick the fruit. They didn't say anything about who would clean up what had fallen. In a gesture that seemed more derisive than helpful, the stranger kicked a handful of the apples aside, wished us *bon séjour* (a good stay) and departed. I stood under the tree, surrounded by some of the rotting apples, as Ken drove into the driveway, squishing many others.

Access to the cottage from there was down a winding path of 28 irregular stone steps. This was not exactly what the website had depicted, though it did include aerial views and indicated that the house wasn't wheelchair accessible, or "suitable for the elderly or infirm." Since we live in a three-story townhouse, I hadn't attached much importance to the last line of our contract with the Douglases, either, which called attention to the stairs. Its reference to "interior and exterior flights" didn't seem like a big deal. We have interior and exterior flights in our house, too.

But not like these. I slowly descended the 28 steps, first hugging the left side where the railing began, then shifting positions where the handrail abruptly switched to the right. I paused on the first landing to survey the garden below. What I saw were only the remnants of the lovingly landscaped property depicted in the website photos.

There was the gazebo – a tiny pavilion surrounded by hydrangea and rhododendron bushes that overlooked the house. Based on the photos, taken when the rose arbor above it was in bloom, I had imagined making this little spot an outdoor writing nook. But in person, it didn't look at all inviting. It was furnished with a stone bench, a very rusty wrought-iron café table and four chairs. Without the roses, there was no shade.

I brushed my hand over a two-foot-high patch of lavender beside the stairs, held it to my nose and inhaled. Like so many dwellings in France, including the château that we drove by on our way into town, the house bore the fingerprints of its various occupants. What was probably once a very modest winemaker's cottage, with a terra-cotta tile roof, was attached to a more elaborate structure, with a blue slate roof characteristic of more upscale homes in the region.

Farther down the steps, Mother Nature had reclaimed the acre or so of terraced former vineyards. The ground cover was choking out the primroses, now past their bloom. Grass, obviously not watered during the recent summer heat wave, had turned to straw. In what might have been a survival of the fittest, geraniums and many varieties of hibiscus were still flowering, and the notoriously invasive wisteria vines had taken over, even enveloping the herb planter directly outside the front door. I lifted it and found basil, chives and parsley thriving underneath. "Great, I can use them in recipes," I thought, still clinging to my fantasy about living in a Loire Valley cottage.

Ken, who by then had caught up with me, watched as I peeled back the acrylic net curtain in front of the door. "Nice touch," he said, pointing to the tears and numerous holes in this poor excuse for a screen. I punched in the secret code to the lock box, retrieved the key and fiddled with the front door. It swung open, and I held my breath as we stepped into a tile foyer, just big enough for the two of us to stand single file.

Several steps beyond it, in what was probably the original one-room winemaker's cottage, was an elegantly designed French country kitchen. It was even nicer than the photos on the HomeAway website, with honey-colored cabinetry made to resemble armoire doors and matching panels that covered the refrigerator, dishwasher, washing machine and dryer. A blue-and-white tile backsplash picked up the flecks of blue in the granite countertops, and there was an under-mounted soapstone sink. The Scholtès oven, microwave, dishwasher and Sauter induction cooktop seemed luxurious for what started out as a very unassuming abode. And many of the copper bowls and pots that hung from the wooden posts in that room were collector's items.

In time I would absorb all these details. But the first thing that caught my eye that day, when I opened the front door and stepped into the winemaker's cottage, was the pile of dirty towels in the middle of the wood kitchen floor.

Could it be that the house hadn't been cleaned?

A steep flight of stairs behind the kitchen, in a spot where there looked to have once been a pull-down ladder and access to storage space, led to what the owners called the loft bedroom. It resembled the picture from the website that I had viewed so many times, except that the bed was unmade, with dirty linen. Another thing, which I hadn't deduced from the website description, now occurred to me: For the next three months, if I needed to use the bathroom during the night, I would have to go down those steep stairs and walk past the kitchen to get there.

I thought of that as I carefully descended, turned left at the foyer, went up a step and through a doorway to the newer house built onto the original winemaker's cottage. To my left was a large living room with a fireplace and French doors that opened onto a flight of stairs leading to the terraced back garden. And there was the fig tree that Oliver Douglas had described to me when I spoke with him on the phone. It was gigantic and covered with fruit that had not yet ripened. I looked forward to having figs for breakfast some weeks hence.

Outside the living room was another interior staircase and, at the foot of it, a rolled-up runner. It had been used to carpet the steps above but was too long for the space and had nowhere to go after that, so the rest of it was just sitting there, like a jelly roll. I stepped over it, thinking what a trip hazard it was – not just for people like us, who were unfamiliar with the house, but also for the owners, who were in their 70s.

On the first landing of this staircase was the Douglases' bedroom – the only one with a door, which was locked and off-limits, as Lisa had said it would be. On the next flight, the stairs narrowed to little more than my body width. As I rounded the corner on the last few steps, I ducked (I am only 5'3") to avoid bumping my head on the loft floor, which extended out to the edge of the house. Around the bend was the tower bedroom. Dirty linen there, too.

The house manual, which I had studied before our arrival, included some hints for maneuvering on the way down: "For many people it seems easier to come down backwards on the narrow part. I usually do the top four forward, then pivot (it is also easier on your head, since you are not so likely to bump it going that way)." These instructions echoed in my mind on that first descent. I was sweating – not just because of the stairs, and the fact that the temperature inside, with all the windows shut, must have been nearly 90 degrees, but also because I was in shock. I just couldn't believe what I was seeing.

My mind drifted to the many months I had spent staging our own house for a long-term rental. We had straightened things up as best we could in our pre-departure rush, but I had arranged for our cleaning lady to come in the day before our tenant would arrive and clean again, with special attention to the kitchen and bathrooms. Meanwhile, the owners of the winemaker's cottage, with whom I thought I had developed such a good rapport, had done nothing to prepare their home for our three-month occupancy. We had paid them $9,000, and they couldn't even make sure the beds had been made. I felt so betrayed.

My body had no idea what time it was, and recent events had a surreal quality. "Let's take it slowly," I said to Ken. "We're going to bring our luggage into the house. And then we're going to call the cleaning lady."

Easier said than done. Ken was still not allowed to bend, lift more than ten pounds or twist, so the job of getting our three wheelies, each of which weighed at least 25 pounds, down those 28 garden steps, fell to me. Already I decided that we had brought too much.

I sat down at the table in what an online photo of the house referred to as the dining room, but it would more accurately be described as a very small dining area between the foyer and the kitchen. On the table was a welcome basket with our names on it, which contained a bottle of Vouvray, a can of pâté and other, more utilitarian, items: several rolls of toilet paper, two packets of tissues, and soap for the dishwasher and washing machine. Clearly someone was expecting us, but why hadn't the house been cleaned?

By then it was noon in Amboise. Our landlords were in California, where the local time was 3 a.m. Surely we two world travelers could handle this situation without waking them. In retrospect, I don't know why I was so considerate. Maybe, in my jetlagged state, I hadn't yet come to terms with the reality. Having spent so much time elaborately embroidering images of what this house would be, I could not quickly let go of them. Not only that. My French fantasy was closely tied to my escape from my staff job and the beginning of a new life. When the winemaker's cottage failed to deliver, that, too, fell apart.

As I dialed the phone number for Madame Lamotte, the cleaning lady, I realized that my hands, which don't ordinarily shake, were trembling. We had agreed, as part of our contract, to engage her services every other week, and Lisa had suggested we call her in due course to set up a schedule.

As I suspected, Madame Lamotte did not speak English, and though we had made every effort to learn enough French to get by, an SOS phone call to Madame Lamotte on the day of our arrival was not one of the dialogues in our conversational French exercises. Still, during the first minute of the call, I deduced that there had either been a lack of communication, or a misunderstanding, or both.

With the permission of our landlords, we had checked in (if one can call it that) three days earlier than initially scheduled, and Madame Lamotte was not aware of the change. So she was surprised to hear from us. But, in any event, she was under the impression that the house was clean: Apparently she also did not know that there had been a booking before us from people who were scheduled to leave two days before we got there.

Not wanting to go off on too much of a tangent, we repeated that the house needed to be cleaned. She replied that she would be very happy to do that, could not come *aujourd'hui* (today) but could be there on *vendredi,* which is Friday – two days later. I had neither the patience nor the facility with the language to describe the dirty towels in the middle of the kitchen floor, the unmade beds and refrigerator full of food, which by then we had also discovered. So I cut to the chase: *"La maison est un désastre!"* (The house is a disaster!)

At that point the voice on the other end of the phone took on a flustered tone, and I did not understand a word of the rapid-fire reply except that it concluded with *tout de suite,* which means at once.

I hung up the phone and told Ken that I thought Madame Lamotte was on her way, even though I wasn't 100 percent certain that was true. But sure enough, 20 minutes later there was a pitter-patter of footsteps growing closer on the 28 stone steps that led to the house, and with a great rush of energy Madame Lamotte burst from behind the torn net curtain and into the winemaker's cottage.

4

TWO FACES of EDEN

MADAME LAMOTTE COULD HAVE COME right out of central casting. She was as humorless and officious as we had imagined, based on no evidence besides the fact that we were to address her as "Madame Lamotte." (We never did learn her first name.) Tall and slender and in her 50s, she had deep brown eyes with a brunette bob that framed her face and was dressed in straight-legged pants topped with a white, short-sleeved blouse. She tsk-tsked repeatedly when we pointed to the pile of dirty towels, the unmade beds and the food in the refrigerator.

In the time it had taken her to travel from her house, directly across the Loire, to the winemaker's cottage, she had devised an explanation. It went like this: Perhaps Madame Douglas had sent an e-mail telling her about our early arrival and she simply did not receive it, since her daughter was always on the computer.

Actually, we had received an e-mail from Madame Douglas precisely a month earlier promising to make the necessary arrangements. So clearly someone had dropped the ball. But we didn't stick around to speculate who that might have been. Leaving our suitcases next to the table in the so-called dining room, we carefully hiked back up the 28 stone steps, got in our car, drove over the carpet of rotten apples, out the green, wooden double gate and set a course to the nearest Carrefour supermarket. Our bodies still had no idea what time it was, but they were telling us that we were hungry.

When we returned, less than three hours later, Madame Lamotte was gone. The beds had been made, there were fresh towels in the bathroom, and the kitchen looked marginally cleaner. Out the window, between two counters that ran at right angles, was a view of the Loire in the distance, much farther away than we had envisioned it.

In a March e-mail Lisa had written, "We're just about to take a long walk on the recently finished walking/biking path that goes from just in front of the house into Amboise along the Loire. It's so pretty just now, with all the almond trees in bloom!" I was still trying to figure out where that path was. The house was in the middle of an old vineyard, from which there was a steep descent to the river. And between the edge of the property line and the Loire was a country road known as the Tours Highway.

As I searched for a place to store our groceries, I felt like I was embarking on an archeological dig. The cabinets and drawers were crammed with every conceivable kitchen gadget, some in multiples. For example, there were three apple slicing/coring/peeling machines. The owners clearly had experience with apple trees. Surely they could have imagined the condition of the driveway.

Though the kitchen was well equipped, what I found there took away my appetite. Two cabinets were filled with staples, spices and condiments of an uncertain age. (Here, too, there were multiples.) Some of these items, which should have been refrigerated after opening, were past their freshness date, or made without preservatives, and were growing mold or oozing rot. On a shelf above the range were Mason jars of home-canned fruit, bubbly with fermentation. The granite countertop around the cooktop was coated with grime, as were the sponges above the sink.

Again, I compared the condition of the winemaker's cottage to how we had left our own house. I had stashed our wok, bamboo steamer and other utensils that I didn't think our tenants would use in the basement, making it easier for them to find necessary equipment. Exotic spices and condiments were stored in plastic bins on a high shelf. I had scrubbed the cabinets and emptied the refrigerator of practically everything, even though it meant throwing out food that we hadn't been able to consume.

I knew that the Douglases had spent time in the cottage during the spring. Could it have really looked much different when they left it? A five-star review on the HomeAway website, by guests who had stayed there for two weeks in June, said, "The house is immaculate." Visitors one month before us raved about the location, décor and well-equipped kitchen.

Perhaps they were the ones who used the barbecue, still filled with greasy charcoal, and maybe it was their clothing – shorts, T-shirt and panties – that Ken found in the loft bedroom as he unpacked the contents of his 22-inch rollaboard bag. What served as a dresser in that room looked like it might have once been a space-saving combination icebox/kitchen cabinet. Clever. But in the bottom-right compartment was a broken safe, its prongs stuck in the open position.

We hung our coats in the musty wardrobe at the top of the stairs. Fashioned out of antique armoire doors, it was creatively tucked under the eaves but, like other spaces in the house, was precarious to reach. The only way to do that was to stand on the top step, trying not to lose one's balance and fall down the stairs. And this compartment, too, contained someone else's clothes: a couple of dirty old bathrobes hung next to the rusty wire hangers available for our use.

There wasn't enough drawer space to keep all of our belongings in the room where we slept. So, bit by bit, I toted my gear up to the bedroom on the other side of the house. My clothes, which had fit easily into a 22-inch suitcase, completely filled the tiny dresser under one of the eaves in the second bedroom.

When we awoke the following day, at noon, having slept around the clock, we were surprised to hear the din of the Tours Highway that separated the winemaker's cottage from the Loire. I went downstairs to make breakfast. The day before, I had noticed that there was a capsule coffee machine and had bought a box of pods when we were at the store. But, as it happened, the machine didn't work. Neither did an antiquated Mr. Coffee machine that I found in the closet. Town was five miles away. It wasn't as if I could run out to the nearest Starbucks for a cup of Joe. Jetlagged and still not sure about whether I could be happy for three months in this house, I made do without my caffeine fix.

Already, the clutter was making me feel claustrophobic. The winemaker's cottage was creatively furnished with reclaimed materials and curiosities from the owners' European travels, many of them to my taste. The trouble was that there was just too much stuff in a very small space – like the collection of old plates, for example. There were hand-painted plates, and others, orphaned from old china sets, on display everywhere: crowded together on the living room hutch; stored sideways in a cabinet in the so-called dining room; hanging on the walls. Under a riser on the stairs leading to the tower bedroom was an arrangement of antique toys, including a precious doll's house–size stove, on top of which was displayed an assortment of miniature pitchers and canisters. It was like a flea market, taken indoors.

Though we could have coped for three months with the stairs, the quirky layout and even the clutter, we couldn't live with the filth. The upholstered furniture in the living room was laden with dust, and the strong smell of mildew there did not dissipate with several days of airing. The best we could surmise, based on 24 mostly positive online reviews for the winemaker's cottage, was that the people whom the Douglases were relying on to maintain the cottage in their absence were neglecting it. This included an English-speaking neighbor Lisa said would be our "welcome committee," but who we didn't initially contact, since we didn't know the precise time when we would arrive and didn't want to inconvenience her. When we later asked a question about making international calls on the house phone, she didn't know the answer and promised to get back to us. We never heard from her again.

Much as we wanted to be fair and give the Douglases the benefit of the doubt, the dust in the living room couldn't possibly be just a function of less than vigilant cleaning between tenants. And, in retrospect, there had been a clue that prior tenants weren't unanimously satisfied with the cottage. In a phone conversation with Lisa two weeks before we left New York, I had asked whether she had ever been burned by a renter. As I told her at the time, I was thinking about writing an article on the sharing economy (I wasn't yet sure of the angle) and wanted her perspective as someone who had been both a host and a guest, many times.

In that interview, Lisa mentioned a recent guest who had, among other things, badly soiled the living room sofa (we found it covered with an old quilt) and protested when Lisa applied his security deposit to clean it. " 'You should pay *me* to stay in that house!' " she recalled him telling her. Given all the positive online reviews, I had thought this case was an outlier. In Lisa's rendition of the story, that guest came across as an inconsiderate boar. Now, suddenly, I found myself wanting to compare notes with him.

We all have our priorities, too. While the Douglases seemed oblivious to the mildewed caulking around the bathtub, for example, in the house manual they included very specific instructions about how to maintain the kitchen, including this request: "We would appreciate it if you would use a dish towel or hot pad for opening both microwave and oven doors, as the brass handles stay shiny a lot longer if they are not touched." We wondered whether we were supposed to use the torn, burned pot holders hanging beside the oven for that purpose.

Instead of taking steps to provide for the comfort of people who were paying a hefty sum to stay in their house, they acted as if we were a friend or relative whom they had kindly lent it to for a short interval. So they had not bothered even to do little things, like empty their toiletries from the bathroom shelves, to make space for ours. And rather than leaving room for miscommunication with Madame Lamotte by e-mail, a phone call to confirm that the house would be ready for our arrival would have been appropriate under the circumstances.

After a sublime afternoon visiting the carefully tended gardens of the château in Villandry, reputed to be some of the most spectacular in

France, the jungle-like overgrowth at the winemaker's cottage seemed even more ridiculous. That evening I sent an e-mail to our landlords. "We have wrestled with what to do about the hundreds of rotten apples that are littering the driveway and overgrown vines everywhere," I wrote. "I opened the kitchen window yesterday and trimmed the creeping vine that was obscuring the view, then emptied the water that had collected in the wheelbarrow and began to fill it with the rotten apples. It was just too much."

Lisa's reply landed in the wee hours of Sunday morning. "We would never have known about the situation if you hadn't written us about it – we do so appreciate knowing what is going on when we're far away," she wrote, and went on to speculate that their new gardener "did the French thing and took the month of August off." She attached an e-mail her husband had sent asking him to work overtime to clean things up.

A day later there had been no sign of the AWOL gardener and no reply to my next (still diplomatic) e-mail about our problems with the interior. That was when Ken lobbed a hand grenade by e-mail. After listing all our issues with the winemaker's cottage and suggesting measures to rectify them, he told our landlords that the place was like the house in the 1960s TV sitcom *Green Acres*. They were certainly old enough to remember the show, starring Eddie Albert and Eva Gabor as a couple who give up their sophisticated Manhattan lifestyle and move to a ramshackle farmhouse.

An analogy between the winemaker's cottage and *Green Acres* could not be mistaken for a compliment. (The show inspired the pseudonym I have given this couple; Oliver and Lisa Douglas were the main characters in *Green Acres*.) Lisa's reply, which landed half an hour later, was terse: "Please let me know where to send your money back so that you can find some other place better suited. Let us know when you will be leaving."

We had been expelled from what was apparently her idea of Eden, but not ours.

What Lisa no doubt realized, having had far more experience with home rentals than we had, was that the success of any deal in the sharing economy depends on mutual expectations. And in this case the gap between "guest" and "host," in sharing economy parlance, was too profound. While we thought the problem could be solved with a couple of days of gardening work and a thorough cleaning, she had apparently decided that nothing was going to make us happy. So she chose not to even try.

We were eating dinner when Ken checked his e-mail, turned to me and said, "They want us to leave." I had cooked mussels steamed in one of the many delicious and inexpensive local wines, seasoned with shallots, plus chives and parsley from the herb box outside the door. And at the moment that I got this news, I had my hands in the soup.

"Where are we going to go?" I asked, reaching for my napkin. The timing could not have been worse. Most rentals run from Saturday to Saturday, and our dispute reached a head on a Sunday. We were also on the brink of the *vendange* (grape harvest), a festival time when it is especially difficult to find lodgings in the Loire Valley.

We arranged to stay in the winemaker's cottage for five more nights and worked out the financial details. Later in the evening, Lisa began steps to wire us a refund from her bank in the United States heartland.

When the money did not land on September 1 as promised, I panicked. Then, gritting my teeth, I sent a polite e-mail confirming the account information. It turned out that Lisa had run into a snafu with the transfer and had to go there personally to straighten it out. So she hopped a red-eye flight from California and traveled to rural Kansas to do that. It took four more days for the money to be shifted, in installments of $2,000 each. We received the last payment on September 5, the day we checked out.

Somewhat shell-shocked, we abandoned the idea of spending three months in one place and, revisiting the sharing economy websites, charted a more itinerant journey. Distances made it impractical to inspect places in advance, but to hedge our bets we decided to limit reservations to two weeks. Starting with alternate accommodations in another part of the Loire Valley, and ending our odyssey with an apartment in Paris, we left open the seven weeks in between.

The disruption in Eden consumed precious time and energy during the first ten days of our French sojourn. For some people that would have been an entire vacation. I suspect that many travelers, not wanting to spoil their holiday, would simply make the best of a disappointing rental and move on. Much relieved once we settled our dispute, though still awaiting our refund from the Douglases, that is what we did during our remaining days in Amboise.

The Michelin Green Guide, *Châteaux of the Loire,* recommends visitors set aside half a day to see Amboise. We explored it at a more leisurely pace. From the terrace of the château, we admired the panoramic view of slate-roof houses overlooking the river, then paid homage to Leonardo da Vinci, who is presumed to be buried in the Gothic Chapelle St. Hubert, on the château ramparts.

On another afternoon, we visited Clos Lucé, the manor house where François I lived, and where da Vinci stayed, at the king's invitation, starting in 1516. Da Vinci is a town hero, and models of his many inventions, built from his drawings, are on display at Clos Lucé. Da Vinci is also credited with designing the double staircase in the château in Chambord, a grand edifice in the middle of a hunting forest that François I built after da Vinci's death.

A longer day trip took us about 80 miles south and east of Amboise to the village of Gargilesse-Dampierre. During our two-hour drive there, we passed apple orchards, as well as fields of corn and sunflowers. Columbine, which I had tried so hard to cultivate in my Brooklyn window box – without success – grew wild on the side of the road to a height of two feet.

Gargilesse-Dampierre, in the lush valley of the Creuse River, measures its population in the hundreds. Long a favorite spot for artists and writers, its well-kept homes and manicured main street convey an aura of affluence. On a visit to the cottage where George Sand supposedly wrote most of her books, I was amused to see that she worked at a very tiny table. Accustomed to my large home office in Brooklyn, I had already adapted to the architecture and furniture in my new surroundings. Our bedroom in the winemaker's cottage had a gait-leg table that I could have used as a desk, but there was no space for a chair, and I couldn't reach it sitting beside it on the edge of the bed. (Another quirk.) Instead, I did all my writing in the tower bedroom, using the trundle bed as a desk and pulling up a chair beside it.

On the other side of the Atlantic, Jack was adjusting to college. Initially, he texted several times a day about what seemed like very mundane issues: how his roommate didn't show up, whether he got to class on time, how he was sitting in the front of the room to make it easier to concentrate in large lecture halls. Did he really need our support, I wondered, or was he testing our response time, trying to figure out just how available we would be to him once we arrived in France?

The day classes began, he wrote, "I got out of my first [class] today, like 15 minutes ago, and it went well. I see a real connection between what we're learning and the real world. . . . It seems that people who actually enjoy learning go on to do better in life." While we were regrouping in France, wrestling with plans gone awry, Jack's transition seemed to be going much more smoothly.

With a bit of reconnoitering, I found the path leading down to the Loire, by then littered with almonds. (More fallen fruit. A metaphor for our dashed expectations?) But access to it was not from "in front of the house," as Lisa had described it in her e-mail. The path began at a neighbor's property line, passed alongside the cottage and ended at the Tours Highway, which separated the Douglases' property from the Loire. The climb back up would have been too steep for Ken while we were there, so we never walked it together.

Instead, we did our strolls along the Loire starting in the village, and in the process we became regulars at a spectacular boulangerie-pâtisserie called Gauvreau. A stop there was the reward for our exercise. By the time we left Amboise, we had partly eaten our way through Gauvreau's display of pastries. They ranged from old French standbys, like éclairs and *tartelettes au citron* (lemon tarts), to an exotic concoction called *Le Thai*, which was mango mousse on a curried ginger biscuit and topped with a crunchy coconut cookie. My favorite was the *Alexandra* – a chocolate cake covered with rolls of meringue that looked like dreadlocks. No matter which pastry we ordered, if we got it *à emporter* (to take out), rather than to eat on the terrace, the clerk would put it on a silver-foil square plate and wrap it like a gift, in the shape of a pyramid.

On Fridays and Sundays we combined our visit to Gauvreau with a stop at the outdoor market along the Loire. All food, except beef, was much less expensive than in the U.S., especially the cheese and pâté, which I could have eaten for every meal. We stocked up on the abundant summer fruits, including the ultra-sweet *Reine Claude* plums, recognizable by their small size (about two bites' worth) and green skins. Cantaloupes were cheaper by the threesome or foursome, and I quickly picked up on the local protocol: Tell the vendor how many you want and when you plan to eat them. With a Magic Marker, the merchant will label the melons with Roman numerals indicating the order in which they should be consumed. Tomatoes were also in season, and we used them to prepare fresh pasta sauce, seasoned with the homegrown basil that the wisteria hadn't managed to strangle.

Once *les vacances* ended, the gardener arrived to clean up the land around the winemaker's cottage, including all the rotten apples. We picked fresh ones from the tree and made applesauce.

The Eden that we had envisioned from the photos, website comments, my correspondence and lengthy phone call with the Douglases fell far short of what awaited us at the winemaker's cottage. My one regret, as we departed, was leaving the sprawling fig tree in the garden, laden with an abundant and not-quite-ripe autumn crop.

5

THE HOUSE
on rue SAINTE

OUR SECOND FRENCH RENTAL was a rambling old family home in Le Puy-Notre-Dame, a tiny village that for centuries has been a stop on the Camino de Compostela – the ancient pilgrimage route to the Cathedral of Santiago de Compostela, Spain, where, according to legend, the Apostle St. James is buried.

While pilgrims may chart a course there, our arrival was considerably more haphazard. Distances in the Loire Valley don't seem big as the crow flies, but traveling through the small towns, with their narrow streets and roundabouts (a quaint and efficient precursor to traffic lights), can be extremely slow. So after our expulsion from what wasn't quite Eden, it made sense to choose a region in the Loire Valley that we hadn't yet explored.

By consulting our guidebooks, we identified the area around Saumur, about 80 miles west of Amboise, as a possibility. Both the *Lonely*

Planet France guide, which I had on my Kindle, and *Fodor's France,* on Ken's iPad, depicted a photogenic city with its own château, at the center of a key Loire Valley wine region. Among the listings in the vicinity that showed up on Airbnb was a house in Le Puy-Notre-Dame that looked spacious and comfortable.

It took us two hours to wind our way to Saumur from Amboise, and another 20 minutes to reach Le Puy-Notre-Dame – it wasn't nearly as close to Saumur as the listing suggested. As one approached, along a road with vineyards on either side, the three stone steeples of the church of Notre Dame became visible in the distance. The village is named for this church, which dates to the Middle Ages, and for the fact that it towers over everything around it. (The French word *"puy"* comes from the Celtic *"peuch,"* which means hilltop.)

About a quarter of a mile before one reaches the town gate is a sign that says *Petite Cité de Caractère* (little village of character), a distinction Le Puy-Notre-Dame shares with 38 other Loire Valley villages, including Gargilesse-Dampierre, the legendary haunt of George Sand, which we had visited the previous week.

From the town gate, our GPS directed us through the labyrinthine streets that project out from the church in all directions, and after a sharp turn onto one of them, appropriately named rue Sainte, announced that we had arrived at our destination.

We sat there, our car motor idling, confused. The Victorian townhouse looked nothing like the photo of the home we had rented via Airbnb – a much older stone building with a garden visible in front. Finally, a door opened and a woman waved, confirming that we were in the right place. This was Virginie, the cleaning lady, who had been assigned to let us in.

She was 42, rail-thin, dressed in straight-leg jeans, high-top wedge sneakers and a light pink down jacket, with purple eye shadow, and purple stud earrings around her eyes and lips to match. Quite a contrast to the prim-and-proper Madame Lamotte.

Our tour of the house on rue Sainte began with the attached stable that serves as the garage. One drives into it from the steep, narrow street that runs in front of the house – a tight maneuver that gave us one more reason to be glad we hadn't arrived in anything larger than a compact Peugeot 308. The next task was to close the two, 20-foot-high wooden doors facing rue Sainte and lock them: Stacked on top of each other were two bolts, and Virginie gave us a skeleton key that fit the lock underneath and turned twice, to the right. Then there was a gigantic iron bar attached to the stone wall of the house that one lifted diagonally across one of the doors and slipped into a slot near the bolts. *Voilà!*

Given that the population of Le Puy-Notre-Dame was a mere 1,300, and that we hadn't seen a soul on our two-minute drive through the little village of character, all this seemed a bit excessive. But it was not our house, so we paid close attention to the instructions.

Next, Virginie led us through the garage, piled with detritus on both sides, past another car parked in front of ours. After exiting out the other side, we watched as she pulled two more large wooden doors, along a rusty track, to close them. This brought us into a garden and courtyard in the back of the house. I recognized it as the vantage point from which the exterior photo on Airbnb had been taken. A wooden door with a lift latch led into the house.

Inside, it was considerably larger and more charming than portrayed in the photos. It had a twisting wooden staircase, with floors of tile or wood throughout. Our bedroom – one of five – was down the hall from a large bathroom with a claw-foot tub. There was a children's room with bunk beds and a play area filled with toys, another small bedroom and the master bedroom, which we were not to enter. A separate small staircase led from the second floor to the attic door.

Downstairs was a large living room with a fireplace and windows facing rue Sainte. The kitchen had a vintage butcher's table that served as a work surface and a high-performance stove installed in the old hearth. An antique armoire held a collection of mismatched bistro-cast-off dishes. Empty wine bottles displayed on top of it, and on a shelf above the sink, suggested that the Parisian-based owners had more than a casual interest in wine.

Adjacent to the kitchen was another bedroom – what was probably at one time a maid's room. It faced the garden and had an en suite bath.

"It's a big house," Virginie kept saying, as she showed us around. (She spoke a smattering of English, which was just a little better than our French.) So much for downsizing, but at $106 a night – a special rate the owner offered us since we would be staying for two weeks – the daily cost was just $3 more than we had been paying in Amboise.

Concluding the grand tour in the foyer, Virginie seemed eager to be on her way. She handed us the front door keys, on a keychain with a four-inch-long stuffed bulldog attached to it. The skeleton key was for the bottom lock, she gestured, and the small round key was for the top. With that, she left us to our own devices on rue Sainte. After a bit of unpacking, we went out to explore the village.

On foot, as by car, Le Puy-Notre-Dame had a ghost-like feeling. There was a boulangerie, a *tabac* (tobacco shop), a pharmacy, a hairdresser, a small grocer, two restaurants and a tourist office. The latter was self-service, consisting of a room on street level with various brochures about the area on display. It probably would not have been there at all but for the fact that the church was a point of interest.

According to an informational trifold available at the church, Louis XI visited often during the 15th century, and "The treasury contained beautiful works of art, jewels, trophies and reliquaries." Inside, it retained its Gothic architecture, but not much else.

Houses, like the church, were an architectural mélange, with historical markers on some buildings (or remnants of them) dating to the 15th century. The Victorian façade and interior details of our house might well have been added to a much older structure. Despite modern updates here and there, it had retained many details of centuries past.

The bottom lock on the front door, for example, still opened with a skeleton key. And when we returned, after our brief stroll, it wouldn't budge. By then Virginie was off the grid. So we phoned Pierre, the Parisian-based owner, for some door-opening tips. He explained that on the second revolution of the bottom lock, you must pull the door toward you.

We felt pretty stupid, but were smarter going forward. From then on, no matter who greeted us upon arrival at a rental property, we did not part ways until we had tested the locks. As for our adventures on rue Sainte, they were just getting started.

6

CUISINE VOLANTE

HE FOLLOWING NIGHT we phoned Pierre again. This time it was about the high-performance stove that wouldn't light.

Designed for restaurant use, this behemoth – a Godin Souveraine – was much fancier than the stove we had at home, and we were excited about the prospect of cooking on it. The wok burner, which extended from the front to the back of the stove, was a novelty, since we enjoy making Asian food. A propane tank that sat under the kitchen counter fueled this burner plus two others. The tank connected to the stove via a narrow pipe drilled through the hearth.

Like the front door, the Godin had its quirks. For example, sometimes it was necessary to push the little button on the propane tank before starting the stove, Pierre explained, during our second call to him in 24 hours. Who knew? We put the potatoes up to boil on the smallest burner and preheated the electric stovetop grill on which we planned to cook our pork chops.

Then all the house lights went out.

"It's your turn to call Pierre," Ken said.

"But you two have such a nice rapport," I whined, to no avail.

The issue, not surprisingly, was a circuit breaker, positioned in a box in the front hall. On the line from Paris, Pierre tried to troubleshoot.

This turned out to be a five-cell-phone operation: While Ken stood on one of the kitchen chairs to reach the electric box, I shone the flashlight app from his cell phone on the circuit breakers, using my own cell phone to talk to Pierre on his cell phone. Fortunately, he spoke English much better than we spoke French. Unfortunately, his recall of the arrangement of the circuit breakers wasn't quite as good.

At the other end of the conversation, Pierre's wife must have sensed the lack of progress. On her own cell phone, she called a neighbor on his cell phone. He arrived within minutes to flip the appropriate switches, and we finished cooking dinner.

As homeowners, we knew that there was a more profound problem that all our cell phones could not solve: The grill needed to be on its own circuit, and wasn't. Surely Pierre knew this already. But perhaps as a goodwill gesture, he scheduled a visit by the electrician/plumber (in rural France, one person often performs both functions) the following day. So there we were, once again sitting in an old house, waiting around for the plumber. We had become so at home in France that we were now doing the same kinds of things we did when we were at home in Brooklyn. Except that this wasn't our house. Or our trusty workman.

In what may be an international custom with plumbers, this one arrived 90 minutes late, and with profuse apologies charmed us into excusing the inconvenience. When Ken explained (using his growing

French vocabulary) that we owned an old house and that appliances should not be on the same circuit as light fixtures, *Le Plombier* (as he introduced himself) heartily agreed. Then, without giving any indication that he would correct the problem, he offered this expert advice: "Do not run the electric grill on the stove at a temperature higher than the No. 4 setting – or maybe No. 3 – or *'Pouf!'*" (I wasn't sure whether this was French or English), the circuit would blow. He also noted, in passing, that the grill was very dirty and suggested that we clean it.

Since we had not actually used the grill yet, I hoped he understood that we were not responsible for its condition, but Le Plombier did have a point. Ken put into the garbage all the greasy black material that was under the electric coils, and the night before the next Thursday garbage day, we rolled that greasy black stuff, in the large garbage can, out onto rue Sainte, where we left it for the garbage men to pick up the following morning.

One month after our departure from Le Puy-Notre-Dame, I got an e-mail from Pierre, saying, "We cannot find the black fake stones that were in the grill. Can you tell me where are they?"

I apologized for our mistake, passed along Le Plombier's opinion that the grill was a fire hazard and offered to reimburse him for the fake stones that we had mistaken for greasy charcoal. Pierre seemed to take it in stride. "No problem for the stones!" he replied.

As we continued cooking on the grill (minus the fake stones), we did not turn the knob above the No. 3 temperature setting, because at No. 4 it did, indeed, go "Pouf!"

I, meantime, had made some progress scrubbing the kitchen sink, which had been coated with grime when we arrived. The kitchen, about three times the size of the one in our Brooklyn house, was extremely attractive and well equipped, but let's just say it was not the kind of place where one could eat off the floor.

Though I would not describe myself as a neat freak, a reasonably clean, functioning kitchen, which had so far eluded us, was a high priority. Part of the plan for our French adventure was to prepare our own meals with food bought at the open-air *marchés volants* (roving markets), scheduled once a week – or sometimes more often – in particular towns. Inspired by the French term for the markets, we called our makeshift meals, prepared with whatever ingredients and equipment were available, *cuisine volante*.

Le Puy-Notre-Dame was too small to have such a market, so we sought out ones in other towns nearby. To find them, we consulted the market schedules posted in tourist offices. Another source of leads were the vendors at food mobiles that made the rounds to various markets throughout the week. I saved the wrappers from the pâté bought from charcuterie trucks, for example, since they listed the other markets where we could find them.

Once we got oriented, we began planning itineraries that would combine a trip to the market in a particular town with touring the nearest château – either in the same village or one nearby. We paired the Monday market in Doué-la-Fontaine (about six miles away) with a visit to the Château d'Ussé, which was the inspiration for the story of *Sleeping Beauty*, and perhaps the castle on *The Wonderful World of Disney* television series. We timed our visit to the château in Chinon to coincide with the huge Thursday market there, held along the Vienne River.

As for operating the Godin, it was not for the faint of heart or mechanically challenged. We never again needed to push the little button on the propane tank, but turning on the stove, like driving a car with a manual shift, required some bilateral coordination. First, you depressed and turned the knob that corresponded to the burner you wanted to light, cocking your head toward the burner until you heard the hissing of gas. Then, with the other hand, you depressed the igniter switch, being careful to move your head away from the burner so that your hair did not catch fire when the flame came on. If, for some reason, the burner still did not start, you needed to repeat the process using a match, instead of the stove's igniter.

No matter what we cooked on these burners, it tasted better than the same items prepared back home. And, with a little practice, I began to feel like I was in charge of the stove, rather than the reverse.

7

WRITER in RESIDENCE

"I have to write to be happy whether I get paid for it or not. But it is a hell of a disease to be born with."
– Ernest Hemingway 1940 letter to Charles Scribner, quoted in
Ernest Hemingway on Writing

SINCE LEAVING NEW YORK I hadn't posted much on social media. I really wasn't in the mood. Between all the time spent online finding alternative accommodations, and dealing with the hassles once we got to each location, life in Europe wasn't anything like what I had imagined it would be. I could visualize a Facebook post, ten days after we embarked on what should have been an exciting new lifestyle. There would have been a picture of me, sweat streaming down my face as I lugged a suitcase up yet another flight of stairs, with a caption that read, "Nothing in France has gone according to plan. Trying to regroup."

But after two days in Le Puy-Notre-Dame, I was starting to feel more upbeat. I posted a photo of the former liveryman's quarters that I had adopted as my workspace. "Here's my office in the rambling Victorian that will be our home in rural France for the next two weeks," I wrote. When we planned to spend three months overseas, I could not have envisioned a more poetic place from which to write.

This room in the house on rue Sainte wasn't pictured in the Airbnb listing, and I was overjoyed to find it beckoning to me upon our arrival. Above the old stable that had been turned into a garage, it was a few steps down from the first staircase landing, in its own little wing. It had a terra-cotta floor, wood ceiling beams, and walls stenciled with vines. The room faced the backyard, with treetops and the red-tiled roof of the garden shed visible from its window. A small attached room, with bookcases and a sofa, was a cozy library.

I photographed my new office from the top of the steps, looking down into the room, the celery-colored door visible on the right. Against the right-hand wall was the small antique desk where I had set up my laptop. Above it hung a framed map of the French wine regions. In the left-hand corner of that little room, under the window, was an old armchair upholstered in velvet to match the door.

My friend Dan, responding to my Facebook post, promptly put up a link to one of Vincent van Gogh's paintings of his bedroom in Arles – the arrangement of the furniture and placement of the window were the same, though it was Provence, not the Loire Valley, that was the subject of van Gogh's painting. Other friends reminded me of literary legends who thrived in France, among them Gustave Flaubert and Honoré de Balzac, and wished me happy writing. It was an absolute delight to hear from them.

This was, in fact, the first time in a year that I had felt inspired to write. The great passion for my work, which had driven me to change careers in 1986 after six years of practicing law, and kept me writing prolifically for more than two decades, had been completely wrung out of me by the time I left my former company. In France both my energy and enthusiasm for work returned – and in a big way.

From the winemaker's cottage, I had sent e-mails to a few friends about all the things that had gone wrong. Initially, those e-mails, along with the replies, were a form of therapy and provided me with a virtual support system. At the same time, I noticed that people seemed intrigued. They wanted to know more, and to hear what happened next. I became so occupied with this correspondence that I put aside other work projects I planned to pursue during our time abroad. The journalist in me couldn't ignore the story that I was living. Of course, I didn't know what lay ahead – or whether the misadventures were behind us. But maybe it would turn into a book.

From the liveryman's quarters in Le Puy-Notre-Dame, I composed essays, in real time, about our daily activities and the emotions that accompanied this huge transition. Instead of pen and paper, I relied on the Evernote app that synced to my laptop, iPad and iPhone. That way, if I thought of something while we were out and about, I could make a note of it on my iPhone and then pull up the same material on my computer later. This enabled me to write more quickly than I could on past trips, when, in order to create articles, I would need to flip through my notebooks and stitch together paragraph fragments. Technology was my friend.

Still, I would be taking a huge risk. Previously, I had generally gone with an assignment in hand. This time I was "writing on spec": without a contract guaranteeing that my work would be accepted and that I would get paid.

With all that was happening in France, there was no time to write a book proposal, and, besides, it would have been premature. I didn't know how the story would end. Rather than submit a half-baked proposal and have it rejected, I forged ahead.

Meantime, I found something about the old liveryman's quarters totally energizing. It was only half the size of my office at home, and, at least on the surface, a lot less comfortable. Instead of my $600 ergonomic desk chair, with its cushioned seat and back that moved with me, I was sitting in a wood café chair with no support for my lumbar – or any other body part. And I had traded my elaborate computer setup, with two screens and an adjustable keyboard tray, for a laptop. Yet while at home I constantly ached from work, especially in my neck and shoulders, in France I felt no such pain.

As at home, I slept in segments, waking up after four or five hours, with my mind racing. But whereas back in Brooklyn it was usually because I was worried about one thing or another, now it was because some thought about all the new stimuli around me had just entered my head. Knowing it would be gone by morning, I got up and wrote for an hour or so until sleepiness returned.

It helped to have a separate room where I could do this without badly disturbing Ken. On past trips, when we occupied smaller quarters, he would occasionally stumble out of bed at night and find me sitting on the bathroom floor, scribbling in my notebook. We would refer to this setup as the "bureau," wherever we happened to be – whether it was Danang, Delhi or Denpasar, for example.

In Le Puy-Notre-Dame I would tiptoe out of our bedroom and,

using the flashlight app on my iPhone, descend the creaky stairs to the old liveryman's quarters and boot up my computer.

Just as I did as a blogger at my previous job, I gave each note a title or headline and would work on several at a time. I knew from that experience that the final product might turn out very differently from how I first envisioned it. Such creative license was very liberating.

Suddenly I felt that latitude again, but this time it was without a steady paycheck. That didn't diminish my morning euphoria, which I have learned to harness in my work. Income from our house rental would cover all our expenses for three months, I told myself, so this was a unique opportunity to experiment. But by late evening, when I was exhausted from the day's activities, pessimism would set in. No matter how productive I had been that day, I wondered whether all my efforts would be wasted.

At least a few times a week, I turned specific notes into e-mails to friends and family whom I thought they would interest. I didn't do that with the expectation that any of them would reply at length, or even at all. But, given the quixotic nature of the undertaking, I found it less intimidating to direct my musings to specific people rather than project them into the vast unknown.

8

HOUSEGUESTS

~~~

W E HAD BEEN in the *Petite Cité de Caractère* for less than a week when our friends Barbara and Ray came to visit.

My friendship with Barbara went back 25 years, to a time when we were both consultants to a non-profit that promoted alternative dispute resolution. Both of our lives had changed dramatically since then. Ray, whom she married in 2012, is a late-in-life love. They had met serendipitously in 2004 while waiting for a plane at New York's JFK airport. He was a corporate executive who had been living in Brussels for many years; she was relocating there for a job. We had last spent time together when they hosted us for several days, in 2013, at their elegant, sprawling central Brussels apartment.

Our French rendezvous, one year in the planning, was originally to have been in the winemaker's cottage. We had invited them to be our guests there and, based on the website photos, had offered them their own room with an en suite bath. After that, they planned to attend a film festival in San Sebastián, Spain, with stops along the way at various high-end hotels and restaurants.

But once we got to Amboise, we wondered how they would react to our lodgings there. During the time that I spent in what would have been their bedroom, writing, and when I showered in the en suite bath, I bumped my head repeatedly, and I am a little over five feet tall. On the HomeAway website, one former guest, who said he is 5'10", had written, "I can't imagine a taller person staying in this room without wearing a hard hat!"

When I sent Barbara an e-mail, very briefly summarizing what had happened and giving her our new address, she replied, "Bet there is a story here." She obviously knew me well!

Ken and I, meantime, had been taking bets about how long it would be until our Brussels friends made their excuses and checked into a hotel, and whether they would have actually spent a single night with us at the winemaker's cottage before they did. (I said yes; Ken said no.)

Fortunately, we could put aside that debate when we moved to Le Puy-Notre-Dame. On rue Sainte they would have their own wing overlooking the garden, again with an en suite bath. Admittedly, the three steps leading up to it from the kitchen were a dead giveaway that it was the former maid's quarters. But, as I explained when I gave them the grand tour, this room and ours were the only two in which Virginie had made the beds – a signal that this was where we were supposed to sleep. The master bedroom, she indicated, was off-limits. If our Brussels friends minded any of this, they were polite enough not to say so.

They arrived with an armful of fresh flowers and an enormous care package. Ken, who is an Asian food aficionado, had asked Barbara to bring oyster sauce and ginger – two ingredients that we so far had difficulty finding in the Loire Valley but which we knew were available at a store down the block from their Brussels apartment. In addition to these items, Barbara had brought many others that she knew we would appreciate: coconut milk, four bottles of Asian beer, sate powder, dried lemongrass and a powdered Middle Eastern spice mixture called zatar (made with sesame seeds, dried thyme, oregano and marjoram). There was even a bottle of Belgian Ketjep, which they insisted bore no resemblance to our ketchup back home, and for which we would ultimately find many uses. Our traveling larder had immediately doubled in size. Fortunately our small car had a large trunk.

As an aperitif, I uncorked a bottle of Champagne, which I served with locally produced goat cheese. The main course was meatless pasta sauce, prepared with tomatoes bought at the previous day's market in Chinon. Dessert was an assortment of pastries from a shop in Saumur.

For the previous three weeks, we had lived in relative isolation, as a social unit of two. Our interactions with other people, limited by language and culture, had so far focused on necessities – like food and electricity. By contrast, being with old friends was a relief.

It was a happy reunion as we lingered at the long, zinc-topped kitchen table, catching up on personal news and comparing notes about our big transitions: Ray's retirement from a high-level post at a Belgian company and my resignation from a dead-end job at The Content Mill. Both he and Barbara, who had retired three years earlier, had positions on corporate boards, but other than that, their lives, like ours, had become much less structured. Some of us were taking it better than others.

The conversation was fueled by glasses of what had already become our house wine: La Cave d'Augustin Florent Bourgueil 2014, a complex, very fruity red with hints of raspberry. Ray, who is a wine connoisseur, praised our selection before Ken gave away my secret: It had been purchased in the local Carrefour supermarket for €4 per bottle. La Cave d'Augustin Florent happens to be the store brand, and Bourgueil is the appellation for Loire Valley wines produced from the cabernet franc grape.

I had discovered it the way I always shop for wine in Europe, which is to shadow residents through supermarket wine aisles and watch what they buy. If the store isn't busy, I look to see which wine selection has the most bottles missing on the shelf. This Bourgueil was so good that I had gone back for more.

By the morning after our welcome dinner, I was concerned about whether our houseguests might find everything else to their taste. During our previous get-together, we were in their home, with surroundings familiar to them. Now they were roughing it in what surely looked to them like a rundown rental, nowhere near the part of the Loire Valley that they had initially planned to visit.

Though we were old friends, we had different budgets and different ways of doing things. Travel together in a foreign country tends to accentuate such disparities. For the rest of their journey, Barbara had prepared a loose-leaf notebook with their itinerary, reservation confirmations, background material and a printout of the two-week weather forecast. Though we, too, heavily researched our travel destinations, our approach to daily activities tended to be a bit more impromptu – to say the least.

Fortunately, our guests were very willing to go along with it. Having maneuvered their car, with considerable effort, into the old stable that functioned as our garage, they left it there for the next two days. On Day 1, we dropped them at the medieval château in Chinon, which we had visited a couple of days earlier after shopping at the town's Thursday market.

The château, which was a favorite residence of Henry II of England, achieved Hollywood fame as the setting of the 1968 film *The Lion In Winter*, starring Peter O'Toole as Henry and Katharine Hepburn as his wife, Eleanor of Aquitaine. A story of family and political rivalries during Christmas 1183, the movie plot is invented but great drama. And though it wasn't actually filmed in Chinon, it does inspire a visit to the château. A six-year, €17 million renovation, recently completed, restored the ramparts and added high-tech exhibits that deliver a historical libretto.

Although they focus on the story of how Henry's three surviving sons competed to succeed him, Eleanor, one of the wealthiest and most powerful women of her time, was for me the far more intriguing character. During a life that lasted more than 80 years, she was, through a tangle of political events, first Queen of France and then Queen of England. She was married twice; bore ten children, three of whom became kings; and went on two crusades. Hepburn won an Oscar for her portrayal of Eleanor, as by then King Henry's estranged older wife (she was 11 years his senior), clinging to control of the vast swath of southwestern France known as the Aquitaine.

These, and other, aspects of her fascinating life, are also the subject of several popular and historical biographies, for sale in châteaux gift shops. We visited her tomb at Fontevraud Abbey, about half an hour's drive from Chinon. Her effigy there portrays the highly educated Eleanor, who was a patron of contemporary literary figures, reading a book. A woman after my own heart.

While Barbara and Ray visited the château in Chinon, we explored the old town, with its twisting, cobblestone streets, stone gables and half-timbered houses. We reconvened for a light lunch and, appropriately enough, a glass of Chinon wine at a bar overlooking a vineyard, before taking off for a visit to the Musée Rabelais, in Seuilly, less than three miles away.

This museum is in the 16th-century country house that was built by Antoine Rabelais, father of his better-known son François I, the French Renaissance man. The old servants' quarters (this seemed to be a continuing theme), with their huge central fireplace, had been turned into an exhibit about his career, as a doctor, anatomist and writer. Perhaps far more impressive were the gardens, which overlooked an apple orchard and a vineyard, both replanted to look as they did in days of yore, and which were heavy with fruit when we visited. The grapes that we sampled from these vines were already beginning to look like those on the front of the Sun-Maid Raisin package.

We got a slow start the next day, since it was pouring when we woke up. Not that there was such a thing as really sleeping late on rue Sainte. The church up the street from our house had two bells. One rang on the hour, the other rang at two minutes past the hour, and once on the half hour. They rang roughly in unison for the Angelus prayer at 7 a.m., noon and 7 p.m. And, mercifully, they both went on hiatus between 10 p.m. and 7 a.m. This was a village for larks; others could treat the morning bells like a snooze button.

When I went downstairs to make breakfast, I found Ray at the kitchen table, contentedly sipping the coffee he had prepared and catching up on world news. Reports of a migrant crisis, which broke a couple of days after we left home, were growing ever more grizzly. Refugees from war-torn Syria who survived the dangerous passage across the Mediterranean were being stranded at European border crossings. The story would continue to unfold long after our return to the U.S., as death tolls multiplied into the thousands. Already, the news was appalling: A truck, filled with about 70 bodies of those who had been asphyxiated in the summer heat, was found on the outskirts of Vienna; another 150 people drowned in the Mediterranean. Photographs of smiling refugees in tattered clothing conveyed their elation at arriving safely to freedom.

Our housing quibbles seemed trivial compared to their travails. Good fortune was such a privilege.

"Have you missed corporate life?" I asked Ray as I sliced a melon for breakfast.

"Not for a minute," he replied.

Because of the weather, we abandoned plans to do a two-hour drive to Château de Chenonceau, which we had not yet visited and were saving to see with Barbara and Ray. Instead, once the skies brightened, we took them to Montsoreau, where on the second Sunday of each month, including this one, there was a flea market along the river. Without question, the setting enhanced the display of many items of uncertain provenance. But it did lend some insight into the source for furnishings of both our Loire Valley rentals.

From the flea market, we drove along the Loire to where it meets the Vienne River in the neighboring former fishing village of Can-des-Saint-Martin, which somehow made it onto the list of the most scenic villages of France, and then to the also overrated Château d'Azay-le-Rideau, set on an island in the middle of the Indre River. It is occasionally described as a small version of Chenonceau. At least at that moment, the analogy seemed undeserved, since one side of it, plus the roof, were under a tarp for renovation and did not show to best advantage. As we well knew, all houses need upkeep, and these establishments needed more upkeep than others. After that, we decided by consensus that a visit to troglodyte caves would be overload. As we got in the car to go home, Barbara said how much she was enjoying our "meandering" mode of travel.

Back at the house, everybody helped cook dinner. Ken made a chicken stir fry using the oyster sauce and ginger that our guests had brought. Ray cut up a huge head of cauliflower, which we had purchased that day at the Montsoreau market, and using the zatar mélange, I prepared a rough approximation of a roasted cauliflower recipe that I make back home. More *cuisine volante*.

Our houseguests went back on the grid the following morning. At breakfast, Barbara showed us a map, on which she had charted the next 11 stops on their two-week journey. Every breakfast, lunch and dinner had been scheduled, with numerical markings on the map to correspond with entries in her loose-leaf notebook.

In a subsequent e-mail exchange, she would describe a Bordeaux vineyard tour, and send the name of a guide she recommended to show us around the *pintxo* bars of San Sebastián. I replied with detailed advice based on our exploration of Angers, where we had seen the 14th-century tapestry of the Apocalypse, on display at the château, and the Musée Jean-Lurçat, a museum of contemporary tapestries housed in a 12th-century hospital. "Because, like you and Ray, we now have what Ken calls 'the gift of time,' we were able to visit these two places on separate days, which was a luxury, since each alone is a lot to absorb," I wrote, describing Angers as a city that looks a bit like a small Paris, on the banks of the Maine. "If you return to the region, I suggest you do the same."

Deep down, I suspect we both knew that I would not take her well-meaning advice, nor she mine. While a guide can point out details we might otherwise have missed, we meanderers fear such rigor will divert us from new discoveries and uncharted paths. As friends, we continue to remind each other of alternate perspectives. How boring life would be if we were all the same.

After two more months on the road, we returned home to find a package from Barbara and Ray waiting for us. Inside were two linen dish towels – one printed with cheeses of France (most of which I had by then sampled); and the other, showing classic French kitchen tools (some of which we had used in our various rentals). I vaguely recalled Barbara buying the towels at the gift shop in Château d'Azay-le-Rideau.

Enclosed was a handwritten note that read:

Welcome back to the U.S.!

Ray and I thought you might find yourselves homesick for France, so maybe this will help evoke fond memories of wonderful kitchen time.

Hugs, R&B

9

SAUMUR SKETCHES

~~~

THOUGH I WAS NEVER FOND of organized religion and hadn't been to synagogue since Jack's bar mitzvah, it was odd to be outside New York during the Jewish High Holidays. For several days leading up to Rosh Hashanah, the start of this eight-day period, I had e-mail prompts from various cooking apps directing me to recipes for brisket – a traditional holiday food. It was a cut of meat that would have been difficult to procure anywhere near Le Puy-Notre-Dame, even if I had the vocabulary to order it. And on Rosh Hashanah morning, as on all mornings on rue Sainte, I was awakened by church bells at 7 a.m. We were spending this Jewish holiday, which focuses on sin and repentance, being called to say the Angelus prayer three times a day.

Not only that. We were living in what folks who knew a smattering of Yiddish would certainly refer to as *Eckveldt* – meaning the boondocks. During most of the day, Le Puy was a ghost town. Traffic picked up at lunchtime, and again around 5 p.m., as people headed home.

Cars moving in opposite directions took turns passing through; the street was not wide enough for two-lane traffic. Except for Friday evenings, when locals gathered for a drink at one of the town's two restaurants, there was practically nothing in the way of village life. I kept thinking it would be the perfect backdrop for a World War II movie set in rural France.

To the extent that the Jewish holiday was a time for reflection and renewal, it found me in the shadow of the Catholic Church, wondering where my latest life transition would lead.

That is more or less what I was doing at my laptop, on the second day of Rosh Hashanah, when the router beside me on the desk gave a little pop and the house went dark. It was neither a bad omen nor divine intervention. "The electric just went off again, and we weren't even *doing* anything," Ken yelled from upstairs, where he was shaving.

"Maybe it's the village," I said, looking for an explanation that would not require another visit from *Le Plombier*. We checked the circuit breakers, which were as we had left them last, then phoned our neighbor across the street – the one who flipped the switch before we flipped our lids during the previous electrical meltdown. We got voice mail, which didn't prove anything about whether it was the house or the village; it was possible that his voice mail was operated by the local telecom company rather than from a device within the house.

Next, Ken texted Pierre, using cellular data rather than the Wi-Fi (which, of course, was off since we had no power). I'm sure he was delighted to hear from us again. But even if he wasn't, he messaged back that, based on the situation we described, it was certainly the village.

By then it was 10:40, and we realized that we had not heard the church bells ring since 10. This confirmed our hypothesis: The ringing every hour, again at two minutes past the hour, once on the half hour, and separately for the Angelus prayer at 7 a.m., noon and 7 p.m., was not done by a modern-day Quasimodo standing up in the bell tower of the 13th-century church of Notre Dame. Much less quaintly, it was preprogramed using 21st-century technology.

We gave the electricity a decent interval (by New York standards) to come back on, which is to say, we waited an hour while I took a hot bath (thanks to what must have been a large hot water tank) in the enormous claw-foot tub and got dressed – two things I had planned to do anyway. Then we decided this was as good a day as any to go to Saumur, see the château and perhaps linger, because Virginie, the French provincial punk cleaning lady, was scheduled to arrive at 2 p.m. to clean the house.

"How will she vacuum if there's no electricity?" Ken asked. "Should we reschedule?"

In my role as what could be mistaken for the family optimist, I suggested that maybe the electricity would be back on by then. But I also noted that, based on what we had seen so far of Virginie's cleaning, it might have been quite a while since she left fingerprints on the vacuum.

Even without electricity, though, she could clean the kitchen and the two bathrooms, which were the areas of the house that most needed her attention.

Shortly before noon we set forth. As we rounded the corner in front of the church of Notre Dame, Ken noticed that the green neon light that said Pharmacie, on the storefront up the block, was on.

"How could they have electric when we don't?" Ken asked.

"Maybe it's solar-operated," I said, racking my brain for every possibility. Then, from high up in the bell tower, the suddenly comforting peels began: first 12 to indicate it was noon; two minutes later, 12 again, and then the bells for the Angelus prayer.

"Just in time for lunch," Ken said. "How French!"

The mention of lunch reminded me that all I had eaten before the lights went out was half a melon, and I began to wonder whether I could manage to visit the Saumur château (or any château, for that matter) on a mostly empty stomach. I programmed our GPS to get us to the château, which was supposedly the inspiration for the castle depicted in the Duke of Berry's 15th-century illuminated manuscript, the Très Riches Heures (on display in the Musée Condé in Chantilly, north of Paris). Then I began to peruse the *Lonely Planet France* guide on my Kindle for other must-see sights in Saumur.

The town, which is a mixture of old and new architecture, was the setting for Honoré de Balzac's 1833 novel *Eugénie Grandet,* which takes place in the early 19th century. It's the story of a young woman's suffering at the hand of her miserly father, who is a wealthy and deceitful winemaker. Behind any number of doors in what remains of the old town, one can imagine what Balzac describes as "that cold dark house, which was to her the universe."

Our guidebook mentioned that Saumur is also a culinary center and that a restaurant called Le Gambetta is "one to write home about." We promptly reset our GPS. The château could wait.

The first thing that happened when we arrived at Le Gambetta is that the maître d' asked us the question one is often asked in establishments that are something to write home about: *"Avez-vous réservé?"* (Do you have a reservation?)

"Non," we replied in unison, wondering if this would be a dead end. But in a flash, we were ushered into a small dining room and seated at a table next to the window, making us the fourth set of diners that day at what we later discovered was a restaurant with one Michelin star.

When the maître d' gave us the menus, mine had no prices, a sexist convention that I didn't realize was still observed in the 21st century. Not having the language abilities to take up the feminist cause at this particular juncture, and not wanting to do anything that might delay eating, I let Ken have a turn at *la carte*. Then I swapped menus with him so that I could consider how much of our nest egg to sink into this. By then he had already discerned that the chef, Mickaël Pihours, prepares French food with an Asian twist, piquing both his curiosity and his appetite.

The fixed-price offerings were only a bit less complicated than certain sections of the Internal Revenue Code, and some of them, like the latter, had serious fiscal implications. Starting at 1:30 p.m. and continuing until 9 p.m., for example, it was possible to spend €105 per person on a tasting menu (and another €49.50 per person to have a different wine with each course). Though we had arrived a bit too early for that, we were in time for what the menu referred to as *Le Panier de Mickaël* (Mickaël's basket) and what back home would be called a lunch special. It cost €28, and included an appetizer and main course, and the choice of a cheese plate or dessert. For an upcharge of €7, I could have a glass of house wine and the coffee of my choice to go with it.

Although the menu described Le Panier de Mickaël as *"La possibilité de déjeuner en moins d'1 heure"* (the possibility to eat in less than an hour), in French fashion, no one gave us the bum's rush. Nor did they insist, as the menu suggested they might, that if one of us ordered Le Panier de Mickaël, the other would also be required to. *En fait* (actually), as the French would say, when I asked if Ken could order à la carte, the maître d' readily agreed without a bit of arm-twisting. He was also kind enough to list every ingredient that would appear on the plate with the turbot stuffed with lemongrass that Ken had ordered; all but the champignons appealed.

Then he explained that I could choose to be surprised, or hear in advance, what was in Le Panier de Mickaël. He seemed relieved to hear that I preferred to be surprised. No doubt it would simplify things in the kitchen.

Before either of our meals arrived, we were served an amuse-bouche: finely chopped seafood with herbs atop a circle of celery mousse, accompanied by lemon sorbet in the shape of half a hard-boiled egg.

Diners at the other tables included two young couples, one of whom seemed to be locals, there to celebrate a special occasion; the Laotian-looking woman was dressed for lunch in a long-sleeved black lace top, though her companion wore jeans. In the far corner were underdressed travelers who, like us, might have been there on a splurge, and who scraped their spoons noisily against the plate while consuming the chocolate-mousse dessert. At the fourth table were two middle-aged French couples, who ordered a leisurely three-course meal. One of the men, who seemed to be the host, especially enjoyed what looked like pheasant under glass, insisting that all the others taste it.

For the most part, though, we were so engaged with both the presentation and the flavors of our own food that we only had time to notice other diners between courses. My surprise meal started with a salad — an assortment of greens and nuts, topped with a warm vinaigrette; and moved on to pork tenderloins served with miniature zucchini, potatoes prepared two ways and a foie gras sauce. Ken shared my dessert of roasted figs with chocolate mousse and vanilla ice cream, adorned with a profiterole and a wisp of spun sugar.

Compared to the meal, which was memorable, the château was a letdown. It had looked so majestic during our many drives along the opposite bank of the river. But with extensive renovations in progress, the other side of it was under a scaffold. We would add this château to the list of those that were best appreciated as part of the Loire Valley scenery. Far more interesting was one just five minutes away, in Brézé, which is known for its 1,000-year-old underground fortress – the largest of its kind in Europe. We had spent a couple of hours there one afternoon, poking around the hidden passageways and chambers where daily living, including an elaborate winemaking operation, could continue while maintaining a defensive posture.

On a subsequent visit to the town of Saumur, the abundant Saturday market was our main event. Held in Place St. Pierre and set against an array of half-timbered houses, it drew shoppers of all ages from the surrounding area, some as intriguing as the produce that was for sale. Mothers with children in strollers, like parents everywhere, bribed them into good behavior with edible treats. An elegant woman of a certain age, wearing large, purple horn-rimmed spectacles, examined the oversize artichokes as her two schnauzers looked on. At a nearby bar, some ruddy-faced men threw back a morning beer, while other shoppers lingered over coffee at the café next door.

For slender women with deep pockets, matchstick leather pants were the attire of choice. One 50-something, with a salt-and-pepper pixie haircut, paired them with a cashmere crewneck and tossed a cashmere cardigan over her shoulders. Another topped the pants with what looked like a Chanel jacket. Just to buy groceries – really? Going to market was a chance to see and be seen, and they were dressed for the occasion.

10

CHEESE IMPRESARIO

———

C HARLES DE GAULLE ONCE FAMOUSLY SAID, "How can anyone govern a nation that has 246 kinds of cheese?" The number varies, depending on where he is being quoted, and is no doubt much higher today.

Compared with other French food vendors, cheesemongers tend to be a dour bunch. Maybe they get as hardened as some of their wares because they attract so many moochers cruising for tastes.

But on a visit to the Sunday market in the village of Montsoreau, I crossed paths with a cheesemonger who was not only generous with tastes but also something of a clown.

By the time he stepped into the picture, Ken and I were standing in line behind what we took to be a sophisticated customer who was being served by a young woman who looked like a modern-day version of a Pieter Bruegel milkmaid. Her wiry customer, with wire-framed eyeglasses, was taking his time with his tastes and his purchases, and with each shaving that the milkmaid offered him, I was getting one, too – not a bad deal.

In France, cheese prices tend to be highest at storefront *fromageries* (cheese stores) and more affordable at the cheese mobiles that make the rounds on market days in various villages and cities. (Imagine a fromagerie crammed into a truck.) Generally speaking, hard cheeses are more expensive the longer they are aged, and soft cheeses are most desirable with just the right amount of mold on their rind. Artisanal cheeses, made by hand, rather than by machine, generally fetch rarefied prices, whether you buy them at a fromagerie or directly from a farmer at an outdoor market.

When packing for the latest France trip, I took along the 2006 book *French Cheeses*, a hard-to-find volume. I had bought it, in English, the previous summer in the souvenir shop at Mont-San-Michel, the dramatic abbey on an island on the border between Normandy and Brittany. So that book had crossed the Atlantic with me twice, even though it is printed on high-quality glossy paper and is not light.

Still, it was worth its weight to educate me about *chèvre*, or goat's milk, cheeses that dominate the table in the Loire Valley from May until October. *Valençay*, for example, looks like a pyramid with the top cut off. Legend has it that Napoléon launched this tradition when he visited the castle in the town of the same name and sliced off the top of a cheese with his sword. Truth be told, though, I don't much care for Valençay, because the ones I tasted were too strong, or in market-speak, *trop fort*.

Far more common is a cylinder-shaped goat cheese called *St. Maure,* but often the cheeses that farmers sell at the market are not even labeled. Ask a farmer the name of a particular cheese, and he might just shrug and say *"chèvre,"* preferring to describe the cheese according to how fort or *sec* (dry) it is, and whether it is in the shape of a cylinder (*un cylindre*) or a small circle, called *un crottin* (a word also used to describe smaller, solid, round excrements, for horses or goats, for example).

If you know the words fort and sec, in fact, you can pretty much make your preferences known at cheese counters, whether or not they offer a taste *(un goût)*.

After inquiring about our nationality, the cheesemonger in Montsoreau complained that many British customers who vacation or have retired in the area don't even make an effort to speak the language. So I apparently scored some points by speaking to him in what might generously be described as rudimentary French. He did seem a bit disappointed when I said I didn't like my cheese fort, though. And on the matter of dryness, he corrected my anglicized pronunciation of the *demi* in *demi sec* (properly said duh-ME).

Once we understood this much about each other, at my request he sliced me *une petite tranche* (a small slice) of a very unique-looking cheese that I had tasted on the coattails of the previous customer. It was firm and cream-colored, with chocolate-colored marbling throughout and a brown paraffin rind to match. The taste was like cheddar, with bitter after-tones, which he said was because it was made with beer.

"Et avec ceci?" he then asked. (Would you like anything else?) I hesitated. What attracted me to his truck was that the selections didn't look like anything I had seen before in the Loire Valley, but I really didn't know what most of it was.

By that time, though, I did know that the cheesemonger's name is Hugues Bocahut and that he has a shop in the town of Closneau, which is about 30 miles from Le Puy-Notre-Dame. He helped me along with a couple of more tastes. His deft handling of the knife with those little pieces was especially impressive, since he had the middle finger of his dominant hand in an enormous splint – the result of a buzz saw mishap, he said, not from slicing cheese.

Once I was done with my selections, Monsieur Bocahut insisted that I step up into the truck and pose for a picture that he carefully choreographed – with me holding up a huge wheel of cheese that looked like a fan. At that point, there was a long line of customers waiting, and I felt a bit like I was part of a circus act.

When we got back to the house in Le Puy-Notre-Dame, I consulted the cheese guide to identify my purchases. It seemed that I had acquired slices of two different artisan cheeses made of chèvre and a tiny crottin that Monsieur Bocahut had thrown in gratis – dryer than I would have liked, but perhaps he was trying to educate my palate.

The marbled cheese that was my first selection had me stumped, though. It was nowhere in my cheese book, and nowhere online, either, when I did a Google search for "cheese AND marble AND France AND beer."

Finally, I ran the search again without the word France, and *voilà!* There was little doubt that the French cheesemonger had sold Irish cheddar with porter beer to *l'Américaine*. This cheese was a delicacy, especially in France. But it was not a *French* delicacy.

11

FRUIT of the VINE

⌒

ABOVE THE KITCHEN HEARTH in our house on rue Sainte was a poster with the caption *"Tous les hommes naissent ivres et égaux."* It was a quote from Sylvie Augereau, a prolific contemporary French wine writer. The translation, "All men are born drunk and equal," was a playful twist on the expression, *"All men are born free and equal,"* attributed to the 18th-century French philosopher Jean-Jacques Rousseau. With a slight spelling change, Augereau turned the French word *libre,* which means free, into ivre, which means drunk. And the sketch above the caption, of many varieties of glasses, suggested that neither all men (nor all wines) are, in fact, born equal.

Although it's possible to find delicious, inexpensive wines in France – my €4 Carrefour-brand Bourgueil was proof of that – the French take their wine labeling very seriously. A wine's appellation, or legal label, refers both to the place where the grapes are grown and to various other criteria, including the alcohol content and type of grapes from which it may be produced. (Wine that bears the appellation Chinon, for example, must be made primarily, if not exclusively, from the cabernet franc grape.) In the Loire Valley, tasting opportunities abound, not only at vineyards but also at cellars on the outskirts of towns where wines are produced – among them the familiar appellations Vouvray, Chinon and Saumur – and even at some of the châteaux.

Ken doesn't drink, so except for when Barbara and Ray visited, I did enough sampling for both of us. Some of the wines I enjoyed most were those ordered by the glass, at wine bars or restaurants, where I simply asked the server for a recommendation based on whether I was in the mood for red or white; dry, sweet or full-bodied; and, if accompanying a meal, what I was eating. Before I took the first sip, I relished their poetic descriptions of the flavors. Ordering wine this way typically cost me between €1.50 and €4 per glass, and I was never disappointed, though I do not pretend to be an oenophile.

For the sake of comparison, I also tracked down some Loire Valley wines recommended by a professional nose. Referring to a recent article by Eric Asimov, a wine critic for *The New York Times,* I scoured the shelves of supermarkets and wine stores for Chinon wines by specific producers and the vintages that he liked. Asimov describes the Chinon red (this appellation is rarely white) as "one of the most overlooked yet thought-provoking reds I know."

My first score was at a tourist shop in Saumur, where I acquired a bottle of Philippe Alliet Chinon Vieilles Vignes 2013 for €16. Then, at the gigantic E.Leclerc supermarket in Thouars – a megastore in an industrial city – I hit pay dirt. There I found four of the Chinon producers for which Asimov said to buy any of the *cuvées* (blends) available. So I purchased these reds: from Bernard Baudry, a Les Granges 2012

(€9.70) and a Grézeaux 2012 (€14.30); an Olga Raffault Les Barnabés 2012 (€11.25); and a Couly-Dutheil 2012 (€12.90).

For my budget, these wines were a splurge – but essential research, of course. And though they were all lovely and about half the price of what they would have cost in the U.S. (assuming one could find them), only the Bernard Baudry Grézeaux 2012 was lovelier than my €4 Carrefour Bourgueil. Clearly, a lot of good, inexpensive French wine never makes it out of France, or even out of the region in which it is produced.

Being in Le Puy-Notre-Dame, however, it wasn't necessary to even *drink* wine to get in the spirit. As we descended from the hilltop and exited the village by any route, vineyards stretched out in all directions. Road signs pointed generally to *"viticulteurs"* (winemakers) and, more specifically, to vineyards by name. Depending on how one counted, there were about 20 vineyards within walking distance of the house on rue Sainte. As the cheesemonger at the Montsoreau market noted, this makes the area *"très jolie"* (very nice). That is, except for the time when I returned from an impromptu walk in a vineyard and noticed that my sneaker was caked with dung. (It occurred to me that this might also be seen as an apt metaphor for my experience renting lodgings on sharing economy websites.)

Though village wine festivals are scheduled far in advance – September 27 in Saumur and October 4 in Le Puy-Notre-Dame during the year of our visit – for centuries winemakers have looked at the sky to determine when to start picking the grapes. Each viticulteur makes their decision based on the type of grape, the vineyard size and the weather forecast – no one wants to pick grapes in the rain – then assembles the necessary labor. Sometimes it's enough to rely on family and friends, but many winemakers also employ migrants for the harvest. As it began, the fields buzzed with activity, and we shared the road with gigantic tractors, some driven by youngsters who could barely see over the steering wheel.

This was not a time for organized vineyard tours and wine tastings, we were advised; winemakers have *real* work to do. But one morning, in glorious sunshine, we meandered to the edge of town, following the tractor tracks and, in one spot, took care not to step on squished white grapes in the middle of the street. There we were, peering into a busy courtyard on rue de la Givaudière, when what turned out to be the lady of the house asked if she could help us.

We replied that we were just observing the *vendange* and did not want to disturb. But she invited us in to watch the work in progress: white grapes being pressed through a machine that extracted the sediment and fed the liquid directly into underground vats. It was like a modern-day version of the caves we visited a week earlier at Musée Rabelais, in Seuilly. Yet what was visible here aboveground bore a very unpoetic resemblance to the fuel delivery tank caps at gas stations back in the U.S.

Madame Jourdain, as she later introduced herself (first name Christelle, "like Christmas," she explained), excused herself to get a glass, then turned a spigot on the bizarre contraption and gave us a taste of a sweet, cloudy, slightly fermented liquid called *bourru*. It's a delicacy available only during the vendange. At shops where it is sold – typically in recycled plastic bottles – one might see a sign announcing, *"Le bourru est arrivé!"* (The bourru has arrived.)

There was not a hint of salesmanship in the manner of Madame Jourdain, who was dressed in blue jeans and a black-and-white sweater, sporting a jauntily tied olive scarf and sneakers that seemed like appropriate footwear for the occasion. But when we started to ask about buying a bottle, she preempted us and offered *"un goût"* (a taste). After sampling three, I passed on the rosé but came away with a bottle of their Domaine de la Salpêtrière Saumur red 2014 (€4.30), and another, of the super-sweet apéritif Coteaux 2009 (€10). She said it paired well with foie gras, which I didn't doubt.

As the conversation turned to the huge assortment of producers in this region, I noted the range of choices on supermarket shelves. Madame Jourdain was quick to say that because of the *Foires aux vins* (wine fairs), in progress, this was an excellent time to buy wine. So we asked what seemed like an obvious question: What was her favorite? It was a question without an answer, though; as it happens, she doesn't drink.

12

LIFE as a LOCATAIRE

B Y THE THIRD WEEK of September, autumn was descending
on the Loire Valley. Ivy vines turned bright red; melons and tomatoes became less plentiful in the markets; and it rained for at least
part of every day. Bare stalks were all that remained in fields where
sunflowers once bloomed. As the grapes were harvested, one by one
the vineyards looked denuded. Pierre and his family planned to attend the upcoming *vendange* festivals. They needed their house back.
It was time for us to move on.

Though we appreciated the spaciousness and charm of the house on
rue Sainte, at times we felt like caretakers, or house sitters, rather than
paying customers. After entertaining *Le Plombier* in rudimentary French
and cleaning the kitchen, we used an entire bottle of DesTop Express Gel
(a drain cleaner) to unclog the shower and one of the bathroom sinks.

Two days before we were scheduled to leave, we had one last incident. It involved the door to the back garden, which also provided our

only access to the garage; on the street-facing side, the garage door was bolted from the inside.

Ken was on his way to check the laundry that was drying on the clothesline in the garden (we had a washing machine but no dryer), when the knob came off in his hand. Without it, there was no way to engage the latch, and since the thread was stripped, it was impossible to reattach the knob. From that side of the house, we were locked in.

I ran to the tool cabinet, which I had discovered when I peeked behind a door one day in the old liveryman's quarters, and grabbed a screwdriver. Ken, meantime, texted Pierre, who replied that he was in a meeting. He suggested that we try to open the door with a screwdriver. At least we were all on the same page about what needed to be done.

Only at first it did not work. As we took turns with the screwdriver, there were some tense moments during which we pictured ourselves not being able to retrieve our underwear from the clothesline or our car from the garage. I imagined us stranded in Le Puy-Notre-Dame, in dirty underwear, for an indeterminate length of time beyond our scheduled departure date, until we could be rescued.

After what seemed like an eternity but was actually an hour, we got the door open, secured the automatic latch with some tape that we found in the tool cabinet, and let Pierre know by text that the latest crisis had passed. He did not reply to the message. After all, it wasn't *he* who would have been stranded in Le Puy-Notre-Dame in dirty underwear. But he did call us the next morning about a subject that was important to him: getting back the keys to his house. In the course of that conversation, he apologized for all our difficulties.

Serendipitously, the lock demons had been doing mischief back in Brooklyn, too. On the day that the town electricity went off in Le Puy-

Notre-Dame, Ward, our tenant, had tried to reach us – first by e-mail, then by text, and finally by calling my cell phone (all this in the space of less than an hour), to say that his wife and two kids were locked out. "The bottom lock on the front door is not working, and my wife cannot get in," he wrote in the e-mail. "She can get into the basement, but she locked the kitchen door so cannot get upstairs."

This was a series of unfortunate events that we had made every effort to avoid. Our house manual included explicit instructions not to double-lock the 100-year-old bottom lock – either from the outside or from the inside. (Though we hadn't said so, it is sometimes temperamental.) Our tenants had obviously overlooked or misunderstood that instruction. As a backup, we had provided them with keys to the basement entrance of the house. But in this case that didn't help, because, as Ward's e-mail indicated, they had locked the door at the top of the interior stairs that connected the kitchen with the basement. We didn't expect them to lock this door – in 17 years we never had. Was it a childproofing measure? And, if so, how had we managed to raise a child ourselves without even *closing* that door, let alone *locking* it?

I felt the slightest twinge of empathy for Pierre. Troubleshooting a problem with an old house – in this case from 4,000 miles away – wasn't easy. Tempted as I was to blame the tenant for the problem (Why didn't he just follow our instructions?), I didn't. "Customer service, customer service," I told myself, pressing the cell phone against my ear as I broke into a sweat. "Handle this the way *you* would like a landlord to react if the roles were reversed."

I gave Ward the name and phone number of the local locksmith, apologized for the inconvenience (even though I thought it was his fault) and offered to reimburse him for any expenses.

He later sent a text saying that, with the help of a neighbor, they had entered the house through a screen and gotten the door open. I replied asking them to test the lock, to make sure it worked, with one person on the inside and the other on the outside. If it still wasn't functioning properly, I reiterated my suggestion that they call a locksmith and offered to foot the bill. Ward wrote back that everything was fine.

Several nights later, I dreamed that I had some reason to stop by our Brooklyn house briefly. There I found that our tenants had rolled up the Oriental area rugs, and put down towels in their place, and on every bed replaced our linens with their own. Did I suspect them of sweeping something under the rug? Clearly I was having a hard time trusting strangers with my house. I wondered if Pierre felt that way about us.

In his public review of us on Airbnb, Pierre wrote, "Thank you for leaving the place in perfect order and for being so patient with our old house." In a private comment, on the site, he added, "Thanks again for your patience with the little troubles you went through!"

I re-read that last sentence. Yep, he really did say, "*Little* troubles." I suppose it depends on one's perspective.

As hosts and guests know, online reviews are the currency of the sharing economy. At the end of each stay, Airbnb prompts them to evaluate each other. For the next 14 days, they cannot see what's been said. When that comment period ends, neither party can any longer post reviews, and what they have written becomes public. This reduces the risk of reciprocal reviews with the implied (or express) promise that "I'll scratch your back if you'll scratch mine."

Hosts' comments about a guest become part of that person's Airbnb profile, which other homeowners can use in deciding whether or not to rent to someone. Another way to brandish one's profile is by requesting references from friends and colleagues, though these are clearly labeled as references, and distinguished from reviews.

I didn't write a review of the house on rue Sainte (or the winemaker's cottage, for that matter). Because I am a journalist, I don't post comments on sharing economy websites, as I explained to Pierre in an e-mail after reading his glowing review of us. In this case, though, I was glad to have an excuse, since I would have been very torn about what to say.

On balance we enjoyed our stay on rue Sainte. I would have been reluctant to jeopardize Pierre's ability to rent to others; for that reason, I have assigned him a pseudonym here. But I didn't think the house was ready to rent. It needed some capital improvements, maintenance and repairs, including an upgraded electrical system and some very basic gardening. Maybe Pierre and his family didn't care about such things – this was, after all, just a country house. Or maybe they could not afford to take the necessary steps. Or maybe it wasn't fair to judge him by my own standards, expecting him to devote as much effort to preparing his house for rental as I had with mine. Maybe I had done too much for our own tenants – much more than I could reasonably expect of our French landlords.

All that being said, again this was a host who hadn't given much thought to the comfort or convenience of guests. In fact, this terminology, unique to the Airbnb website, seemed ill-suited to our financial arrangement, as did the expression "sharing economy." We were paying to use his house, not *sharing* it.

Like many old houses, the one on rue Sainte had practically no closet space, and the owners compensated for it with armoires. None was provided for guests. A simple solution would have been to put a small garment rack in the guest bedroom. Without one, the best we could do was to leave most of our clothes folded, in a suitcase, and hang our outerwear on the coat rack in the front hall, draping it over the belongings of Pierre and his family.

Likewise, the refrigerator and kitchen cabinets were crammed with their food. This was understandable, since they used it as a weekend home and rented only occasionally. But one morning, while Barbara and Ray were visiting us, Ray called my attention to some liquid seeping out from under the curtain in front of one of the counters. I traced it to a bulging juice carton that hadn't been refrigerated after opening, and seemed to have exploded from the fluid fermenting inside of it.

Though linens were included in the rental fee for this house (in some rentals they aren't), there was no top sheet and no cover supplied for the polyester duvet – on our own bed, or the one that had been designated for Barbara and Ray to use when they visited. We preferred not to think about how many skins they had touched before ours. When the weather got cold and I fished out a couple of blankets from the hall cabinet, I found an old cover in there – too small for the duvet on our bed, but we made do with it.

In a country where few homes have dryers, supplying linens requires the extra work of hanging sheets and towels out to dry, or the additional expense and effort of taking them to one of the many establishments that wash and press bed sheets. And, of course, there's the risk that guests will stain the sheets, take a bath towel to the beach, or walk off with an item that's a bit softer or fluffier than what they have back home. So it's understandable that this is an area where homeowners tend to skimp.

By the time our 89 days in the European Union were over, I had resolved that if I ever again wound up at a place with grungy linens, I would buy my own. Depending on how much I had spent, I would either leave them for the next guest at my final rental of the trip, or add them to my stash of souvenirs.

Such was the life of what the French call a *locataire* (tenant). This was a word I learned from Lisa Douglas, the retired professor who was our landlord in Amboise. She used it in a couple of e-mails that she sent to friends in France, introducing us in advance of our arrival. In them, she described us as "a couple from Brooklyn who seem delightful." I'm assuming she subsequently changed her mind about the delightful part.

We thought we had put that whole experience in the rearview mirror, but it crept up on us again, shortly before our scheduled departure from rue Sainte when I received an e-mail from Lisa. In it, she said that she planned to apply our entire $200 security deposit to pay Madame Lamotte, her so-called cleaning lady.

The message was unwelcome, to say the least, and it arrived at a moment when I was already feeling fed up. Just hours before, we had been wrestling with the jammed back door on rue Sainte. Now, suddenly, I was engaged in another round of bitter e-mails with Lisa Douglas, about our *previous* accommodations. When would the housing hassles stop?

Three weeks earlier, in the course of settling our dispute, Lisa had offered to tear up the check for the security deposit and send us a photograph of it. Now she was reneging on that promise. What prompted it was a bill, from Madame Lamotte, for what under current exchange rates equaled $220, reflecting 11 hours of cleaning time associated with our stay in the cottage.

This was hard to fathom, since Madame Lamotte had spent less than three hours at the house the day we arrived. We had left the house cleaner than we found it, by, among other things, stripping the beds, neatly piling up the sheets and used towels, and putting up the dishwasher.

Though our lease had included a provision for us to pay €12 per hour, plus benefits of 83.9 percent, for biweekly cleaning during what was originally to be our three-month stay, we had never engaged those services. If Madame Lamotte spent 11 hours there after we departed, that would have made the house much cleaner than it was when we took occupancy. Perhaps she was billing the Douglases for the house-keeping that should have been done before our arrival, or just capital-izing on our falling-out.

What's more, as I explained in my e-mail, Lisa had broken the lease by kicking us out, and after that we no longer had an obligation to pay Madame Lamotte. Without any discussion of cleaning – except for our complaints that the place was filthy – we had settled up by prorating the rent for the time we stayed in the winemaker's cottage.

Without any comment on Madame Lamotte's moral compass, I suggested that Lisa ask her for an explanation of the charges. Then I booted up my computer, signed on to my bank account and put a stop payment on the check for the security deposit. I did not hear from the Douglases again and have no idea whether they attempted to cash the check.

Except for trying to pass along the cleaning fee, I think they did the right thing, and what I would have done under the circumstances; no homeowner wants her house occupied by a tenant who is unhappy there. But had she behaved differently, we might have been stuck.

In our last e-mail exchange, Lisa also said something that stayed with me as I reflected back on this enormously unpleasant experience and as we moved on to other rentals. "I think you were confusing the condition of a vacation rental with a regular home rental or with a hotel room," she wrote. In other words, we had expected too much.

Her comment raised questions both about the standards that apply in the sharing economy and what protections are available to travelers. Though we were able to resolve our dispute satisfactorily, if not amicably, it cost us considerable time and angst. It also illustrated how vulnerable travelers can be in these situations, when conceptions differ about what's "good enough."

After our return to the United States, I looked into both issues more thoroughly.

Although this area of commerce is evolving, I found that consumers' recourse depends on a combination of factors. They include: your negotiating skill; which online platform you use to book the reservation; and the payment method.

It's always best when you can resolve disputes, as we did, directly with the owner. In telephone interviews, representatives of both HomeAway and Airbnb told me that we should not have stayed a single night at the winemaker's cottage. Exhausted as we were when we arrived, we should have immediately gone through the place from top to bottom, decided that it was uninhabitable, and never dragged our suitcases in from the car. We should have contacted the owners immediately, even if, because of the time difference, it meant waking them up. And if that didn't work, we could have called HomeAway for help.

It was also a mistake to pay offline rather than using the site's "checkout" system, Jon Gray, chief revenue officer at HomeAway, told me. By doing so, we lost the right to rely on the company's so-called "Book with Confidence Guarantee." It covers a variety of situations, from fraud to being unable to gain access to the property, reimbursing travelers for up to 100 percent of what they have paid.

Though the fine print makes it impossible to get one's money back purely for lack of cleanliness, Gray said the mold we found in the cottage went far beyond that, creating a "safety issue." In such cases, the Book with Confidence Guarantee would have covered the cost of emergency lodging and help rebooking, he said.

He didn't buy Lisa's argument that we expected too much of a vacation rental. More than 90 percent of the listings on HomeAway are such properties rather than people's primary residence, he said. Typically they are less cluttered than the place where people live full-time, with empty closets where guests can put their belongings. But again, Gray said, there was no excuse for the mold. He kept coming back to that.

Our recourse probably would have been comparable with Airbnb. As it happens, the winemaker's cottage was not listed on that site. On Airbnb no money is supposed to change hands directly between guest and host; though guests must pay in full when they make the reservation, Airbnb does not disburse the funds to the owner until 24 hours after check-in. Meanwhile, we could have tried to address the problem with the company's 24-hour hotline.

Minimally, they would have put us up for the first night someplace else, said Nick Shapiro, global head of crisis communications and issues management at Airbnb. That would have saved us the trouble of having to deal directly with Madame Lamotte.

Both Gray and Shapiro also told me that our experience in the winemaker's cottage was an anomaly – that such problems rarely occur. When they do, though, as we discovered, it can trigger a bundle of legal issues that may require interpretation of: the rules of a particular platform (which customers agree to when they use the site); the contract, if any, between the traveler and the homeowner; and local law (perhaps in a foreign country). Uncertain standards and divergent expectations further muddy the waters. When things don't go well, the sharing economy may turn out to be much more complicated than it seems on the surface or than its name implies.

Legal issues can crop up when you least expect them, too, as they did at 10:52 p.m. on our last night in Amboise. And this time the Douglases had nothing to do with the problem.

I was sitting in the tower bedroom in the winemaker's cottage, writing, when an e-mail from Pierre landed. It finalized the arrangements for Virginie to meet us at the house in Le Puy-Notre-Dame, give us the keys and, in his words, "show you how to live in the house." (How ironic that turn of phrase seemed in retrospect.) The e-mail was written in English. Attached was a seven-page lease, in French. "The contract (attached for infos) will be given later, to be signed from your side," Pierre wrote.

It had been three days since we had made the reservation for the house on rue Sainte. There was no reference to a contract on the Airbnb listing. (The site recommends one for stays of 30 days or more, but we would be there for less time than that.) Nor had there been any mention of it in our previous correspondence with Pierre. We were packed and ready to move to our new lodgings, and suddenly there was yet another potential glitch.

Springing the contract on us, I would later learn, was against the Airbnb rules. Hosts who require their guests to sign a lease must indicate that in the "house rules" part of the listing, so people will know about it before they book. What I ought to have done in that situation was to immediately reply to Pierre, saying, "'I don't speak French. This would be difficult for me to do,'" Shapiro told me, in our interview four months later. If the host had a negative reaction, we should have immediately contacted Airbnb's 24-hour hotline for help.

I didn't realize that at the time. Nor, after all we had been through, did I want to jeopardize our reservation or get into an argument with our next landlord before we had even arrived. So I opened the contract on my computer, launched the French dictionary app on my iPhone and began to read the document.

As a former contracts lawyer, I had an advantage over other travelers. Though I didn't speak much French, I knew enough legalese to surmise that this was not a contract written from scratch. Portions of it seemed to have been cribbed from other sources and weren't relevant to our situation. For example, it included an inventory of the furniture and electronic equipment – in case we might be tempted to walk off with a kitchen armoire, for example. Various other provisions, like one saying this wouldn't be our principal residence, and another, indicating that the lease couldn't be renewed, seemed designed to prevent us from staying on past the end of the lease term, as squatters. (No danger of that.)

There were a couple of bloopers, too. A section about utilities provided that our landlord would pay them and bill us for them, but the listing on Airbnb said that they were included. Another provision required a €500 security deposit, to be returned 48 hours after checkout. But this violated the Airbnb rules: The company doesn't allow hosts to collect a security deposit upfront; all claims for loss or damage must be submitted through the Airbnb platform. Since elsewhere in the contract references to Airbnb had been inserted, I assumed these inconsistencies were just oversights.

Pierre clearly meant business, though. The day of our arrival, after showing us around the house, Virginie (no doubt as instructed) presented us with a bottle of wine that she said was a present from Pierre, put two copies of the contract in front of us and waited for us to sign. It was the first time I ever put my John Hancock on something that would be interpreted under French law. It was also the last time (until now) that any of us mentioned that contract. But just for the record: Nothing in it required a locataire to perform or supervise home repairs.

13

SECOND THOUGHTS

TEN DAYS BEFORE our departure from Le Puy-Notre-Dame, we booked our next accommodations, in Sare – a one-street village in southwestern France, five miles from the Spanish border, in Basque Country. This was a part of France that we had never been to, and didn't initially plan to visit during our three months overseas. With the luxury of time, we could explore the unique culture and cuisine of the region. We later discovered that it isn't readily accessible from international hubs, and therefore attracts fewer Americans than other parts of the country.

Weather, too, played a role in our decision. Since we would be 500 miles farther south, it would be warmer in Basque Country than in the Loire Valley. We would be chasing the season change, giving us a chance to experience autumn all over again. At this new rental, we would also get another shot at making our financial strategy work. But based on our experiences at the previous two, I was beginning to have my doubts about the viability of our plan to live on the sharing economy.

The idea of going to France for three months was to make a temporary home there and lower our expenses while I continued writing. I never envisioned what had turned into an itinerant lifestyle, as we changed accommodations three times during the first month.

Though online platforms made it possible to easily find other housing, these moves were a time-consuming chore. Our misadventures had given me plenty to write *about*, but they had also cast a shadow on the oft-romanticized sharing economy and left me appreciating the convenience of checking into a hotel.

During the week leading up to our relocation from Amboise to Le Puy-Notre-Dame, and again, from Le Puy to our next destination, in Sare, I spent an entire day online, looking for potentially suitable places to set up house next, then contacting the owners of those places to perform my due diligence and negotiate a favorable rate. On more than one occasion I thought to myself, "I can't believe we're in France, and *this* is how I'm spending my day."

After we arranged for each rental, there were housekeeping issues associated with our move. For example, there was the question of when we could do the last load of laundry and have it dry on the clothesline by the time we departed. As the weather changed in Le Puy, I kept one eye on the sky, dashing out to the garden several times to retrieve our freshly washed garments before a sudden autumn shower drenched them. (This dynamic just raised the stakes the day the door handle broke.)

To minimize the amount of food we needed to transport, we tried to consume as much of it as possible before we moved. But by the time we left Le Puy, we had accumulated enough staples to fill an entire kitchen cabinet.

We transported our expanding larder in three large, lightweight duffle bags that were previously used to store Aerobeds. After owning three of these inflatable beds, each of which had ruptured for no good reason, we had invested in a more durable variety. But we saved the storage bags, with the Aerobed name emblazoned on one side, thinking that they could be repurposed. At the last minute, we had stuffed them into our suitcases.

In France we kept the Aerobed bags in the trunk of the car. When not deployed to tote Asian ingredients, toiletries or cleaning supplies from one rented home to another, we took them to the supermarket. (As in the U.S., many food stores either did not supply bags or charged extra for them.) There was no hiding the word "Aerobed," in large letters, as I carried those bags over my shoulder. I joked that perhaps we would start a trend.

In choosing our lodgings so far, I had followed what both Nick Shapiro of Airbnb and Jon Gray of HomeAway would later describe to me as best practices: Carefully peruse the online photographs; read between the lines of the owner's description; and look for recent reviews by other travelers. The most helpful reviews would theoretically be those that said the property was just as it was described on the website (or better); and gave details about the pros and cons (including how the owner addressed any deficiencies).

I say *theoretically*, because this approach is anything but fail-safe. It's hard to evaluate the credibility of the person doing the rating. Maybe they have different standards. Maybe they escaped any mischief by the house demons on rue Sainte, or didn't look inside the kitchen cabinets at the winemaker's cottage. Or maybe guests were just reluctant to tell the whole story. There's room in the system for shilling, too, by having a friend spend a weekend in one's home and write an ecstatic review.

Or perhaps our troubles were a function of what Michael Klein, of the short-term vacation rental company Onefinestay, would later describe to me as a lack of "professionalism, quality and trust" in the sharing economy. That's the premise behind the concierge-style service that his company offers. Nightly fees for the properties that Onefinestay manages, so far all situated in big cities, are about twice what one pays renting from homeowners directly. Its business model has been appealing to investors: In April 2016, AccorHotels, the large European hotel group, bought Onefinestay for $169 million. Six months earlier, while we were in France, the travel website Expedia acquired HomeAway for $3.9 billion.

Legacy companies clearly see a business opportunity, but they are latecomers to this market. Sharing economy platforms got their start giving amateurs entrée to the hospitality business, just as disruption in the media industry made wannabe writers into "content creators." In both contexts, quality has suffered.

Malcolm Gladwell, the journalist and author, famously wrote that to become an expert in something, one must do it for 10,000 hours. By that standard, online platforms have catapulted us into an age of amateurism. As hosts in the sharing economy, we were among the neophytes. Yet we held ourselves to a higher standard than the owners of the homes we occupied in either Amboise or Le Puy-Notre-Dame. That just compounded our disappointment with these two rentals.

Still, the house in Sare looked beautiful – online. Though the text said nothing about the owners, the triplex was furnished in exquisite taste and expertly photographed. It lacked a track record: The property had been listed for only six months, and during that time there had been just one (albeit glowing) online review. As new landlords ourselves, we could empathize, so decided to take a chance. Besides, after the past two rentals, how much worse could it get?

But after making the reservation, for a two-week stay, I felt less optimistic about what awaited us. What concerned me was the Airbnb headline, which advertised the house as a *maison mitoyenne*.

A quick check of my French dictionary, while I was surfing for rentals, had revealed that the word mitoyenne could refer to a common party wall or something that is semi-detached. My frame of reference was our Brooklyn row house.

A chatty e-mail from the owner, confirming our booking, made me wonder whether something had been lost in translation – which is to say, my translation. The note, from Laurence Chambon, was written in French. She described the house as *"une grande maison familiale"* (a big family home), dating from 1619, that she, as an architect, had renovated.

There was good news in one respect: This was the work of a pro. However, what came next in the message threw me into a panic: *"Nous avons 4 filles qui ne vivent pas avec nous, c'est pourquoi nous en louons une partie."* (We have four daughters who no longer live with us. That's why we are renting part of the house.) Then she asked if we spoke a little French.

What difference did it make whether or not we spoke French? I began to worry that this was not *attached* housing, as I had initially assumed, but, using another possible definition of mitoyenne, *shared* housing. Perhaps Laurence was wondering whether I spoke enough French to understand the living arrangements.

Could it be that she was renting out her daughters' former bedrooms, and we would be sharing all the other living space? I pictured passing these strangers in the hallway at night on my way to the bathroom; storing our food in their refrigerator; having to take turns using the kitchen; and all lounging around together after dinner. At other times in my life, I would have relished such a "homestay," but that was not what we envisioned for two weeks during our French adventure.

There should have been no room for that possibility. The Airbnb website gives users the option of using "filters" (specific criteria) to narrow their search results. By checking a box labeled "whole house," as we searched for potential rentals in Basque Country, we should have eliminated any offers to rent a room in someone's home.

But after receiving this most recent e-mail from Laurence, no amount of staring at the online photos, translating the description using my dictionary, or putting that text through Google Translate, could quell my anxiety. So from my cozy little office in the house on rue Sainte, I composed a note to her, in French, trying to resolve the ambiguity with as much diplomacy as I could conjure up under the circumstances.

Then I checked the refund policy for the maison mitoyenne. It came under the Airbnb category of "strict," providing for a 50 percent refund if we canceled seven days before our scheduled arrival. We were on the cusp of that deadline. That meant the best we could do was forfeit half of the $2,804 that we had paid upfront, or $1,402. I was a wreck.

Four hours later, when I had not received a reply, I wrote again, this time in English, and more bluntly:

"Laurence, Can you please tell me whether this is a private space or a shared one? Your listing on Airbnb indicates that we would have the whole house ALONE. In your message of earlier today, you suddenly suggest that is not the case – that we will be renting the rooms your daughters used to occupy and sharing the kitchen, the living room and the office. Your listing shows pictures of a living room, kitchen and office that would be entirely ours – not shared with you. If that is not what you are able to offer, please issue us a full refund immediately."

I also sent a message to the Airbnb help desk saying that I was afraid the property had been misrepresented. They responded within 24 hours, with a voice mail. By then I had already sent a follow-up e-mail, indicating that there had been a miscommunication with the host and that everything had been resolved. Even though they had received that e-mail, someone from Airbnb still called to confirm. This was my first experience with the help desk. I was impressed with their service.

Meanwhile, Laurence had allayed my fears with an e-mail that said, *"Oui! Vous avez tout pour vous. La cuisine est toute neuve. Nous venons de la faire pour les locataires. Toutes les pièces de la maison sur les photos sont pour nos locataires.*

Je pense que vous ne serez pas déçus."

Translation: Yes, it will all be yours. The kitchen is all new. We did it for our tenants. All the rooms in the house in the photos are for our tenants. My guess is that you will not be disappointed.

PART THREE

THE BOUNTY of BASQUE COUNTRY

14

THE SHIPBUILDER'S MANSION

"A well-spent life, like an outstanding trip, is made up of unexpected turns, strange encounters and priority-changing experiences."
– Darrell Wade, chief executive of Intrepid Travel, quoted in *The New York Times*, September 18, 2007

OUR USUAL METHOD of GPS navigation – starting with the street name – wouldn't get us to our accommodations in Sare. The address was *Maison Ihartze Beherea, Allée des Platanes.* Maison is the French word for house. Ihartze Beherea is its name in the Basque language, known as *Euskera.* Allée des Platanes refers to the street, which is lined with plane trees. When our GPS came up blank, we charted a course south and west to Sare, from Le Puy-Notre-Dame.

As we got closer, we followed the precise instructions that Laurence had sent by e-mail (in French), routing us either from the village of St. Jean-de-Luz, if we were approaching from the northwest, or St. Pée-sur-Nivelle, if we were coming from the northeast. But an apparent wrong turn at one of the roundabouts landed us in a parking lot near the campgrounds on the outskirts of Sare rather than at the one she had directed us to, across the road from the house.

I phoned Carmen Amestoy, the cleaning lady, who was scheduled to welcome us, since, as Laurence had obtusely indicated in an e-mail the day after we booked, *"Nous venons d'avoir confirmation que nous serons absents pour quelques jours lors de votre séjour, et nous en sommes désolés!"* (We've had confirmation that we will be away for a few days during your stay and we are sorry!) Where were they, for how long, and what misadventures awaited us at our latest lodgings, we wondered. The six-hour drive had given us plenty of time to speculate, and the last half hour of it, on mountain switchbacks, had depleted our reserves of both patience and optimism.

When I tried, in French, to tell Carmen that I was calling from the campground parking lot, standing in front of a recycling bin, she gave no indication of knowing where we were. But she had a practical suggestion: Meet in front of the boulangerie in Sare – almost every French town, no matter how small, has a bread shop. So we followed the road signs back into the village, where we quickly spotted the boulangerie.

In this one-street village, in addition to the boulangerie, there is one pharmacy, one beauty shop, one butcher shop, a church, two cemeteries and two fronton courts with bleachers, used for games of *pelota* (jai alai). Set in the basin of La Rhune, the first summit in the Pyrenees mountains, Sare is surrounded by green rolling hills dotted with traditional Basque-style houses, with their whitewashed exteriors; red-tiled roofs; and wooden shutters, roof and trim, all painted green or chile-pepper red. Originally, the whitewash was made of chalk, and the paint was tinted red with cattle blood.

After Carmen retrieved us at the boulangerie, we caravanned to the house, following her car along the route that we would get in the habit of walking round-trip at least once a day, in 20 minutes, to buy bread or cake. The house had its own parking lot – a quarter of an acre lined with plane trees and rosebushes. We left our suitcases in the trunk and followed Carmen across Allée des Platanes to an enormous whitewashed house with a sign over the entrance indicating that it was built in 1619. I gasped.

The 11,000-square-foot structure was for many years the manor house of Basque shipbuilders, the largest of four homes on an estate that was ultimately divided. As Mark Kurlansky notes in his 1999 book *The Basque History of the World: The Story of a Nation*, "A central concept in Basque identity is belonging, not only to the Basque people but to a house." Rural houses always have names "because the Basques believe that naming something proves its existence," he writes. "Even today, some Basques recall their origins by introducing themselves to a compatriot from the same region, not by their family name but by the name of their house, a building which may have vanished centuries ago."

Ihartze Beherea, the name of the manor house that we would occupy, means "the patch of ferns below." That distinguished it from a house facing it, uphill, on the other side of the street that bisected the former estate (and where there may have at one time been a patch of ferns). Now situated on nearly an acre of land, Ihartze Beherea has working farms on two sides.

The Basques were expert carpenters and masons, and Ihartze Beherea was evidence of that. Built in the style typical of the Labourd province in which it is located (one of the seven historic Basque provinces), it has dovetailing stones at each corner, wooden shutters, painted green, and a red tile roof. An elaborate timbered façade faces east, in Basque tradition, in the direction of the rising sun.

The previous owner inherited the house during the 1960s from his mother, who bought it after World War II. Laurence and her husband, Emmanuel, purchased it in 2000 and moved there from St. Tropez. While raising a family, they spent two years renovating it, starting in 2001, separating the eight bedrooms and six bathrooms that comprised the family's living quarters from a three-story antiques shop that she operated for 14 years. After closing the store, in 2014, she adapted that space into a 2,000-square-foot triplex apartment with hardwood floors, its own garden and a separate entrance.

Her good taste, talent and ingenuity were apparent everywhere. On the entry-level, which functioned as a basement, were various curiosities from the shop, including a player piano, a sideboard hutch fully loaded with silver spoons and an antique doll's carriage. An old armoire had been turned into storage for the vacuum and cleaning supplies. Under the stairs, separated from the rest of the room by a curtain tastefully suspended from the ceiling, was a washing machine and ironing board. As in many French homes, there was no clothes dryer, but there were two retractable clotheslines that could be extended the length of the room, as well as a large, freestanding drying rack.

Covering the window at the foot of the staircase that led to the second floor was a linen curtain, embroidered with the family monogram. A shelf above the stairs held antique farm tools, and at the top were three oil paintings, each depicting an old man in a traditional Basque costume. The second-floor landing opened into a loft-like central room. It was furnished with antiques and family heirlooms that divided the space into living area, dining room and a galley-style, fully equipped kitchen. From the lampshades and custom-made draperies, to the throw pillows and artwork on the walls, everything was done in coordinating tones of red, white and beige. A bureau in the living room held two drawers full of Basque table linens and kitchen towels to match.

The mezzanine overlooking the living room was designed as a recreation area, with a baby grand piano, card table, two sofas and an enormous flat-screen TV. Like the two other stories, it connected to the owner's side of the house with a latch-lift door that was locked from the other side. We now understood the meaning of the word *mitoyenne*, used on the description of the house on Airbnb.

Within our own apartment, a large oak door separated the second-floor living space from a corridor that led to the two bedrooms, a bathroom (with both a tub and a shower stall) and a separate toilet cabinet called the WC (very typical in France).

Once Carmen had finished showing us how everything worked, including the pop-up exhaust fan and electrical outlet behind the propane-fueled stove, she let herself out through the latch-lift door on the first floor. We looked at each other, all smiles. This was exactly what we had in mind when we had envisioned living in France.

After we heard the door lock behind Carmen, we went out to the car to retrieve our belongings and get settled in our new home. I had a bit of buyer's remorse as I carried a dozen bottles of the Carrefour-brand Bourgueil 2014, which we had wedged between other items in our car trunk, roughly the distance of one city block, from the parking area to the front door. The more belongings we accumulated, the more manual labor was involved each time we relocated. I put all those bottles into a laundry basket on the first floor of our apartment, so I would not have to carry them upstairs.

Then we took another lap around the apartment to soak up the details. There was cross-stitched embroidery everywhere, from the family monogram on the lampshades and window shades to the hand towel in the WC. Laurence had left us a jar of homemade pâté, a basket of walnuts (the tree in front of the house was dropping its fruit) and a bottle of 2008 Bordeaux. She had stocked the refrigerator with bread, butter, juice and jam for our first breakfast. We compared this generosity with the "gift basket" at the winemaker's cottage, mostly filled with toilet paper, tissues, dishwasher soap and laundry detergent.

I was completely chagrined by my display of mistrust a week earlier in the e-mail correspondence with Laurence. Before I could compose an e-mail trying to make amends, I received one from her. It began, *"Content de savoir que vous êtes bien arrivés."* (Happy to know that you arrived well.) If her trusty servant, Carmen, had given her the full report (we assumed she had), there was no mention of how we had lost our way and no doubt inconvenienced her with our late arrival.

Laurence went on to clear up the mystery of their whereabouts. She and Emmanuel were walking part of the Camino de Compostela and wouldn't be back until October 4, unless their legs gave out sooner. For the next ten days, we would be all alone on this 17th-century Labourdine estate.

Not only had Laurence entrusted us with her historic home. She had also made at least as much effort to ready it for our arrival, as we had to prepare our Brooklyn home for our own tenants. On our pillows were tiny boxes of chocolates from Pariès, a gourmet shop with boutiques throughout Basque Country and a store in Paris. And on each of our night tables was a little square dish with a message written around its perimeter in script: *"Bonne nuit. Faites de beaux rêves."* I didn't need my French dictionary to translate: Good night. Have sweet dreams.

15

MOUNTAINS and OCEAN

～

I N AN E-MAIL sent on September 27, the day before my birthday,
my friend Wendy, who lives in Seattle, called my attention to the
much-anticipated lunar eclipse that evening. "Even though you probably
can't see this in France, it is an auspicious time for a birthday," she wrote.

I woke up early the next morning and checked. There, peeking
through the silhouetted trees, was the very visible surface of the moon,
partially eclipsed. Soon after, a rooster began to crow.

The choice of Sare as our home base had been fortuitous, and a
product of internet surfing. Having decided to explore Basque Country, I went on the Airbnb website and looked for lodgings in the vicinity of two small cities with names that I recognized: Bayonne and
Biarritz. We wanted to live in proximity to these places without necessarily being in the center of town. The Airbnb platform flags nearby
properties as well as those that satisfy the search terms one enters, and
gives the distances between them.

Though clicking on these other possibilities takes one farther afield from the original destination, that proved to be a marvelous research tool. During many hours of browsing, I read what guests had said about villages where we hadn't previously considered living. In the context of reviewing home rentals, several people, who didn't sound like they were shills for the tourist industry, portrayed Sare as a tranquil and scenic place. A search on Google revealed that it was on a list of the most beautiful villages in France.

From our experience in the Loire Valley, we knew that these lists are marketing hype, and the towns on them don't always measure up. However, in this case there were corroborating online sources. Though the full-time population of the village was only 2,100, it had two hotels and a tourist information office, suggesting that it had enough visitors to merit both. During the spring and summer, Sare was the site of numerous festivals. It got barely a mention, if at all, in our English guidebooks. Given our desire to go off the beaten path, this was a good sign. Between the location and the house, we thought we might have finally found a place to live out our French fantasy.

More comfortable in our new surroundings than we had been elsewhere, we began to reflect on the life stage that had brought us to France in the first place. As we age, we lose parts of ourselves. No matter how healthy our lifestyle, we can't turn back the physical decline. We feel less wanted – or not wanted at all – in the workplace. In cruel moments our kids accuse us of living in the previous century. They have their whole life ahead of them. We have more yesterdays than tomorrows.

Ken had made peace with these issues, but, with my impending birthday one short of 60, I was still struggling with them. Separated from the familiar, in new surroundings, immersed in a different language and culture, I began to rebuild.

From our bedroom windows in Sare, on the northwest corner of the house, we could see mountains, horses and free-range chickens. With a little head-cranking from a west-facing living room exposure, we had a view of La Rhune, shrouded in fog most mornings.

One day, after the morning fog lifted, we dashed to the nearby cog railway and took the lumbering, 30-minute ride to the top of Mt. Rhune. From there we could spot the beaches of Biarritz, France in one direction, and the forests of Spain in the other.

Regardless of the weather, tour buses deposited hordes of visitors at that little railway station each day. On weekends, when the weather cooperated, the adjacent parking lots were filled with cars, as hikers came to traverse the mountain by foot. We couldn't hike – just walking on cobblestones was painful for Ken. But we felt extremely grateful that, thanks to modern surgical techniques, he had enough mobility to make the trip to France.

It was a blessing to have a car, too. Through a sale-buyback plan available only to people who are not residents of the European Union, we had the use of a brand-new Peugeot, and unlimited mileage, for about $1,000 per month. It even came with a GPS, which, at least until we got to Sare, was good for marital harmony: We could blame the machine, rather than each other, when we lost our way. But it was an unreliable navigation tool for the zigzagging mountain roads in Basque Country. Its computer couldn't even get us back to Ihartze Beherea from the traffic circle just down the hill from our house.

By prowling local tourist offices and bookstores, we gradually assembled an impressive collection of maps, which also helped us orient ourselves. Basque Country comprises about 8,000 square miles on the Atlantic seaboard, in southwest France and northeast Spain. It is divided into seven provinces – four of them in Spain, where it is referred to as *El País Vasco*, and three in France, where it is called *Le Pays Basque.* Together they make up a territory that the Basques call *Euskadi.* Ask for a map of the area at a Spanish tourist office, and you are likely to get one focusing on the provinces in Spain: Alava (Araba in the Basque language), Guipúzcoa (Gipuzkoa), Vizcaya (Bizkaia) and Navarra (Nafaroa). Not surprisingly, maps from the French tourist offices give greatest prominence to the provinces in France: Basse-Navarre (Benafaroa), Labourd (Lapurdi) and Soule (Zuberoa). We ultimately purchased a detailed road map of the entire *Euskal Herria,* as it is known in Euskera, the Basque language. That means "the land of Euskera speakers."

Though we often had our GPS running in the background, we second-guessed the instructions it blared out in a disembodied female voice with a British accent. "She's WRONG!" I would exclaim, consulting the map spread across my lap, and checking the signs at various roundabouts – sometimes in French, sometimes in Euskera, and occasionally written in both. Fortunately for me, Ken did all the driving, since I found the twisting roads in Basque Country unnerving.

Even taking our time on them, we could drive in 45 minutes or less to the exquisite beaches of Biarritz, San Sebastián and St. Jean-de-Luz. Although they would have been mobbed during the summer, they were much less heavily populated in the fall as the owners of homes and condos boarded up their summer residences for the winter. I figured this was one reason that in Biarritz, for example, several had responded to my housing inquiries indicating their place was unavailable. It was too cold for swimming without a wet suit, but on many days during

September and October, it was warm enough for us to make day trips to one of these three places, explore the town and walk either on the sand or on the promenade.

We may reach a point where age makes this type of travel impossible. But for now, having wheels gave us freedom we didn't have when we were young and relying exclusively on public transportation. In those days we thought transiting overnight was a great way to save money, because we wouldn't need to pay for a hotel.

On one such night, in 1994, we rode the Mandalay Express – the train in Myanmar that goes from Rangoon to Mandalay. At the time, the Burmese government segregated tourists in a separate car, in seats that did not recline, and kept the overhead fluorescent lights on all night. During those sleepless hours, I read most of Paul Theroux's 1975 book *The Great Railway Bazaar*, about his Asian train odyssey, including experiences many years earlier on the Mandalay Express. Even with that distraction, I can remember few occasions when I was so happy to see the sun rise.

Now we could get in our rental car and easily leave an inhospitable situation. Our physical limitations, which had forced us to slow down, in effect made us appreciate the less frenzied, more gracious lifestyle in France. Everything, including the boulangerie, closed for at least two hours at lunchtime. Each transaction in the market started with bonjour and ended with *bonne journée* (have a good day), and on Fridays, *bon weekend.* On our first Saturday in Sare, as we traversed the mountain roads that led to St. Jean-de-Luz, we passed a couple picnicking on the side of the road. They had brought their own table and red-checkered tablecloth.

St. Jean-de-Luz eventually became our go-to place for everything from coffee beans to haircuts. And that is where we headed on the first morning in Basque Country, to provision ourselves for our latest French home. The ten-mile trip from Sare, which we would ultimately travel in 20 minutes, took considerably longer the first few times we did it.

To get there, one descends along twisty mountain roads with hairpin turns, then passes through the outskirts of town, dense with modern, low-rise buildings along the Nivelle River. They reminded us of Del Boca Vista – the fictitious Florida condominium complex where Jerry Seinfeld's parents lived in *Seinfeld*, the popular television sitcom.

The opposite end of St. Jean-de-Luz is much more upscale. Art Nouveau and Art Deco beach houses painted in pastel colors line the promenade that runs along the Grande Plage. Sandwiched in between is the port, with its crayon-colored fishing boats reflecting in the water. A 17th-century Italianate mansion that looks out on this scene was once the home of Maria Theresa of Spain. As part of a peace accord with that country, in 1660 the French King Louis XIV married her in St. Jean-de-Luz, at the church of St. Jean Baptist, which is still standing. A model ship hangs from its ceiling – believed to invoke God's blessing for the local fishermen.

St. Jean-de-Luz was, at various other times in history, an ancient port, a whaling village and a center of the French Resistance movement. During the Spanish Civil War, it became a base for expats who were known enemies of dictator Francisco Franco, notes Adam Hochschild in his 2016 book *Spain in Our Hearts: Americans in the Spanish Civil War, 1936–1939*. Among them were foreign embassies to the Spanish Republic and the trailblazing journalist Virginia Cowles, who was known for covering the war from the Republican perspective.

Today some of the cobblestone streets in the old town have been turned into pedestrian walkways, where it is possible to spend €800 on a cashmere cardigan or €1 on a single chocolate truffle that takes less than 30 seconds to melt in the mouth.

For lower Maslowian needs, visitors swarm the outdoor market on Tuesdays, Fridays and Saturdays. Food vendors set up their stands around the perimeter of the covered market called *Les Halles,* on Boulevard Victor Hugo, and shoppers from the surrounding area jockey for the town's woefully inadequate number of parking spots.

This market was far less abundant than our Loire Valley favorites, and the prices noticeably higher. Lush though the land looked around our house in Sare, it was primarily for cattle grazing and for growing corn used as cattle feed. (Corn on the cob is rarely seen in stores or on menus.) Not surprisingly, then, the market featured many preserved foods, sometimes labeled *produits du terroir:* The French word terroir means soil or region. The cookbook writer David Lebovitz defines it as "a confluence of elements – soil, atmosphere, weather, and other factors – that gives something a certain taste or flavor to foods and wine."

At the market, produits du terroir included *saucisson* – air-dried, garlicky pork sausage that looks like salami; cured ham from the nearby city of Bayonne; jars of duck confit and tuna; and preserves of fig, cherry and myrtle. Accustomed to shopping at markets for fresh foods, rather than preserved ones, I initially turned up my nose at these products.

Only later, once I better understood the region and its people, did I realize what I had been missing. The home-canned preserved tuna, for example, bore no resemblance to the tins of tuna fish sold in U.S. supermarkets. In Basque Country, canning, done in homes and factories, was a practical way of making certain ingredients, like peppers and white asparagus, available when they are not in season.

Those black cherry preserves, ubiquitous in Basque Country, were no ordinary jam, either. They are made with cherries from the village of Itxassou, where the spring crop is abundant enough to supply the whole region. When I finally succumbed and bought a jar of it, I found it paired well with the region's piquant sheep's milk cheeses, and when spread on French butter cookies known as sables.

Given a potentially overwhelming choice of merchants at large markets like this one, many selling the same items, I routinely looked for the longest line. That first morning in St. Jean-de-Luz, I relished a 30-minute wait to buy cheese from the farmer who seemed to have the best prices in the market. All around me, there was much air-kissing and gossip, to the extent that I could understand the banter. By the time my turn arrived, I could practically sound authoritative as I ordered the most popular sheep's milk cheeses, though many of them looked indistinguishable from one another.

My facility with the language, begun with podcast French, had improved with practice. Now I could shop as the locals do, asking for small quantities of everything: *un petit morceau de fromage* (a little piece of cheese), *une petite tranche de pâté* (a small slice of pâté) or *une poignée de haricots verts* (a handful of green beans).

With nouns, which are either masculine or feminine, I still used the wrong form at least half the time. How to explain that lettuce (*laitue*) and tomato (*tomate*) were both feminine, but that the cucumber (*concombre*) that went with them in the same salad was masculine? Oh, yes, and *salade* was also feminine. Sometimes I felt like a hopeless case.

I had worked especially hard on numbers, too, with mediocre results. Fluency with the numbers from one to 100 is essential for shopping in a French market, especially now that digital scales have become ubiquitous. These had tripped me up the previous year, when we traveled to Normandy and Brittany. So to prepare for the latest trip, during sleepless nights, or as I swam 40 laps at the gym in Brooklyn, I would count in French, sometimes starting with the number one, and other times beginning at 60, to get extra practice with the mind-bending use of 20 as a base in the French number system. The number 80, for example, is *quatre-vingt,* which signifies 4 (*quatre*) times 20 (*vingt*), and 90 is *quatre-vingt-dix* (a shorthand for 4 times 20 plus 10).

Though I thought I had mastered the numbers up to 100, on location they continued to confound. When quoting prices generated by those digital scales, merchants would slur together the number, followed by the word euro. The result, especially with an overlay of a regional accent, could be difficult to understand. So I found myself repeating the number, visualizing the numerals, then fishing through my change purse for the correct amount. Sometimes they would print out a receipt from the digital scale that I could use to verify I had heard them correctly. It was very humbling, at this stage of life, to feel so incompetent.

Ever patient, the French merchants were always happy to help. It was also immensely satisfying, on occasion, to ask a question and realize, from the answer, that I had actually made myself understood.

One Sunday we traveled the same route a bit farther, to the beach town of Socoa (its name in the Basque language is Zokoa). As we sat on a bench overlooking the ocean, having our own picnic of take-out paella, a stranger walked by and called out, bon appétit. Back home in New York, we would have thought that she was some kind of nut. But such gestures are so common in France that we assumed she was perfectly normal.

After lunch we walked along the beach and then to the fortress that juts out of the promontory. On the way back to our car, we perched on the stone wall overlooking the water, to rest. The beach had gotten more crowded, perhaps with others who had finished their picnics. Children played in the sand, and a few hardy swimmers headed out into the chilly water. One of them was a woman in a wheelchair being pushed by two men. Once the water was up to her shoulders, she slid off the chair, and the men took it back to shore. I watched her swim far out into the distance, her electric-blue bathing cap bobbing.

Though I was concerned for her safety, her two male companions didn't seem to be. They stood at the shore, next to the wheelchair, chatting, at times looking inattentive, as I watched her swim for 20 minutes. Then, she turned toward shore and, with a strong but awkward dog paddle, began swimming in. At that point, the two men monitored her progress more closely and, at just the right moment, came out to meet her with the wheelchair. It was a lesson in how to savor liberty to whatever extent we have it.

16

LET THERE BE LIGHT!

ONE EVENING, after we had been in Sare for about a week, the lights suddenly went out in half (but not the whole) house.

"Not *again!*" we exclaimed, practically in unison. Laurence and Emmanuel were still on the Camino de Compostela. Thrilled with our new digs, we had already committed to an additional week in Sare. But here we were, once more, being inconvenienced by a mechanical problem in someone else's old house. Things had been going so well lately, too. Before this happened, we were actually starting to feel relaxed.

Ken had made ginger chicken for dinner, using the ginger that Barbara had brought from Brussels to the Loire Valley, and which had traveled another 500 miles with us to Basque Country. Like so many recipes that we had cooked in France, it tasted much better than what we prepared back home – something we attributed to freshness of the ingredients. In this case, we had bought both the chicken breasts and the green beans that went into the stir fry at the morning market in St. Jean-de-Luz.

As we polished off the last morsel, we congratulated ourselves on how well we were adapting to the equipment in our various rental houses. Before making a recipe, my job in each place had been to survey the stove, oven and larder (both what was supplied and the expanding number of ingredients we had acquired along the way), to be sure we had everything we needed. Ken's role, as we got oriented in each new house, was to figure out how to operate the dishwasher and the washing machine – the theory being that, given the brevity of our tenancy, it would not be productive for both of us to master this new skill set.

So after dinner, in what had become our division of labor, Ken started up the dishwasher and put up a load of laundry. I, meantime, toted up the vacuum that Carmen, the cleaning lady, had called to our attention more than a week earlier, and ran it quickly around the kitchen and dining area.

I was downstairs, putting the vacuum away in the armoire near the washing machine, when Ken yelled down, "We've got a problem." After 25 years together I realize that sometimes when he says this, there really is a big problem, but other times there is a relatively quick and easy solution.

Though we disagreed about how to characterize the latest events, there was no disputing the facts: As Ken flipped the wall switch to turn off the candelabra over the dining table, there was a momentary loud pop and a flash of light from the fixture. After that, the electricity in half the apartment went off.

Based on my experience during the previous few weeks with electricity in rural France, I began to think in the manner that was becoming my habit when the power went off, which was to ask, "How does this affect me?" Both the desk lamp, and the electrical outlet in the second bedroom that I had made into my latest office, were still in working order, as was the Wi-Fi. Half the living room was lit, the refrigerator was on, and the dishwasher and washing machine had continued running. And though the bedroom was dark, the outlet we used to charge our iPhones (at that moment being deployed as flashlights) was functioning. Things could have been worse; I hadn't forgotten *Le Plombier* from the Loire Valley.

During our brief orientation with Carmen, when she met us upon our arrival the previous week, she had pointed out the main electrical switch, in a box outside the house. Why did I have an inkling that we might need this information? Though the contents of the box were of recent vintage, the key to it had the appearance of coming from at least one century earlier. Carmen had demonstrated how it worked, and how to turn the knob inside it for the main power switch. She didn't show us anything resembling a circuit breaker, though, and lacking the ability to get that granular in French, we did not pursue it.

When half the lights went out, I looked for clues in the loose-leaf notebook that contained the house manual. Laurence had thoughtfully included essential information in two hand-printed columns, with French on one side and English on the other. But on matters of electricity, it was not terribly, um, illuminating. All it said was, "If there is no more electricity, just have a look on the general electricity meter outside the house." So I went out in the dark, had a look and turned the dial, thus confirming that it was, indeed, the main switch.

By then Ken had deduced that there was some other switch, on the owner's side of the house, which we could not access. And the fact that we had been left in the dark about this, so to speak, tripped his personal circuit breaker.

In the welcoming e-mail Laurence had sent the evening of our arrival, she had said we shouldn't hesitate to contact her. But since our latest electrical crisis had erupted at 10 p.m., I suggested that perhaps we should wait until morning to take that liberty. I pictured Laurence on the Camino de Compostela, exhausted after a day of hiking, and being awakened by our phone call. But this was *her* house, and we couldn't address the problem without her.

While Ken composed an e-mail message in French, using Google Translate, I tried calling Laurence on her iPhone, left a voice mail and then sent a text.

If my carefully composed e-mails in our previous correspondence had led Laurence to believe that I could communicate in French, the latest messages most likely cleared up any misunderstanding about that. But 15 minutes after I sent the text, my cell phone rang. *"Déborah,"* said a husky voice on the other end (by then I knew from our correspondence that my name in French is spelled with an acute accent on the first syllable). *"C'est Laurence."*

However humbling that phone call might have been for the chagrined and very apologetic Laurence, linguistically speaking it was completely humiliating for me. It accentuated the fact that facility with a foreign language is inversely proportionate to the speaker's stress level. And whatever competence I had achieved during the past five weeks seemed to evaporate as I struggled to explain the rooms that had electricity and those that did not. Inconveniently enough, the *salle de bain* (bathroom) and the WC (the separate room with a toilet), neither of which had windows, fell into the latter category.

Even with the language barrier, I got the feeling that the problem I described in halting French was not foreign to Laurence. The good news was that it was easily fixed. The bad news was that fixing it did, in fact, require access to her side of the house. By the time she called, at 11 p.m., she had established that neither Carmen nor a friend nearby, both of whom had the house keys, could be reached that evening.

I held my cell phone at a distance as I translated this information for Ken. His reaction included a four-letter word that starts with an "f" and which some people might preface with, "Pardon my French." If Laurence did not know how to translate that word, she certainly understood that he was not pleased. After a bit of uncomfortable laughter, she spoke slowly, enunciating each word, as a mother might when explaining a difficult concept to a young child. The bottom line: She said that she and her husband were five hours away and could not do anything that evening but would leave first thing in the morning.

Just as daylight was breaking, she sent a text saying, *"Nous partons maintenant et serons à Sare vers 13 h 30. Encore mille excuses pour ce désagrément."* (We are leaving now and will be in Sare at about 1:30 p.m. Another thousand apologies for the inconvenience.)

The one logistical hurdle that remained was how to do our morning necessaries in a totally darkened bathroom. I told Ken, paraphrasing a famous quote from John F. Kennedy, that it would be better to light some of the many decorative candles around the house than to curse the darkness. He replied that he would rather curse the darkness. We compromised and did both, cursing the darkness in mid-morning as we brushed our teeth and showering by candlelight.

That afternoon, as I was sitting in the garden working on my laptop, a woman who could only have been Laurence blew through the gate. Petite and about 60, with golden hair pulled back to accentuate her high cheekbones, she was remarkably peppy for someone who had just walked nearly 140 miles of the Camino de Compostela in 11 days, and then traveled five hours back to Sare. *"Je suis très, très désolée,"* she said (I am very, very sorry), taking my hand. With the ice thus broken, and the lights back on, the French words flowed more easily. Ken came out to say hello, and between the two of us we managed to hold up one person's side of the conversation.

In the course of it, Laurence assured us that, for the rest of our stay, this would never happen again. She was rarely more than ten minutes away, she said. And if she ever went farther than that, she would leave the basement door that separates our two parts of the house open, so we could flip the appropriate switch ourselves. We thought of the classic movie line from *Casablanca,* when Rick (played by Humphrey Bogart) turns to Captain Louis Renault (Claude Rains), the French-man, and says, "I think this is the beginning of a beautiful friendship."

17

SIGNPOSTS

WHILE OUR LANDLORDS were still on the Camino de Compostela, we embarked on a *pèlerinage,* or pilgrimage, of our own, but one of a culinary rather than a religious or spiritual nature.

If our focus in the Loire Valley had been on housing – from opulent châteaux to our considerably less lavish rentals – in Basque Country the emphasis shifted to food, which has always been one of my favorite subjects. In foreign travel, observing how people eat and drink gives us more insight into their culture than we could possibly glean from any guidebook. And since we all need to eat, food is a great conversation starter, even when you don't speak the language very well.

In Basque Country, of course, we didn't speak the official language at all. Though *Euskera* uses the Roman alphabet, it makes heavy use of letters that rarely occur in English and score high points in games of Scrabble – most notably, "z" and "x." It also combines these and other letters in completely unfamiliar ways, for instance, by putting a "z" next to a "k," as in *Bizkaiko,* which means Biscay-style. On a menu, this word signals anything served in a pepper sauce. So if you don't like peppers – or especially do like them – it is very helpful to know that.

But whether you like peppers or not, you might wind up with them on your plate, since they are a key ingredient in Basque cuisine. Our arrival in Basque Country coincided with the pepper harvest. And it was a rare stew, braise, sauté or casserole that wasn't threaded with julienned strips of sweet or hot peppers in shades of red and green. When peppers are out of season, they are available in jars and continue to be used extensively in Basque cooking.

As for other ingredients, they were as diverse as the topography. From the sea there were many kinds of crustaceans, and less abundant but much prized (and pricey) hake. From the mountains came lamb, beef and free-range chickens. In the forests hunters shot game. Mushrooms grew in fields, woodlands and even along the road. Instead of butter, olive oil was the primary fat; though Italian brands dominate store shelves in the U.S., Spain happens to be the largest producer in the world. Pork dishes were an economical staple, incorporating nearly every part of the pig. There were *produits du terroir* in the markets, and *menus du terroir* in restaurants, featuring dishes with Basque names that were unfamiliar to us.

Deciphering them was a constant guessing game that we lost at least half the time. If we correctly deduced that *xardinak* meant sardines, or congratulated ourselves for figuring out that *txipiroiak* was the word for squid (I speak Spanish and took a gander at this one, since it sounded a bit like the Spanish *chipirón*), we would be stumped by the next puzzler: *xerrak* (filets).

We needed something to help us get oriented – maybe a cookbook. I stopped at a souvenir shop in Ainhoa, another one-street village about five miles from Sare, to inquire about whether there was a definitive guide to the local cuisine.

As I was mentally rehearsing how to pose my query in French, the saleswomen in the store, as one of them later confessed, were taking bets on whether or not I was Spanish.

This would become a common occurrence in Basque Country: On the French side, when I spoke halting French, I was mistaken for a Spaniard; in Spain, they thought I was French. *"Ce n'est pas mal."* That's not bad, the saleswoman told me, admitting that she had me pegged for a Spaniard.

Before I could express a jot of interest in the hefty volume she was recommending, she had removed the shrink-wrap from the 2006 book *Recettes des Sept Provinces du Pays Basque* (Recipes from the Seven Provinces of Basque Country), by Juan José Lapitz Mendia and Jeanine Pouget.

My father, who taught me to cook, always said that if you get one good recipe from a cookbook – what Ken and I refer to as "a keeper" – it has earned its place on your bookshelf. But in this case the first question was whether the book deserved a place in our suitcase. That tome weighed at least two pounds, which was more than any other single item I had packed. And it wasn't small, either – it measured about nine by eight inches.

After the shrink-wrap removal, I felt obliged to seriously consider a purchase that I would have otherwise dismissed out of hand. In fact, had it not been for the saleswoman's intervention, I never would have opened that book. I would have walked right by the table on which it was displayed, and not even put a single finger on it.

Though I pride myself on being able to go anywhere with nothing but a carry-on bag, for our three-month French adventure, I exercised less than my usual willpower. Instead of one 22-inch rollaboard bag apiece, we left New York with a total of three of these suitcases. Of course, we made our excuses. Since temperatures and weather conditions would change during our stay, we needed clothing appropriate for everything from a European heat wave to the potential early arrival of winter. And we figured things would be easier with a car.

After carrying those suitcases up and down the stairs at our first rental, I knew we had made a big mistake. Things hadn't gotten better with the expanding larder and supply of household items now filling all three of our gigantic duffle bags imprinted with the Aerobed logo. (Not to mention all the bottles of wine I had brought from the Loire Valley.) And now I was thinking about buying a two-pound cookbook.

The saleswoman may have been wrong about my nationality, but she was right about one thing: I was a sucker for a beautiful book. And *Recipes from the Seven Provinces of Basque Country* certainly was one. The binding was elegantly stitched, rather than glued, with thread in red and green – the Basque colors. It had a green cloth cover to match. The 176 pages inside were heavy, glossy stock. A mouthwatering photograph illustrated almost every recipe.

Both France and Spain were represented, and there was a brief historical or regional note at the foot of most recipes. In the back was a glossary and an appendix with advice about various kitchen techniques – for example, how to peel a pepper.

Most of the recipes were attributed to well-known chefs. Though surely some things had changed since this book was published, I figured that it could offer signposts for our culinary pilgrimage. Before I had even tried the first recipe, and arguing strenuously against Ken's sound-minded protests, I pronounced the book a keeper.

18

CAMINO FEVER

W E BEGAN our culinary pilgrimage, auspiciously enough, in St. Jean-Pied-de-Port, the most popular of five starting points for pilgrims on the Camino de Compostela. (The name of the town means St. John at the foot of the pass.) Situated about 30 miles southeast of Sare, in the Basse-Navarre province, St. Jean-Pied-de-Port is in a basin where three rivers, running down from the mountains, converge. Brick-and-stucco houses in the center of this picturesque town have their foundations on either side of the Nive River and are connected by a bridge.

At various times in history, the citadel that towers over the village was a military stronghold, since it provides a panoramic view of the surrounding countryside. When France and Spain were at war – and they were, often enough – this vantage point was used to spot attackers.

Centuries-old brick-and-timbered houses still line the narrow cobblestone streets that wind down from the fort. With a little imagination, one can envision the bustle of markets and hear the clip-clop of horses' hooves. Today, though, it is teaming with backpackers on their way to hike the Camino, a spiritual journey popularized by the 2011 movie *The Way.*

The film, adapted by Martin Sheen and his son Emilio Estevez from the book by Jack Hitt, depicts St. Jean-Pied-de-Port in one of the opening scenes. Sheen plays Tom Avery, an ophthalmologist who has come to retrieve the remains of his son, Daniel, who died on his first day on the trail. On a whim, Tom makes a pilgrimage to Santiago, along the 500-mile route from France, scattering his son's ashes and acquiring friends during the journey.

Among those whom the movie inspired was Denise Thiem, 41, an American tourist who had been missing on the Camino for five months when her body was found, in northern Spain, 18 days before our arrival in St. Jean-Pied-de-Port. The owner of a farm near the village of Astorga was arrested and charged with her murder. Thiem had quit her job in Phoenix the previous year to travel, and had begun cycling the Camino in St. Jean-Pied-de-Port.

Even without that sobering news, we had no plans to hike the Camino. We admired those who made the trip – not just the fictional characters in *The Way* but also those portrayed in Lydia B. Smith's 2014 documentary *Walking the Camino: Six Ways to Santiago.* (Santiago means St. James in arcane Spanish, and in English the road is called St. James's Way.) After his most recent back surgery, Ken wasn't up to it, but for me, especially, this arduous journey was ill-advised. For nearly 30 years, I had waged a battle against recurrent systemic infections that entered through the foot. Blisters, like those that hikers develop on the Camino, could be perilous.

Nor did we find the Camino fever in St. Jean-Pied-de-Port at all contagious. Despite its visual appeal, the old town was overrun with tourists, some of them hikers, and seemed to be profiting handsomely from 21st-century capitalism. A camping store, housed in a 16th-century building, sold everything from hiking boots and down sweaters to souvenir hats and pilgrim ponchos emblazoned with a scallop shell or sunray – both symbols of the Camino.

As for lodging, innkeepers had employed what Ken called a "market segmentation strategy." For those on a budget, dormitory-style accommodations, labeled *"refuge,"* fetched €10. But modern pilgrims with deeper pockets didn't have to rough it. For €76 they could spend a more restful (and private) night in a double room with an en suite bath. And just in case the Wi-Fi at either place happened to be malfunctioning, pilgrims could log on for free at the super-high-tech Tourist Information office.

Conveniently enough, it was directly across the street from Arrambide, the restaurant in Hôtel des Pyrénées, which we had identified, referring to our new Basque cookbook, as a potential lunch spot.

Neither the restaurant's chef, Firmin Arrambide, nor the recipe featured in the book – for *tartare de thon* (tuna tartare) – was anywhere in evidence. We ate there anyway. The €42 menu de terroir that I ordered was a terrific value compared to the prices back home but expensive for Basque Country, and the part I liked best were the complimentary hors d'œuvres. First came the goose bouillon with goose foie gras, which Ken fortunately didn't care for, so I ate two. Then, on a separate plate, were bite-size servings of smoked salmon with a dot of rémoulade sauce, trout with pepper sauce and a crispy cheese wafer. (I ate two portions of these, too.)

My first two menu items (more smoked salmon, followed by hake in green sauce), though beautifully presented, were unremarkable. For obvious reasons, I was stuffed by the time dessert came, so turned over the madeleines with apricot and raspberry confiture, vanilla ice cream and profiteroles to Ken, who had ordered the restaurant's send-up of steak frites à la carte. Our waiter, upon observing this contra dance, decided to make great fun of it, teasing Ken that he was eating my dessert, bringing an extra set of dessert cutlery, and serving up not only two plates of petits fours but also more sweets (these coffee-flavored), on the house, with my espresso.

Although our leisurely lunch had been delicious, it was a €90 splurge that neither our wallets nor our waistlines could afford to often repeat, and we came away no more enlightened about Basque cuisine than we were when we walked in the door.

We hoped for a more authentic experience at Zuberoa, in the Spanish Basque village of Oïartzun, about seven miles from San Sebastián. Our cookbook included a recipe by award-winning chef Hilario Arbelaitz for squid in its own ink, and I was eager to try it. (Squid ink is the dark liquid that these mollusks release as a defense when they are chased.)

We arrived in the rain to find Zuberoa, in a 600-year-old house, closed for vacation. Our grumbling stomachs matched our mood as we drove off until, around the next bend at the edge of a stream, I spotted a small red building with a sign that read "Matteo Taberna-Jatetxea." We could see that the lights were on. This was a good sign.

Lunch starts a bit later in Spain than in France, and, at 1 p.m., we were the first customers of the day. The middle-aged proprietor, who spoke Spanish with what I took to be a Basque accent, showed us to a table for two on an enclosed terrace, overlooking the stream. She asked whether we wanted to see the menu in Spanish or Basque, though the answer by then was probably self-evident. We later learned that the restaurant, which she and her husband now run, has been in her family for four generations, since 1902.

We opted for the fixed-price lunch, which was a bargain at €18 apiece, including: three courses, a bottle of wine, a bottle of water and a glass of Coke for Ken. No surprise that the place soon filled with locals who seemed to be on a leisurely lunch break, some of them dining alone.

I ordered squid in its own ink (*calamares en su tinta*) – a thick brown sauce that looked like chocolate and tasted intensely fishy – but the best item was the appetizer: *Huevo a baja temperatura con cremoso de patata y txistorra.* The centerpiece of this luscious ensemble was a poached egg, cooked at a low temperature (about 145 degrees Fahrenheit) in its shell, either in the oven or at a simmer, on top of the stove, for 45 minutes. This one was served in a thick, creamy potato soup that tasted like warm vichyssoise. It was topped with half a dozen chunks of cooked chorizo. (The menu had used the Basque *txistorra.*)

Our waitress said that, on weekends, when the fixed-price menu includes an extra course and costs €35, they do a more upscale variation, serving the egg in a creamed asparagus soup with truffles. I still regret that I didn't go back to try it – white asparagus is a specialty of the Basque province of Navarra. Even if I could master the technique for cooking the low-temperature poached egg, between that and preparing the soup in which it was served, this would be a very time-consuming recipe to make at home.

When we got back to Sare, I went online to look more closely at the menu for Zuberoa, the restaurant that had been closed. I noticed that they do their own version of the low-temperature poached egg, with foie gras cream, celery and truffle. It's available as a starter on the €130 tasting menu or for €31 when ordered à la carte. That's just a little less than it cost at Matteo Taberna-Jatetxea for the two of us to have a three-course meal. Again and again, since we left home, the most pleasurable experiences of our French adventure were not the ones that we had carefully planned but those that happened serendipitously.

19

HOMESTAY

~

A FTER LAURENCE AND HER HUSBAND returned from their
pilgrimage, we not only became acquainted with her charm but
also discovered the benefit of having a landlord on the other side of
a wall, rather than on the other side of an ocean, on the Camino de
Compostela, or a few hours away, in Paris. When something went
awry, as was inevitable in an old house, it was no longer our problem.

One evening, immediately after the electricity went off again, I
heard a noisy lifting of the door latch on the ground floor. When I
ran downstairs, I found Laurence holding two battery-operated lamps,
which she had brought for us to use.

I wasn't surprised about the power failure (this time it was the whole
village) – we were getting used to this aspect of life in rural France. But
I was touched by her thoughtfulness. It was also amusing to see this very
fashionable *parisienne* (though she hadn't lived there in decades, she still
described herself as a Parisian), with fingernails carefully painted Basque

red, standing in the shadows holding two plastic lamps. I wondered whether it had been too dark on the first floor of the apartment for her to notice our underwear hanging on the long indoor clothesline. She would have brushed by it as she rushed into our apartment.

The previous evening, from the other side of our *maison mitoyenne*, Laurence had sent the following text:

Bonsoir Déborah

Cela nous ferait plaisir que vous veniez dîner chez nous lundi soir, 12 oct. Est-ce possible pour vous?

Laurence et Emmanuel

(It would be our pleasure if you would come to dinner at our house Monday evening, the 12th of October. Is that possible for you?)

Excited as we were to receive the invitation, when that day came, we had some trepidation. Would we like her cooking? How would we communicate for an evening, given that we spoke very little French, and Laurence, at least, seemed to speak no English? To further complicate the situation, we had learned, in a couple of conversations with her, that Emmanuel, like Ken, was hearing-impaired.

With some hesitation, we paused outside the door on their side of the house at the appointed time (we were invited for *vers 20 h*, or around 8 p.m.). Standing in a drenching rain, I was holding a bouquet that we had bought several hours earlier at a florist in St. Pée-sur-Nivelle, a village about six miles northeast of Sare. We didn't know whether the evening would be a bomb, or a bust.

I had tried to psyche myself – and Ken – up for the occasion by reminiscing about other times when I had operated at what might be called a language deficit. I could still remember being left alone, at age three, with a woman whom I would come to call *Eichin*, a few

146

days after our family moved to Germany, courtesy of the U.S. Army. Although I spoke no German, I walked around our little apartment, in a German farming village, pointing at things and asking my new babysitter, who spoke no English, *"Was ist das?"* (What is that?)

As a mother, I harkened back to that day when our son, Jack, approaching his first birthday, was in the habit of pointing to things and saying, "That!" until we told him the word for the item at which his little finger took aim. Until then, I had no idea that my own approach to learning a foreign language as a child had been equally intuitive.

Fast-forward more than five and a half decades. Now, speaking a foreign language required one to let down adult inhibition and risk total humiliation. I kept telling Ken, as we struggled to speak French, that there was no need for perfection with either grammar or vocabulary. We could consider ourselves successful with a foreign language if we made ourselves understood.

In that respect, we surprised Barbara and Ray, when they visited us in Le Puy-Notre-Dame, and we all went out to dinner one night. Ken and I spoke to the waitress in stumbling French, while our dear friends, who had lived in Brussels for so many years and no doubt knew far more French than we did, spoke in English. By the next day, they told us that they had decided, much to my delight, "Heck, if they can speak French, we can, too!"

But while ordering from a restaurant menu involves a brief exchange, spending an evening trying to communicate with Laurence and Emmanuel might be far more challenging.

My first glimpse of their side of the maison mitoyenne left me tongue-tied. Their front door, on the same level as the area we were using as a basement, opened into a formal living room. From there, the house seemed like a vast expanse, in which rooms flowed into one another. The walls were painted a pale gold color, and almost all the furniture was white.

After a kiss on both cheeks, Laurence introduced us to Emmanuel, whom we had not met previously. He looked younger than he appeared in the postage-size photo of the two of them together on Airbnb, with a round, ruddy face, graying hair that might have once been red, horn-rimmed glasses and an avuncular manner.

Laurence served Champagne aperitifs, as we sat in what back home might be called a family room, and we made the first attempt at conversation. We started with an easy topic: the weather.

"À Sare, nous avons quatre saisons en un jour," said Emmanuel, who knew enough English to translate (and seemed to be able to lip-read in both languages): In Sare we have four seasons in a day.

During our first two weeks there (we had by then extended our stay to six), we had already noticed that, and knew enough to always have sweaters, raincoats and sunglasses in the car. But this expression was the perfect metaphor for more profound topics that dominated both the evening and our lives at this stage.

Emmanuel was born in Annonay, a small town 40 miles from Lyon, in Ardèche, a region in south-central France. They both spent summers in Sare as children and met at his cousin's wedding when they were in their 20s. They had raised four daughters, ranging in age from 24 to 34, whose faces beamed out from a framed photo they proudly showed us. Laurence ticked off their names, in birth order. The eldest, Elodie, lived in Toulouse and had two children who were coming the following week to visit them *sans parents* (without parents). They hoped the pitter-patter of little feet on the other side of our *maison mitoyenne*

148

would not disturb us. Marie, *numéro deux* (Laurence held up two fingers), lived in Nantes and had a toddler.

The two youngest were single. Justine, an aspiring comedienne, lived in Paris. Pauline, who we would later discover was the family linguist, was the youngest and was then living in Melbourne, Australia.

I figured this must have been what Laurence meant when, in the course of our initial, awkward e-mail exchange, she wrote, *"J'ai juste voulu vous parler de nous et de notre famille pour faire un peu connaissance."* (I just wanted to tell you about us and our family so you could know us a little.) Again, I felt ashamed for my earlier suspicions.

As we chatted about the number of babies she had in a short space of time, Ken sat silently with a blank look on his face. Classical music was playing on the stereo. I knew that, with this ambient sound, he couldn't hear a word of what we were saying. Even with a high-tech hearing aid in each ear, he couldn't decipher dialogue when there was background sound. At a party, in many restaurants, and even at small social gatherings when more than one person was talking at once, he couldn't comprehend anything. It was very isolating.

This happened in the U.S., too, when we got together with friends. When people entertain they set a mood with background music. It's awkward to ask them to turn it off.

And try to explain that in French. I couldn't. Pointing at my own ear, I simply told them that Ken could not hear with the music playing.

Laurence jumped up from her chair. *"Désolée! Pas de problème,"* she said. (Sorry! No problem.) In a flash, the music was gone, and we began to talk about what we had in common at this stage in our lives.

Ken and Emmanuel, who is two years younger than he, compared notes about their sudden hearing loss. Emmanuel thought his was age-related. With Ken, a bout with pneumonia and an ear infection following our 2010 trip to Tibet had a domino effect. For both men, it created an insurmountable hurdle in the business world. After working most of his life in the family food-distribution business, in 2016 Emmanuel told us he would be – we learned the French word for retired – *retraité*. Easy to remember: It sounded like the English word retreat. Too much so.

Ken might be retired, but we weren't ready to retreat. He was determined to keep traveling, and I was prepared to do whatever was necessary to make that possible while I continued to write from wherever we happened to be. Travel was an important part of our life together, and we both thrived on the stimulation. I carried batteries for his two hearing devices in my handbag. They needed to be changed every couple of days. We deposited the many used ones in the battery-recycling containers at tourist offices all over Basque Country.

After so much hard work in his French course, Ken could make himself understood, but he had great difficulty deciphering the replies. When asking directions, or checking in at an airport, he would motion for me to come close and serve as interpreter, even if the person on the other side of the conversation was speaking English. Whether in French or in English, many conversations in France were one-way.

When Ken described to our hosts how he had taken a college French course to prepare for our three months in France, Laurence exclaimed, *"Quel courage!"* (such courage). We were so moved when we realized that they completely understood.

We ate dinner in the kitchen at an old refractory table, facing an enormous hearth, reminiscent of the one in the house we had rented in Le Puy-Notre-Dame. The appetizer was a luxury item: grapefruit (from Spain) stuffed with avocado and shrimp. The next course was a home run: *axoa*, the chile-like local specialty that had already become our favorite. Laurence had bought it at the butcher shop in nearby Espelette and was amused to learn that we had already discovered this item there. (Axoa is widely available as a prepared food, not only by the kilo at butcher shops but also, home-canned, from farm stands, as well as factory-bottled, at supermarkets.)

From then on, the discussion continued without a lull. Like me, Laurence was born in 1956 and had a 60th birthday approaching – almost six months to the day before mine. To celebrate, she and Emmanuel were planning a trip to Australia. The walk on the Camino de Compostela, from which they had recently returned, was partially spiritual, they said. It was an expression of gratitude.

Like us, they were in transition and were monetizing their house. Income from their tenants helped pay for repairs and gave them a chance to meet new people.

For dessert, Laurence brought out a homemade lemon meringue pie. As perfect-looking as it was delicious, it was obviously one of her specialties. We couldn't refuse her offer for a second slice.

While we lingered over it, Laurence and Emmanuel asked whether we were warm enough on our side of the house. With the high ceilings and unheated third-floor loft, staying warm could be an issue, even though the house had many radiators. We were used to living in a cold house, though, and the temperature had not yet dropped below 45 – the threshold for turning on the heat in our house in Brooklyn. So for the most part we had been very comfortable putting an extra blanket on the bed at night and wearing sweaters during the day.

But given a segue into landlord-tenant matters, we mentioned that, ever since our arrival, the little door on the freezer compartment had been broken, and the bathroom radiator was now leaking. After our experience with our Amboise landlords, we didn't want to be blamed for any damage that might be attributed to us and debited against our security deposit, especially since the deposit in Sare was much larger – $1,116. And as cordial as our relationship with Laurence and Emmanuel seemed to be at that moment, we had also started out on good terms with the Douglases, owners of the winemaker's cottage. Laurence promised to address both problems during the next couple of days.

For the first time since leaving New York six weeks earlier, we were free of housing hassles. Not only that, but this part of our journey had turned into a grown-up version of the homestay I had experienced as a teenager, when I lived for two summers with Mexican families. Now, while maintaining our privacy, we were actually living with French people. And, as luck would have it, they were kindred spirits. Emmanuel observed the wonderful coincidence that had brought us together. *"La vie est belle,"* he said. (Life is beautiful.)

As we got up from the table, we thanked them for their hospitality and said how wonderful it was to spend a quiet evening in conversation. They knew that this particular comment was more than polite chitchat. At a wedding the previous weekend, Laurence noted, Emmanuel had been miserable because he couldn't hear anything that was going on.

"If I'm blind, people can see that, and they know what it means," he elaborated. "When you're hearing-impaired, people don't know." Unless, of course, you tell them.

Making new friends takes time and energy. When language is a barrier, it also requires considerable patience. After we returned to our side of the maison mitoyenne, Ken and I recalled key snippets of the conversation. Then we realized that most of it had been in French.

20

SATURDAY HAUL

⁓

OUR GPS INDICATED that it would take 27 minutes to get from Sare to Bayonne. It wasn't sophisticated enough to predict when we would get stuck on a narrow road behind bikers, or a slow-moving tractor, either of which could delay our arrival by as much as ten minutes. During this time we might appreciate the autumnal landscape, or find amusement in the road signs, like one that said *Chevaux!* (horses) and another, without any writing, that simply had a picture of a sheep.

Built at the confluence of the Adour and Nive rivers, Bayonne was for several centuries a major commercial center. Today artisans' studios line the cobblestone streets of the old market area. A three-story riverfront house holds the Musée Basque, an ethnographic museum with rooms devoted to various themes, including domestic life, sports and religion. In a nod to the Jews who once inhabited the city, there is a showcase with some largely unimpressive religious items, including a New Year's card and a couple of *ketubahs* (marriage contracts) from couples who were probably long forgotten. The Sephardic Jews fleeing the Spanish Inquisition are credited with bringing chocolate to Bayonne, and the city's reputation as a chocolate center has survived their dwindling population. But when we inquired at the Musée Basque about the best place to buy chocolate there, the staff recommended Pariès, the boutique where Laurence bought the welcome treats she had left on our pillows.

We became regulars at the Saturday morning market in Bayonne. On the first trip for this weekly event, we followed the traffic to what became our parking lot of choice – under the Tour de Sault. Built in the 12th century by the Viscount of Labourd, that tower once supported chains on a wooden landing that could be used to close off access to the Nive. Underneath it today are 490 covered parking spaces, where the first hour is free. From there, it is a five-minute walk to the Saturday market, first on a winding path that leads to the Ardour, and then down a dark alley of the old city that lets out on the Quai de la Nive.

Of all the markets I have been to in the world, the setting of this one is among the most beautiful. Vendors put up their stands along the river, creating an explosion of colors, the predominant ones in autumn being the green, red and orange of the squash and pepper harvests. While waiting to be served, shoppers have a view not only of the produce but also of the river and half-timbered four- and five-story Basque city houses on the opposite bank.

Unlike many of the markets we had visited in the Loire Valley, this one was a wonderful mix of generations. At the charcuterie truck, the vendor handed a taste of salami to a little girl wearing a blue-and-white-striped shirt and purple-framed glasses. The cheesemonger flirted with a golden-haired boy shopping with his father. And at one of the many vegetable stands, an elderly woman in an apron left a line of customers waiting as she came out from behind the counter to play with a baby in a stroller.

Though we were in a city, rather than in a small town, even here, no one was in a hurry. That was especially true at one farmer's stand where we waited to buy eggs while a woman in a dusty-pink down sweater had an animated conversation with the vendor. Though we were not close enough to eavesdrop (and probably would not have understood the exchange even if we were), it seemed to involve the condition of the *lapin* that she was purchasing. She came away with that rabbit, in a very unappetizing state of rigor mortis, tucked underneath her arm in a clear plastic bag. Completely skinned, from head to foot, its flesh was about the same color as the woman's jacket.

Upon arriving in the market, Ken and I would separate, agreeing in advance what we would each buy, and giving both of us the freedom to explore at our own pace and practice our French. We rarely lost each other for long enough to necessitate a phone call or text, asking, "Where are you?" I knew that I could usually find Ken staring longingly at a showcase of prepared Asian foods. He knew that he could find me queued up to buy cheese or *saucisson*.

Generally speaking, saucisson is garlicky dried sausage, unless you happen to be in a butcher shop or in front of a charcuterie truck looking at raw meat. In that case, I have heard uncooked sausage called saucisson if it is in links; or *saucisse* if those links are small. When ordering loose sausage meat (for example, to make stuffed peppers), one asks for *char*. This much is clear: There is no uniformity in the lexicon, and that gives foodies something to chew on. If there is any room for confusion, a simple hand motion in the direction of the desired item resolves any ambiguities.

As with so many other matters involving the use of language, the most important thing is to communicate your preferences. When discussing dried saucisson, those preferences involve shape, degree of dryness and the presence or absence of chile pepper. The slightly piquant saucisson made with chile pepper is called *chorizo*, possibly the one Spanish word that everyone in French Basque Country understands.

Dried saucisson is usually cylindrical but also comes shaped like a disk. The latter is called a *béret Basque*. Use this term in a hat shop, and you get something a little larger than the classic French béret. Ernest Hemingway sported one of these toppers on frequent trips to Basque Country as a young man. But nowadays, outside of folk festivals, one rarely sees a person younger than 75 wearing a béret Basque.

In the market, the charcuterie stands that sell saucisson are seductive, since they put out samples that get snatched up by hungry shoppers. And after that, the vendors assume, correctly, that you will not be able to resist buying the whole salami, as it were.

No matter the weather, the vendors were on the Quai de la Nive each Saturday, from 6 a.m. until about noon, under their market umbrellas, with each of them occupying the same spot from week to week. One exception was during the last two weeks in October, until *La Toussaint* (November 1 – All Saints' Day), which is a popular vacation time in France, and many schools are closed. In anticipation, those who would be *en congé* (on vacation) posted a notice of that the week before.

Though it didn't take much for a vendor to win our loyalty, the occasional curmudgeon could just as easily turn us off. That's what happened at the poultry stand where I had initially observed the lapin purchase. I had not brought empty egg crates with me, and the vendor refused to provide me with more than half a crate for my purchase of six eggs.

Without a covering, even though fresh eggs have harder shells than those we buy in the supermarket back home, two eggs broke in transit.

On future trips to the market, I took my business to another farmer, on the Pont Marengo. He gave me a starter set of egg crates that I brought back on subsequent weeks to refill. At his stand I also discovered *mamia* – a junket made by adding rennet to fresh ewe's milk. It is sold in portion-size ceramic containers that I returned on a weekly basis.

Also on the Pont Marengo, Ken began to frequent a stand that sold kiwis from the South of France, which were the best we had ever eaten, and another that sold nothing but clementines, which were in season in Spain. With their leafy tops that were an indication of freshness, the tangy tartness of this fruit made our mouths pucker. Our initial two-kilo Saturday purchase lasted only three days, so the following week we upped our order to three kilos.

My market splurge each week was a single perfect *cèpe* – a woody-tasting mushroom from the Irati Forest. The largest beech forest in Europe, comprising more than 42,000 acres in the Pyrenees, it straddles France and Spain.

The fall crop of cèpes, with their reddish-brown caps and dense stems, are prized items at the market. Fetching €28 per kilo, they are out of reach for many shoppers. On one occasion I observed a man fork over two €20 bills for a medium-size plastic bag of them. More often, they were purely a source of curiosity; passersby would just glance at the posted price and tsk.

A sign next to the cèpes read, *"Ne touchez pas. Merci"* (Do not touch. Thank you) When I told the mushroom vendor that I wanted just a single cèpe that was not too large, she held up a specimen that she pronounced *"très joli"* (very nice). I saw no room for argument.

I intended to make an omelet out of that cèpe, but after sautéing it in butter, I tasted one slice, and then another, until the mushroom was gone more quickly than I could scramble an egg.

My one cèpe quandary was how to clean them. Even the most jolie cèpe is streaked with dirt; the mushroom vendor wore white rubber gloves that had become tinged with brown from handling her wares. Real chefs do not submerge cèpes in water because they act like little sponges and absorb the liquid, reducing the intensity of their woody flavor. Our very thorough Basque cookbook suggested cleaning them with a wet dish towel, something I didn't think Laurence would appreciate my doing with her fine linens. The mushroom vendor recommended using a damp brush, which I thought only partially did the job; I scraped off the residual dirt with a knife.

As for cheese, in Basque Country *brebis* (sheep) was essential vocabulary, and it was a farmer who taught me how to pronounce it. We had taken a turn off the road into Sare, following handwritten signs that said *"fromage brebis"* (sheep's milk cheese) and led us to a ramshackle farmhouse. The place was locked, and a very frisky puppy ran over to great us. Just as we were about to give up on this latest pursuit of local color, an ample-size man drove up on an even larger tractor and called out, *"J'arrive!"* (I arrive.) Unfortunately, the cheese we bought from him had a lot less personality.

Going forward, I found it much more efficient to let the farmers bring the cheese to me rather than traveling to the farmers. And there were plenty of opportunities to do that at Basque markets and festivals. In Bayonne my favorite one set up a table on Saturdays at the foot of the Pont Marengo. After I had made several small purchases from her, one week she asked me, *"Est-ce que vous êtes seule?"* (Is it only you?) I explained that my husband did not like cheese. Though she clearly understood what I said, this seemed to be an alien concept.

I also patronized George & Co Bar à huîtres, an oyster bar on rue Bernadou adjacent to the market. Before, during or after shopping, the ritual at weekend markets includes stopping at the nearest café for coffee, or at a bar for a glass of beer or wine, even if it is only 10:30 in the morning. Since we were in Bayonne during months that include the letter "r," considered the prime time for oyster consumption, I availed myself of one of the specials at George & Co: six oysters, bread and butter, and *un verre de blanc* (a glass of white wine) for €10.

This repast was served to me by a waiter who could have passed for a young George Clooney. He was dressed in a pumpkin-colored apron and a natty neckerchief, with narrow pinstripes in orange and blue. I still associated those colors with the 1964 New York World's Fair. He was much too young to have appreciated the reference, but he wore those colors well and understood my French.

21

FRENCH COIFFURE

WHEN IT COMES TO HAIRDRESSERS, I tend to be a serial monogamist, but during our French adventure, it was inevitable that I would cheat.

As I explained in advance to Sonja, my loyal Brooklyn hairstylist, I would be living overseas for three months, working on a book, and there was no way I could go that long without a haircut and, more importantly, a dye job.

Sonja was very understanding. After what we agreed would be "one for the road," she handed me a Post-it note with the formula for my preferred shade of brunette. It looked like an eighth-grade algebra problem, but she assured me that nothing would be lost in translation: The most important thing, apart from this mix of color, was how long to leave it on.

But whom could I trust with my tresses – and with Ken's (he, too, needed some grooming)? After eight weeks away from home, I posed that question, loosely translated, to Laurence in an e-mail sent to the other side of our *maison mitoyenne.*

Laurence had lived in the South of France for several decades but had reminded us more than once that she was a native Parisian. And though you could take the girl out of Paris, you clearly could not take Paris out of this girl. For example, on one occasion we observed her raking leaves, dressed completely in white. On another, she showed up in suede and cashmere and, with gold bracelets dangling from her wrists, applied a rubber plunger to a clogged sink in our apartment. Her bluntly cut, chin-length blonde hair was testament to the fact that she knew where to find good grooming in rural France.

And it was not in Sare, a village with one boulangerie, one pharmacy, one butcher shop and one beauty shop that never seemed to be open. Instead, she referred us to what turned out to be the Chambon family's longtime coiffeur, in St. Jean-de-Luz.

Knowing what good taste Laurence had in everything from clothing to home furnishings, I feared her salon of choice might be one of the costly upscale establishments we had already observed in this beach resort. So, with some trepidation about that (and everything else), I phoned Pascal Coiffure and said she had sent me.

It seemed to be going okay until I said I wanted an appointment for about 3:00 the next day. Big mistake. Time in France is expressed using the 24-hour clock, and there is not much, if anything, open in St. Jean-de-Luz at 3:00 a.m. The man with the booming voice on the other end of the phone, who turned out to be Pascal himself, booked us for a cut and color at 15:30.

We arrived at Pascal Coiffure, which is half a block from the beach, at the appointed hour and got a warm greeting from both Pascal and his assistant, Chris. I'm not sure if that was because they had found my phone call so amusing or because I had been referred by Madame Chambon. But, really, it didn't matter. I was relieved to see that the salon, despite its proximity to shops where one could spend €800 on a cashmere crewneck, was totally no-frills.

First I asked Pascal, who looked to be about 50, had a two-day stubble and wore a black-and-white-striped apron over an all-black outfit, if he spoke Spanish. That was a fair question, since the salon's website indicated that Spanish was spoken. *"Un poquito"* (a little), he replied, which turned out to be an accurate assessment. My Spanish was slightly better than Pascal's, and my beauty shop French was considerably worse than his Spanish. So, as the conversation progressed, we defaulted to Spanish for most of the essentials, supplementing when necessary with French, facial expressions and hand gestures.

For the color, I showed him the recipe I had brought from Brooklyn. Pascal nodded approvingly at the formula, and disagreed with Sonja's note to leave it in for 45 minutes – that was too long, he said.

While I sat with the goop on my hair (he ultimately agreed that 45 minutes was right), I researched the French words I would need for the haircut. The most important one was "curly." Two possibilities, both easy to remember, popped up on the Collins French dictionary app on my iPhone. One option, *frisé*, sounded a bit too much like frizzy, so I went with *bouclé*, even though it might have described curls tighter than mine.

The other important thing I needed to convey was that I do not use a blow dryer, so I needed a low-maintenance cut. Pascal understood. *"Au naturel"* (literally, as it occurs in nature), he said, teaching me the essential vocabulary. His only question, which he used hand motions to indicate, was whether to cut it straight or, as he recommended instead, at an angle. Suddenly it dawned on me that this was not the first time Pascal had seen a head of naturally curly hair. I exhaled, sat back in the chair and relaxed – a bit.

He worked quickly. The place was hopping with women of a certain age, who seemed to be regulars. Judging from what I could hear of the conversations, some of them came every week for a coiffure. Most paid by check (Pascal doesn't take credit cards), leaving their payment on the counter. When Pascal got around to it, he would retrieve the check, stamp the back of it and put it in a drawer behind the counter. There was no slipping the hairdresser folded-up bills as a tip, either. At most, customers seemed to just put a few euro coins into the little pot on the counter.

After I sat under the heat lamp for about 20 minutes to dry my hair, Pascal came over and fluffed up what he said was my *cheveux bouclés* (curly hair). The cut, especially, was the best I had gotten in years.

Unlike Pascal's other customers, we did not pay by check. Instead, I left Ken, equally pleased with his own coiffure, in the shop as collateral as I went to the nearest cash machine. The total for the two of us came to €137 – less than I pay in Brooklyn, just for myself. I handed Pascal three crisp €50 bills and, with as much savoir faire as I could muster, deposited several coins he gave me as change in the little pot on the counter. As we turned our freshly coiffed heads and walked out of the shop, I heard his voice behind me say, *"sympathique"* (nice people).

I was in a tough spot when I got home and went back to Sonja, however. Clearly, she knew that someone else's scissors had touched my head. But I don't imagine she expected me to say, a bit sheepishly, "Do you think you could just follow the same lines?"

22

UNACQUIRED SKILLS

W E REACH A POINT in life when we are forced to acknowledge that there are some skills we will never acquire. For example, though I love learning foreign languages, I will never speak *Euskera*.

The origin of Euskera, like that of the Basque people, remains a mystery, and there are at least seven dialects. During most of Francisco Franco's long regime, speaking Euskera was prohibited, and even in the French provinces it was not spoken in public. So at least two generations grew up without learning it.

Today an estimated 700,000 people speak the language, and some of those words are coming straight from the mouths of babes. At the elementary school in Sare, at least half the children's signatures on the artwork displayed are Basque names. Parents who want their youngsters to have more instruction in the language than the school provides send them to afterschool programs, the way Jewish children in New York (and elsewhere in the United States) might go to Hebrew school.

For those getting a later start, there is the 2009 book *Le basque pour les nuls*, by Jean-Baptiste Coyos and Jasone Salaberria-Fuldain, widely available in bookstores and souvenir shops. Its bright yellow cover, with a black banner in the middle, is a tip-off that it is part of the "Dummies" series. The iconic Dummies mascot on the bottom edge of the cover wears a red béret and neckerchief – a traditional Basque costume. The word *nuls* means useless or hopeless. That seems to be as close as the French language can politely get to dummies. The fact that such a book, and many others on the Basque language and culture, even exist, is a sign of the enormous changes this region has undergone in the last 50 years.

Sufficiently challenged with French, we were not even tempted to buy the book. But we did find it helpful to learn a handful of words that are rarely translated. Not surprisingly, these words involve food.

They include *kokotxa* and *koka*, both of which might sound like they are somehow related to coconuts but aren't. The latter is the Basque word for what the French call crème caramélisée and the Spanish call flan. Kokotxa (pronounced ko-KO-cha), as a waitress indicated, pointing to her own corresponding body part, is the fleshy underpart of a fish's jaw.

To put it in the vernacular, kokotxa means double chin. And while most humans might not consider this a desirable trait, on menus in Basque Country, kokotxa, made with cod or hake, is a prized item. In their 1998 book *The Basque Table: Passionate Home Cooking from Spain's Most Celebrated Cuisine*, Teresa Barrenechea and Mary Goodbody note, "So desirable are these morsels that they often are removed from the fish while still at sea and sold right from the boat as soon as it docks."

For us, the most essential Basque word turned out to be *axoa*, one of our favorite regional dishes. The pronunciation (AH-tcho-a) roughly approximates the sound of a sneeze. To the American palate, it is reminiscent of chile but without the beans, and there are probably as many renditions of it as there are varieties of chile in the U.S.

Axoa can be made with either roughly chopped veal or beef, and an ingredient in many recipes for it is Espelette pepper – either whole or in powdered form. Chile peppers are not indigenous to France but were brought back long ago by the Basque seafarers. And they have since become widely used in Basque cuisine. Though not nearly as piquant as the chiles we are accustomed to in Mexican, Indian and American Southwestern cooking, they are so prevalent in Basque Country that it's easy to get caught up in chile pepper worship. And the great shrine of chile peppers is the town of Espelette. So it seemed appropriate to eat axoa in what Ken called "the point of origin."

It takes just ten minutes to drive to Espelette from Sare, first following the signs to Ainhoa, past sheep grazing, and then taking the first turn where the routing to Espelette picks up. Though the town, like Sare and Ainhoa, has just one curving street, it was hard to miss. The day we went there to eat axoa, in late September, the roundabout at the entrance to the village was planted with bright red begonias arranged in the shape of a chile pepper. The peppers, which start out green and sweet, turn red and piquant as they ripen in August. There is an Appellation d'Origine Contrôlée – a French certification of geographic origin – for Espelette peppers, just as there is for certain wines, cheeses and butters. Peppers are serious business.

Espelette, too, is surrounded by green hills and Basque-style whitewashed houses – these, trimmed in red, like the ripened peppers. People do seem to live there, but mostly it gives the impression of being a chile pepper theme park. Tour buses pull in each day, depositing hordes of day-trippers to have lunch and patronize the souvenir shops selling Basque linen, espadrilles and tacky chile pepper souvenirs. Peppery items for sale include: chocolate, ice cream, mustard, sheep's milk cheese and, of course, jars of powdered Espelette pepper. Tourist shops are decorated with strings of chile peppers, hung outside in the sun, which makes an attractive background for a photo; though this was the traditional way of drying peppers, today that process takes place mainly in hothouses.

Axoa is the house specialty at Hôtel Euzkadi, which also has a large restaurant. On the Saturday we ate there, it was filled with families, and with good reason: The portions were huge, the food was delicious, and it was possible to get a three-course meal for €20. At Euzkadi, axoa is made with veal.

But why go to the effort of all the chopping, pepper peeling and simmering to make the perfect axoa? This delicious concoction is widely available not only on restaurant menus but is also sold as a prepared food at butcher shops and in bottled versions at supermarkets. Even Laurence, who made lemon meringue pie from scratch, had served us takeout axoa for dinner. After that I decided there was no need to try my hand at it. We enjoyed takeout axoa from a variety of purveyors for the remainder of our time in Basque Country.

On the subject of salt cod, I reached the same conclusion for even better reasons. This ingredient, which is integral to Basque cuisine, is so different from fresh cod that in France (but not in Spain) it has a different name. The French word for fresh cod is *cabillaud*; once it has been salted and dried, it is *morue*. (In Spanish the only word for cod is *bacalao*; in Euskera it's *maikalao*.) Drying hardens the skinned fish, and salting preserves it further. The French refer to salt cod as *poisson des terres intérieures* (fish of the interior), since it could be transported inland and consumed far away from the sea. For Basque seafarers, it was also an important protein source onboard.

Ironically, Basque cod fishing has never taken place in local waters, as the journalist and author Mark Kurlansky notes in his 1997 book *Cod: A Biography of the Fish That Changed the World*. Four centuries after the Basques became associated with this precious catch, an omnivorous, shallow-water fish, in 1497 John Cabot inadvertently discovered what until then had been their secret source. He named the area New Found Land and claimed it for England. Jacques Cartier, arriving at the same spot, at the mouth of the St. Lawrence River, 37 years later, claimed it for France. "He also noted the presence of 1,000 Basque fishing vessels," Kurlansky writes. "But the Basques, wanting to keep a good secret, had never claimed it for anyone." By the mid-1990s many more centuries of politics and economics had just about put the Basque cod fishermen out of business.

Still, their rich legacy of salt cod recipes endures. Most begin with the instruction, *"dessaler la morue"* (desalt the cod). The gist of it is that if you can't find a fish store that has already reconstituted the fish, you need to soak it for 24 hours in freshwater or milk, changing the liquid three times before cooking the cod. To prepare it Biscayne-style requires even more advance planning, since one must also soak six dried peppers for 12 hours.

Salt cod happens to be available in New York, and used in a variety of ethnic recipes (among them Italian and West Indian), so I make a policy of eating it out rather than going to the trouble of preparing it myself. I saw no reason to vary this practice simply because we were in France. And, as luck would have it, morue, prepared various ways, was also available as takeout food. For example, René Massonde, the Espelette butcher shop that was Laurence's preferred source for takeout axoa, sells scrumptious *piquillo farcis à la morue*. These are sweet red peppers, grown in the Basque province of Navarra, that are stuffed with codfish. For €18.90 per kilo, or about €2.29 apiece, I could apply my energy to eating this labor-intensive delicacy rather than preparing it. It was money well spent.

But for me the cod recipe to end all cod recipes is *morue au pil-pil* (pronounced peel-peel). Some say this onomatopoetic term comes from the cooking process, in which the pan is vigorously rotated until the oil, drizzled in a little at a time, emulsifies with the gelatinous liquid given off by the fish as it cooks. Depending on the chef, garlic, chiles or parsley may be sautéed in a little oil before adding the fish.

Pil-pil was traditionally prepared in all-male Basque cooking clubs, known as *txokos* (txoko means a cozy place), the theory being that brute strength was required to get the liquid to emulsify. Sexism aside, a perfect – or even passable – pil-pil is not easy to produce, as I would later discover when I tried it in my Brooklyn kitchen. If the flame is too high or you add too much oil at a time, the liquid will separate, and you may not be able to reverse the damage. And while all this is going on, you want to make sure the fish is fully cooked.

"You must watch, listen and learn from your mistakes with this dish," writes Alex Raij, co-author of the 2016 cookbook *The Basque Book*, published after our return to the U.S. Owner of the New York restaurant Txikito, with her husband, Eder Montero (she's an Argentinian Jew and he's Basque), Raij offers an alternative to turning (or shaking) the pot. It involves removing the fish from the pan after cooking, and dealing separately with the sauce. To do this, you first pour off most of the oil in which you've poached the fish, so you can harvest the fish gelatin that collects under the oil. Then you put the gelatin in a bowl, together with the juices that the fish has released while it's sitting on a plate (tented). And, finally, you slowly whisk in the warm oil in which the fish has cooked, until the sauce emulsifies – you hope.

Raij warns readers that they may not have success until they have made this dish a dozen times and learned to control all the variables. "But don't worry: You can make all kinds of things from broken pil-pil," she adds in a not very comforting note. "I have made a career of it."

I'm sure Raij means well. But this is where she lost me. She is a restaurant owner, who could pass the broken pil-pil off to the next customer. What were all the rest of us supposed to do with about eight ounces of greasy glop? I served it with pasta, spread it on toast and folded what was left after that into the next pil-pil recipe.

It didn't take me a dozen tries to finally get it right. (I stopped counting – it was just too discouraging.) But the number of my failed attempts came pretty close to that. Every time that liquid separated yet again, I would repeat my favorite quote from Julia Child. As she dropped a lamb, a turkey or an omelet on the floor, she would tell her television audience, "If you're *alone* in the *kitchen*, nobody will know." I wondered what she would have said about pil-pil.

23

CAKE CULTURE

M OST PEOPLE THINK OF CAKES as something they buy, or bake, for a celebration. In Basque Country there's an annual celebration of the cake itself. Not just any cake. This is a festival for the *Gâteau Basque* (Basque cake), which is so lacking in visual appeal that it could easily earn a label as the ugly duckling of French pastry.

Compared with the delicate confections we sampled almost daily in the Loire Valley, the Gâteau Basque (or *"pastel Vasco,"* as it is called across the border in Spain) seems crude. The smallest one, meant as an individual portion (though two people can easily share it), resembles an oversized hockey puck. Larger ones bring to mind the cakes in a Bruegel painting. The Gâteau Basque looks like peasant food.

Basic ingredients of these cakes, which have the consistency of shortbread, are: eggs, sugar, vanilla, baking powder and flour. Traditionally, they were filled with cherry preserves. Later, chefs began to use the same pastry cream one would find inside an éclair.

Mark Kurlansky, in his 1999 book *The Basque History of the World: The Story of a Nation*, writes that the origin of the cake is uncertain but that it may date to the 18th century. In any event, it has so much folkloric importance that there's a Gâteau Basque museum, in Sare, set up for group visits, especially by schoolchildren. The Musée du Gâteau Basque is situated in an old farmhouse, and going there is like being on the set of a cooking show. You won't come away with a recipe – families zealously guard them – but you can see the technique demonstrated, and patiently explained:

Mix all the ingredients together to form a dough (called a *pâte*). Roll it out to a thickness of about one-quarter inch. Use a large, round cookie cutter to create a circular cake to fit your pan, which has been buttered and lined with parchment paper. In the pan, insert two layers of the rolled-out pâte, spread with the desired filling in between. Then bake for 35 minutes, if you are using cherry, or 45 minutes, if the filling is cream. Some chefs add a little almond powder to the pâte, or a dash or two (or three) of rum to the cream. The crystalized sugar, which is a key ingredient, acts as a preservative.

At first I didn't understand what all the fuss was about or why the Gâteau Basque ought to be a proper noun – in Basque Country, the name is always capitalized. In a New York minute, I would have traded a Gâteau Basque for any one of the pastries in the display case at Gauvreau, the Amboise pâtisserie that I had been so reluctant to leave behind. Maybe an appreciation of the Gâteau Basque was an acquired taste.

But within ten days of our arrival in Sare, I had acquired that taste, along with some preferences and what might pass for culinary insight. It seemed that the chewy texture I preferred was the result of bakeshop recycling – the pâte being rolled out again and again until it was used up. With each successive rolling, the cake got a bit denser.

As for filling, I favored cherry, as most women do, Laurence told us. Men, she said (including Ken), go for the cream. Either way, whatever was in the middle of that cake was as vital to the Gâteau Basque experience as the sweet cream filling is to an Oreo cookie. Without it, one would just be eating a dry biscuit.

When we told Laurence that we were looking forward to the *Fête du Gâteau Basque*, she glanced at us askance, as we might react to New York visitors who were bubbling over with enthusiasm about the Ninth Avenue International Food Festival. After attending this raucous event held in the neighborhood known as Hell's Kitchen many years ago, on an unseasonably warm Sunday in May, I decided never again.

The Fête du Gâteau Basque, which is low-key by comparison, is one of many festivals in Basque Country devoted to a single food. It is held on the first Sunday of October in Cambo-les-Bains, a village better known for its ostensibly curative thermal waters. (Edmond Rostand, who wrote *Cyrano de Bergerac*, reportedly went to this spa town in 1900 to treat his lung disease, and his home, Villa Arnaga, has been turned into a museum.) At the festival, there is a Gâteau Basque contest in which local bakers compete for top honors. Results are mostly a matter of proportions but also depend on how many times the pâte has been rolled out and the weather. While we were at the Fête du Gâteau Basque, it began to drizzle. That caused the cakes to absorb moisture from the air and softened them slightly, which was not necessarily a bad thing.

Just as the rain started, I overheard a French woman offer the following summary to her friend of what one does at these festivals: eat, drink, buy a Gâteau Basque and go home. At that moment, I happened to be sitting across from her at a long communal table, eating some very greasy paella out of a Styrofoam container. Apparently I was on the right track.

After that, Ken made the rounds at the various bakers' stands offering tastes, while I queued up to sample the wares of yet another farmer selling *fromage brebis*. Dressed in a Bretagne stripped shirt, red apron and *béret Basque*, the vendor was waiting on other customers when I slid into the line behind them. I thought I had gone unnoticed. Then he interrupted his sales pitch, picked up a wheel of cheese from which he had cut a large wedge, held it close to my face and said, *"Madame, posez votre nez dans ce fromage!"* (Put your nose in this cheese!)

I did as I was told, wondering who would want the cheese after I had put my nose in it. Apparently it didn't bother the customers ahead of me. They bought half the cheese. Then I bought what had become my usual amount, which was *"une petite tranche"* (a small slice).

Ken asked me why I needed another petite tranche of sheep's milk cheese, when I already had five others back at the house. I told him it was for the same reason that he needed to taste so many Gâteaux Basques.

When we asked Laurence and Emmanuel about their favorite send-ups of the Gâteau Basque, they named two producers that we had already discovered. One was at the Hôtel Arraya in Sare, which has a Gâteau Basque concession stand outside, supplied by a baking operation down the street. On walks into town, we often stood next to the open door of that little kitchen and inhaled deeply.

Our other favorite baker was Maison Pereuil, a sixth-generation family business in St. Pée-sur-Nivelle. In Basque tradition, they turn scraps of leftover pâte into cookies. These ultra-firm buttery rounds, which are easy to store, provided sustenance for the seafaring Basques — like a dessert version of hardtack.

With each purchase, the sales clerk at Maison Pereuil hands customers (and the mailman) one of those scrap cookies, "on the house." We looked forward to them as much as we did to the cakes. But when I tried to buy a half-kilo, the clerk explained that not a single one of these cookies was for sale. They are reserved as *"un cadeau"* (a gift), she said, and were disbursed just one to a customer. There was no room for negotiation about this. And, as we were yet to discover, like so much else in Basque Country, custom and culture were baked in.

24

CULINARY BOUNDARIES

W E HAD COME THIS FAR in our culinary journey when we
returned to the village of Ainhoa, this time for an annual festival. Autumn folk festivals in various villages coincided with our six
weeks in Basque Country. Printed signs for them were posted several
days in advance at crossroads, at local tourist offices and in town cen-
ters. And after enjoying all the local color at the *Gâteau Basque* festival,
we made a point of seeking out others. In Ainhoa, the big event was the
Fête de la Palombe, on the second Sunday in October.

Ordinarily I would have jumped at the chance to attend a village
festival. Such events provided one more way to observe local customs
and culture. But my enthusiasm for this particular fête waned when
I looked up *palombe* in my French dictionary and discovered that it
means pigeon. I have early childhood memories of feeding or chasing
pigeons in various piazzas all over Europe, when my family lived in
postwar Germany. Yet I grew up to find them distasteful. It's not just

that my hair seems to be a magnet for pigeon poop, but also that, in Brooklyn, I must routinely thwart the attempts of pigeons to nest in our window air conditioners. I tend to think of pigeons as flying rats.

In Basque Country, though, wood pigeon (and other game birds, including woodcock and partridge) are considered delicacies. Hunting season begins in mid-October, as the pigeons migrate south. Soon after, a sign appeared in front of the restaurant of the Hôtel Lastiry in Sare, announcing, *"Les palombes fraîches sont arrivées."* (The fresh pigeons have arrived.) At the Fête de la Palombe, some lucky pigeons are set free before others are turned into lunch.

In anticipation of this tradition, we joined the locals at high noon sitting on the pelota court in Ainhoa, waiting for the festivities to begin. The music started with a couple of songs by the church choir. Then a folk group came on stage and performed in front of a large, rectangular plywood box. It was followed by a benediction by the village priest, who wore a Basque green scarf over his white robes for the occasion. He led the audience in a responsive blessing of domestic animals, before opening the box and releasing a flock of pigeons that scattered into the sky.

At that point the crowd, too, dispersed. Some folks headed to La Maison Oppoca, a restaurant at the hotel of the same name across the street from the pelota court, where the first three courses on the €40 lunch menu were pigeon consommé, pigeon *salmi* (the bird is roasted and then served sliced in a sauce) and half a roasted pigeon. We left them to their gustation and headed home for a less elaborate lunch.

In his 2015 book *Around the World in 50 Years: My Adventure to Every Country on Earth*, a pilgrimage that included a lot of Third World travel, Albert Podell catalogues all the exotic foods he has eaten. The long list includes Mekong rat, elephant dung beetle and the brains of a freshly killed monkey.

There is not much overlap on our lists. Like Podell, we had eaten bird's nest soup and shark fin jelly, which were part of a Chinese banquet at a wedding we attended in Thailand. And the month before we met, Ken tried fruit bat soup on the Micronesian island of Palau – he told me about it on our first date. (I was impressed, not because it sounded appetizing, but because it established his credentials as a world traveler.) We probably ate dog meat on the island of Sulawesi, in Indonesia; the curry was so spicy, who could tell? What we took for beef rendang in Bali was more likely water buffalo. And we had allowed Jack, then seven, to eat fried crickets at a Bangkok night market.

Podell, not surprisingly, ate pigeon in France, but that is where I drew the line. I did carefully consider it: After all, on the plate, it looks a lot like chicken. But then, at the Saturday market in Bayonne, I saw several pigeons for sale, feathers and all. They looked just like the pigeons that we see all over New York, except that they were dead.

I realized that there's a difference between having an eclectic palate and being a truly adventurous eater. On our culinary pilgrimage, there was nothing to prove.

25

FROM a DISTANCE

⁓

I HAD BEEN SO PRODUCTIVE in the old liveryman's quarters in Le Puy-Notre-Dame that I was afraid of losing momentum when we moved on. In Sare I created a new workspace, in the second bedroom, where there was a writing table just double the width of my laptop. And, to my surprise, I continued the narrative with even greater intensity.

My workday started later than it did in Le Puy. We were too far from the village church to be awakened by the 7 a.m. bells. On many mornings, after a restful night's sleep, one of us would stumble out of bed, and the other, who had been disturbed by that stumbling, asked, "What time is it, anyway?" thinking surely it was the middle of the night, when, in fact, it was almost 8. The darkness was a result not only of the days getting shorter as autumn progressed, but also stemmed from the fact that France is on Central European Time rather than on Greenwich Mean Time.

As the morning fog burned off, the view outside our bedroom window looked like a painter's palette. In the garden the hydrangeas were fading to pinks and purples. The plane trees were brushed with fiery red and orange, while the rolling hills all around us were still a deep emerald. Even the sky was many hues of blue.

I spent most mornings writing, then joined Ken for an afternoon activity, which was sometimes just lunch in St. Jean-de-Luz and a walk on the beach. At La Boïna restaurant, on Boulevard Thiers, a main commercial street, we discovered what we called the "blue plate special" – a daily reduced-price main course. It might be fried hake one day and roast beef another. The special wasn't advertised outside, but as soon as we were seated, a waitress would arrive with a plastic holder containing a printout of the daily deal.

At lunchtime on weekdays, the place was filled with pensioners eating whatever that special happened to be. We wanted to think that was the only thing we had in common with them. "We're younger than they are – right?" we asked each other rhetorically.

During late afternoons, back at our house, when the weather cooperated, I carried my laptop to a café table in the garden, where I could smell the roses still in bloom and enjoy the shade of a giant walnut tree.

We adopted that tree. Its branches overhung the gravel path leading to our entrance, and during our first few weeks there, we had delighted in the windfall of nuts. We gathered our little harvest, shelled them, and munched on them as snacks or sprinkled them on top of salads.

In the European tradition, "to plant a tree was a sign – and it still is with many farm families – of settling down, of taking possession of a piece of land," notes John Brinckerhoff Jackson in his 1994 book *A Sense of Place, a Sense of Time.*

Laurence didn't know anything about the age and history of our walnut tree. Trees and houses guard the secrets of generations past. A note in our newly acquired Basque cookbook indicates that a walnut tree has special significance to the Basques. There's a tree planted on each farm to supply nuts for the whole family. They were food for thought, too, as journalist and author Mark Kurlansky notes in his magnum opus on the Basques. "Europeans believed that the physical appearance of food indicated hidden properties," he writes. "Walnuts enhanced intelligence because they resembled the brain."

On a clear evening, La Rhune might be capped with cottony clouds and backlit by the setting sun. I would move back inside, to my makeshift office, and write for a little while longer before dinner.

I had always fantasized about getting a fellowship to one of the well-known writer's colonies. But this was even better than that. Although the rent ($175 per night) was considerably more than our previous lodgings, our triplex in Sare was still within our budget. And it had most of the comforts and amenities we had missed since leaving home.

For the first time in several years, I felt happy. What was the French word for that? I observed, in eloquent e-mails from Laurence, both during our time in Sare and subsequently, that the language provides various ways to describe life's joys. There's "content," spelled and used the same way as it is in English, and *"plaisir,"* as in, *"C'est une grande maison familiale qui date de 1619, et que nous avons rénovée avec beaucoup de plaisir."* (It's a large family home that dates to 1619 that we have renovated with much pleasure.) Another possibility is *"bonheur."* For example: *"Nous continuons notre voyage avec autant de bonheur!"* (We continue our journey with the same happiness!) It had been a long time since I had needed any of this vocabulary.

Still, there were moments when I worried that I was spending too much time during our French adventure writing a book on spec. I did not want to look back on this interlude and wish I had spent less of it working. Part of what kept me going was the sheer pleasure that came from having a sense of purpose, even if the "assignment" was one of my own design. Having left a job that I abhorred, I had created one that I loved.

What's more, I believed in the adage, "The worst pencil is better than the best memory" – though I happened to be using more high-tech tools. If I didn't write about the sights, sounds, smells and emotions as we were experiencing them, I would lose the richness of the detail.

As my investment in the story grew, I became anxious about losing it in an even bigger way. The tens of thousands of words that I had written existed only in digital form, stored on electronic devices and backed up on a thumb drive and in the cloud. What if, through some freak event, I lost all that work?

Such concerns are nothing new, of course. Technology just gives us new ways to lose – and preserve – our creations. Ernest Hemingway famously lost what he called his "starter novel" and other material in 1922, when a suitcase full of his manuscripts disappeared. His wife, Hadley, en route to meet him in Lausanne, Switzerland, was carrying the unpublished manuscripts, including carbon copies, so Hemingway could continue his work on them and show them to an editor at a conference he was attending. As the oft-told (and psychoanalyzed) story goes, she stowed the suitcase in her train compartment, stepped away briefly to buy water, and came back to find the valise gone before the train ever left the Gare de Lyon station, in Paris. The suitcase and the manuscripts were never recovered. One wonders how Hemingway's literary legacy might have been different if there had been such a thing as thumb drives or, better yet, cloud storage.

My assumption that I could work from anywhere was certainly true, but the headaches and complications did not stay in New York. After going paperless in preparation for our journey, I was still getting used to paying bills and reviewing monthly financial statements, online, from overseas. Another Deborah, who had been my muse since I worked at The Content Mill, observed in an e-mail that our latest sojourn was dramatically different from when we backpacked as students and could "be away for long periods of time, with no bills to pay, no cell or computer, only the day-in-and-day-out of a new life."

As members of the "sandwich generation," we were both keeping an eye on an aging parent and parenting a college freshman from half a world away. As the only one of three siblings who lived in the same city as my mother, I had been most actively involved with her during the 18 years following my father's death. In my absence, and without being asked, one of my brothers, whom she favors, played a much more supportive role. The fact that she is relatively self-sufficient and fiercely independent made this easier. We were very pleased with how well it worked.

Our role as parents was by far more challenging as Jack made the transition to his first semester of college. Miraculously (or so it sometimes seemed), he gave every indication of managing just fine with such daily necessities as food, clothing and shelter. When we spoke via FaceTime, he looked happy and well groomed. There was no sign of weight loss or weight gain, and as he sat at his desk in front of his computer, in the background the bed was always made.

Though he texted us at least once a day, with an eight-hour time difference between Sare and Boulder, it was harder for him to call spontaneously. By late afternoon Boulder time, when he felt like talking, we were getting ready to go to sleep.

One day he texted, asking us to stay awake a little longer, so we could connect by phone. He had more than schoolwork on his mind. After saying throughout the college application process that he had no interest in Greek life, he had suddenly decided to rush for a fraternity. At first he was rejected by the frat that he had thought was courting him. He received a bid, or invitation to join, only once others had declined.

I was surprised that Jack would even consider a frat. Four years earlier, a 19-year-old Cornell student named George Desdunes had died in a gruesome alcohol-related hazing incident at the Sigma Alpha Epsilon frat house. George, who was from Brooklyn, had been a counselor at Jack's sleepaway camp the summer before, and the two of them had apparently bonded on the basketball court.

The morning that I took Jack, then not quite 14, to the funeral, was one of the most wrenching of my life, and the experience haunted Jack for years. When we spoke to him from France, the question running through my mind was, "After what happened to George, why would you ever want to join a frat?" But that was not how I phrased the question.

"What about that frat appealed to you?" I asked, trying to appear neutral. His answer sounded like something straight out of a frat's sales pitch: help with academics and time-management skills; career connections; and camaraderie that lasts a lifetime.

As he separated from our household, Jack had thought this band of brothers could give him another way to belong. By the time he called us, he had already turned down the bid. We were delighted that he had made his own decision.

The next morning, as day broke on the verdant hills of Sare, I flashed back to a conversation I had with Jack's third-grade teacher a decade earlier. When I went for a routine parent-teacher conference, he told me, "Jack's doing fine academically, but you must send this child to sleepaway camp ASAP. He needs to learn to live in a community that doesn't consist of his two adoring parents." We had followed his advice. Now Jack was at the next stage of the process. Our hermit crab was looking for a new home.

26

BORDER CROSSINGS

"The real voyage of discovery consists not in seeking new landscapes but in having new eyes."

– Marcel Proust

ONE OF THE BENEFITS of living in Sare was being able to sleep in France and spend at least part of the day in Spain. From Sare we were seven minutes to the Spanish border, and we had occasion to cross it regularly.

These were nothing like the European border crossings that I remembered from my childhood living in postwar Europe. My father, who fulfilled his two-year Army obligation in Germany, had been stationed, starting in 1959, at Käfertal Wald, outside of Mannheim. Instead of living on the base, we resided for two years in the attic of a two-family house over a butcher shop in Viernheim, then a village of potato farmers. And, during that time, I crossed many European borders.

Our travels, from the time I was three until I was almost five, consisted of what seemed like endless hours riding in an Opel station wagon, its backseat lowered to create what my parents thought was a reasonable facsimile of a playpen. In the days before seat belts, my brother Dan, who is 16 months younger, and I were supposed to quietly play with our toys, while my father drove and my mother navigated, holding our younger brother Paul, then an infant, on her lap. (Sometimes we cooperated.)

We moved to Germany just 14 years after the end of World War II, and I can still recall my father trying to explain the war to me. In Berlin, he pointed out bomb craters. When we visited Amsterdam, he took me for a walk along the Prinsengracht Canal and showed me the house where diarist Anne Frank and her family had hidden.

My other memories of our travels include eating double ice cream cones in the Tuileries Garden in Paris; walking around Madurodam, a miniature city in The Hague; and observing Dan, then about two, with his leg caught in a radiator in Madrid's Prado Museum. The hero of the rescue effort was a museum guard who extricated the child.

Those were very formative years. Most notably, I learned, from my parents' example, to go off the beaten path – to cross borders and test boundaries, both literally and figuratively. This would become a continuing theme in my travels and in my life's work. As I would later tell my own child, each of us is a product of our experiences. Remove any one of them and we are a different person.

Though I was too young to understand the military, I remember being frightened by men in uniforms, even when my father dressed in one to go to the Army base each day. And I found the guards at Spanish border crossings especially scary. With their three-cornered black-patent-leather hats, they were members of Francisco Franco's militia – the so-called *"guardia civil."* Future historians would tell of the atrocities committed during his 36-year reign.

"Franco's rule became less murderous and repressive in its later decades," writes Adam Hochschild in his 2016 book *Spain in Our Hearts: Americans in the Spanish Civil War, 1936–1939.* "But torture was routine, the regime remained a police state, and until 1974, a year before the dictator's death, it continued to execute prisoners with the garrote" (an iron collar used to strangle its victim). This included the time when my family lived in Europe and we traveled in Spain.

I would later learn that, during World War II, some Basques had collaborated with the French underground, transporting British and American pilots shot down in enemy territory, as well as Jews fleeing Nazi-occupied France, from St. Jean-de-Luz (a center of the Resistance movement) to Sare, and through the Pyrenees, which separate France and Spain. Today tour operators organize treks that retrace various escape routes along mountain passes, and there is little evidence of the old border patrols between the two countries that I recall from my early childhood. The only evidence that one has crossed the border tends to be a change in the language and color of the signs (yellow for France, red for Spain) and, in some spots, the condition of the road.

One exception is in the village of Dantxarinea, where one day we came upon a little building that quaintly said *"Douanes Françaises"* (French Customs). We were on our way back to Sare from the *Fête de la Palombe*, in Ainhoa, when we reached that triangular intersection. Normally we would not have come this way, but, because of the festival, we had wound up on what the French call *une déviation* (a detour).

By then it was Sunday afternoon, when nothing is open in France. On the Spanish side was a large Biok supermarket, which was doing a brisk business. In front of it were many cars with French license plates. (Prices for food are noticeably lower in Spain, both in supermarkets and at restaurants.) Ken, who calls himself the "Will Rogers of supermarkets" – he visits them everywhere we travel – went in to try to locate decaffeinated Diet Coke.

Meanwhile, I walked back to poke around the boarded-up old Customs station that had triggered powerful memories of my childhood. The white paint on its exterior was chipped, and inside were a couple of abandoned chairs and Formica and metal desks. Nearby was a patch of butternut squash ripe for picking. Beyond it, a red-and-white sign for Navarra identified land that belongs to Spain.

Across the road from the supermarket was a bank, now called Caja Rural de Navarra, which I imagined was a remnant from the days when one used to have to change money after crossing the border.

Such sites gradually disappeared after the Schengen Agreement went into effect, in 1985, opening borders between signatory countries, including France and Spain. And with 19 of those countries now using the euro, adopted as a unified currency in 1999, it is no longer necessary to change money when moving between the two countries.

I, too, was crossing borders, both physical and emotional. While living on the sharing economy, I had begun to discover new ways to work, without constraints. It was a world without boundaries.

27

THE SEDUCTION
of PINTXOS

WHILE ON A PILGRIMAGE along the Camino de Compostela, Tom Avery, a character in the 2011 movie *The Way*, stops at a Pamplona restaurant and tries to order tapas. Both a fellow hiker and the waiter tell Avery (played by Martin Sheen) that he's using the wrong word; in northern Spain bar snacks are called *pintxos*. Though the two are practically the same, the waiter says, he babbles on (in Spanish) about what seem like trivial differences: Tapas come on a big plate, while pintxos are smaller, served separately and are more work to prepare, he says. Misinformed by his American guidebook and thus humiliated, Avery decides to skip it.

About 50 miles north of Pamplona, in the coastal city of San Sebastián, he might have had a harder time resisting. Platters of these delectable finger foods are displayed in buffet-like fashion in bars all over town. And, as I discovered on multiple visits there, it is almost impossible to eat just one.

During the six weeks that we spent in French Basque Country, we traveled weekly to San Sebastián (Donostia is its Basque name) – to eat. Situated along three beaches, the most spectacular of which is Concha Beach (in a bay), the city is a favorite spot for surfers, who come for the giant waves at Zurriola Beach. Foodies know it as the place where pintxos are thought to have originated. And with some 200 pintxos bars to choose from, it is a grazer's heaven.

The 45-minute drive to San Sebastián from Sare took us along the edge of a forest and through the foothills of the Pyrenees. On one of those trips we stopped outside the Spanish village of Bera, to admire the mountaintops ringed in fog. En route home the same day, we slowed down to let a flock of sheep cross the road and, at the edge of a forest, drove by a couple who might have been foraging for mushrooms; they had their haul spread out on a picnic table beside the road.

In San Sebastián we would leave the car at one of the numerous underground parking lots and explore the city's pintxo bars by foot. With a little legwork and sampling, we recognized the standard offerings: stuffed mushroom caps; croquettes (made with beef, sausage or salted cod); and *tortillas*, which in this case are omelets, typically filled with potatoes and served in wedges. Hard-boiled eggs took on new personalities, stuffed with tuna or topped with shrimp, for example. Many pintxos looked like open-faced sandwiches and were constructed of toasted baguette slices covered with a spread such as crabmeat, or Russian salad – a mixture, of potato, egg, peas, tuna and mayonnaise.

And then there was the ubiquitous *Gilda*: a stack of *guindillas* (skinny pickled green hot peppers) threaded through a toothpick with an anchovy and an olive. Meant to resemble a shapely woman, it is named for Charles Vidor's 1946 film noir starring Rita Hayworth as a seductress and Glenn Ford as the love of her life. Legend has it that Casa Vallés, on Calle de los Reyes Católicos, a bar founded in 1942, invented this pintxo.

In the long history of the Basques, the one- or two-bite finger foods called pintxos are a relatively new phenomenon. The Spanish word *pincho* (pintxo is the Basque spelling) comes from the verb *pinchar,* which means to prick, because originally pintxos were skewered on toothpicks. There is no mention of them in Ernest Hemingway's novel *The Sun Also Rises,* published in 1926, though Jake Barnes, the protagonist, like the author, visited both San Sebastián and Pamplona, two places where today pintxos are commonly served.

By some accounts, they became popular in the 1940s, as train and car travel made San Sebastián easily accessible to vacationers. La Espiga, the San Sebastián bar on Calle de San Marcial, founded in 1928, is credited with inventing the *banderilla,* which is a pintxo on a skewer-length stick. In Spanish bullfighting, a banderilla is an ornamented dart thrown into the neck or shoulder of a bull to make him angry. At San Sebastián pintxo bars, wooden banderillas are embellished with more palatable substances, such as shrimp, squid or a combination of the two.

Many bars are situated in the medieval part of the city (the *Parte Vieja*). There are dozens just on 31 de Agosto, a street named for the day in 1813 when most of San Sebastián was destroyed by fire during the Peninsular War, and this street was reportedly the only one in the old city that wasn't affected.

A few blocks away, at a branch of Elkar, the largest publisher of books in *Euskera,* we armed ourselves with the 2015, second, edition of *The Pintxo Trail*, by Josema Azpeitia and Ritxar Tolosa. But within minutes of buying the book, which features about half the pintxo bars in San Sebastián, I had violated the authors' prime directive: "Say no to the plate!"

We had followed the lunchtime crowds into Casa Bartolo on Calle de Fermín Calbetón, where the garrulous bartender handed us a large plate and encouraged us to fill it from the platters of mouth-watering pintxos on the bar. This was good for business but apparently ran contrary to the tradition of San Sebastián bar crawling – the Basque word for it is *txikiteo*. Rather than fill a large plate, the idea is to sample just one item at a place, perhaps with a drink, and then move on.

Though soft drinks were available, it's more common to wash down pintxos with a bottle of hard cider; a small cup of beer; or a non-alcoholic grape juice, known as *mosto*, or *Txakoli* – a slightly sparkling white wine with acidic overtones. When pouring cider or Txakoli, bartenders hold the bottle a full arm's length above the glass, aiming the flow at the interior side of the vessel. They are not just being dramatic: This aerates the liquid.

To specify the size beverage we wanted, terminology was important, but inconsistent. This much was clear: The smallest portion of draft beer is a *zurrito*, served in a short, straight glass that holds up to about four ounces. Wine or Txakoli in the same glass is referred to as *un chiquito* or *una caña*. As a waitress explained to me, people who prefer to drink their wine in a goblet ask for *una copa*, but that leaves the portion ambiguous.

The best way to figure out the convention in a particular place is to stand at the bar for a few minutes before you place your order and watch how other people do things. Or, you could become a repeat customer.

Another benefit of the latter is that you discover the best items at each place. We returned to Casa Bartolo on several occasions just to eat what we called "the pickle-tuna thing": preserved tuna sandwiched between sweet-and-sour pickles, with a green olive on either end, all held together with a toothpick.

As a source of information about house specialties, *The Pintxo Trail* led us to nothing but dead ends. On several occasions, we sought out establishments based on the tantalizing pintxos featured in the book's photos. These items were either not available when we asked for them, or the bar was closed when we got there (some are open only in the evening).

To be fair, the book includes a recipe to correspond with each picture. So if we were really disappointed – say, we had our hearts set on pork tenderloin stuffed with duck mousse, or a chunk of veal sirloin with foie gras and a reduction of forest fruits – we could have gone home and cooked it ourselves. But it was a lot easier to just move on to something else.

Indeed, part of the fun of grazing our way through San Sebastián was how one thing led to another. The city had an air of spontaneity, especially on Friday afternoons, when it resembled a giant party. On one such day, in the residential neighborhood of Gros, which is on the opposite side of the Urumea River from the old town, I was sitting at a table outside La Plata, on Calle del Padre Larroca, eating a tiny plate of very tender squid in its own ink, when I noticed a shop, across the pedestrian walkway, with cured ham legs (*jamón*) hanging from the ceiling.

In the time it took me to consume my squid and a café con leche, I got the impression that Abacería Balanzategui, as the shop was called, was popular with middle-aged women who wear a lot of makeup and gold jewelry. And though age was the only obvious thing I had in common with them, I began to think that taste in cured ham might be another. So when we had finished our pintxos (Ken had fried cod with tomato sauce), I entered the shop and tried to talk the talk.

The cured ham, which comes from Extremadura, near Andalusia, is sliced off the entire leg, including the hoof, which is held in place with a vice. The slicer, dressed completely in black, wears a tight black glove on his left hand, which he uses to grasp the hoof, while he slices with his right.

The man with the black glove gave me a taste and told me in Spanish that this was the best ham in the world. Before I knew it, I had forked over €10.20 for jamón with a posted price of €22 per 200 grams. Even without seeing the price list or doing the math, I knew ahead of time that this pleasure would not come cheap, for I had seen the heavily made up middle-aged women handing over large denominations of euros as they made their purchases and had decided that my order would need to be proportionately smaller than theirs.

After I completed my purchase, of ten slices, the man with the black glove offered that, if I wanted more of it, he could ship it to me in France within 24 hours. Good to know. As it happened, that wasn't necessary. I made it last for three days, by which time we were almost ready for what was becoming a weekly outing to San Sebastián.

The man with the black glove was not there on our next Friday visit, or the one after that. In his place was a much less pleasant slicer who did not offer me a taste and refused to sell me anything except presliced, vacuum-packed ham. It did not taste like the best ham in the world. Maybe it wasn't.

A stroll on the boardwalk along Concha Bay soothed my disappointment, and we ambled over to the Bretxa Market, figuring we would take advantage of Spain's lower food prices before heading back across the border to France. It was late morning, and there was a lively crowd at Gorriti Taberna on San Juan Kalea, opposite the market. I suddenly realized I was hungry, so we crossed the threshold and squeezed into a sliver of space along the bar. There was much eating, drinking and chattering in progress. I noticed that no one seemed to be dashing off to do the txikiteo.

There are no plates at Gorriti Taberna, and everything is on the honor system. You help yourself to whatever looks good, eat standing up and toss your small napkin on the floor. Then you tell the guy behind the bar what you ate and ask him what you owe.

I started with a toast topped with goat cheese and tomato marmalade. The bartender insisted that it needed to be heated, and he did that just enough to soften the cheese so the two blended together in my mouth in a sweet and pungent swirl. Next, I couldn't resist the Russian salad, which looked so fresh. And, oh, well, no harm having that prawn brochette, followed by a Gilda. The total tab for the two of us that day came to €12, including drinks. Pintxos are traditionally people's food.

Not so, though, at the constellation of Michelin-starred restaurants in and around San Sebastián, where elaborate renditions of pintxos appear as complimentary appetizers.

We sampled this miniature cuisine at Arzak, which was the big splurge of our trip. Juan Mari Arzak, the owner and a pioneer of nouvelle Basque cuisine, cut his teeth at this family establishment, which currently holds three Michelin stars. And his daughter Elena, who presides with him in the kitchen, is, by some accounts, one of the best female chefs in the world.

Situated on the outskirts of San Sebastián, on Avenida Alcalde in the Alto de Miracruz neighborhood, Arzak is not the sort of place travelers might stumble upon. It occupies a salmon-colored building, with a brick façade on the first story, and boasts a red-tiled roof. Long before pintxo bars, Juan Mari's grandparents built the structure in 1897 to house the wine cellar and tavern of the village of Alza, now part of San Sebastián.

According to the detailed chronology on the restaurant's website, his parents turned it into a more upscale establishment, which his mother renamed Viuda de Arzak (Arzak's Widow) after his father's premature death: "It was claimed in those days that wedding dates were decided more according to the availability of the restaurant than of the parishes."

We, too, had difficulty making a reservation. When I called Arzak to do that, several days before my late September birthday, I was told nothing was available until the middle of December. They advised me to put my name on a waiting list. Instead, we spent my birthday at the beach in Biarritz, where we picnicked on bread, cheese, *saucisson* and fresh figs.

One month later, at 11 a.m. on a Friday, I phoned Arzak and, without any trouble, made a lunch reservation for 1:30 that day. We were seated at the kind of table you would give to someone who calls to reserve at the last minute rather than several months in advance: next to a window, but directly in line with the toilets and close enough to the kitchen that we could hear the clatter from within. Despite what might be considered our second-class dining quarters, there wasn't a pinch of pretense about the service.

Sensing we had no interest in the tasting menu for €199 per person, our waitress offered another way for us to eat a variety of items: Order half-portions of appetizers, main courses, or both. "If you don't like anything, we will bring you something else," she added. "And if you haven't had enough to eat, you can order more." I ordered three half-portions of appetizers.

Arzak's rendition of a slow-cooked poached egg, made with red peppers, fermented cereal and crispy pig's trotters, was a lot fancier than the version I had eaten at Matteo Taberna-Jatetxea, the mom-and-pop establishment in the nearby town of Oïartzun, at a fraction of the price.

Crab over seaweed with *huitlacoche* (corn fungus) sounded more intriguing than it tasted, and the presentation, in a salt rock, did not make up for that. Another of my appetizers, the foie gras, was chewy, rather than creamy, and got lost on the plate beside the apple slices injected with beetroot. The garnish, a paper-thin fried slice of "mother of pearl" potato, was intriguing but tasteless.

Ken said the tuna he ordered as a main course, which arrived covered with a wine-tinged tamale, was some of the best he had ever eaten. His other demi-size main course was a steak, ingeniously delivered. First, a digital picture frame with a blazing fire was brought to our table. After that, the steak was served, on a glass plate put over the frame, making it look like the meat was ablaze. Call it a digital flambé. When the server poured on the green tea sauce, it sizzled, giving off a small cloud of smoke – an effect that can be created with liquid nitrogen. As it subsided, the photo under the plate switched from fire to a tranquil mountain scene. Ironically, this was the menu item that seemed to be designed for less adventurous eaters.

But the star of the show turned out to be the pintxos, brought to each table with compliments of the chef: bright orange, prawn-flavored gyoza (wonton wrapper) with a juicy piece of prawn at its center; chopped squid cooked in its own ink, served on a banana fritter; marinated white tuna stuffed with cheese and topped with a strawberry; and a tiny bottle of what looked like gazpacho but was actually a raspberry bitter. The most creative item was *txistorra* (the Basque word for the spicy sausage the Spanish call *chorizo*), wrapped in mango and served on top of an inverted mini (squashed) beer can in a tiny puddle of sweetened beer.

The total tab came to €172.70, including tax and beverages (a glass of house wine for me and a soda for Ken). Theoretically, the pintxos were free, but we had paid dearly for everything else.

28

PHARMACIE FRENCH

~

E VENTUALLY, I was able to find my way around any French market, but I never achieved the same level of competence in the French *pharmacie*. The most embarrassing example of that was the time I tried to buy gauze.

Of course, I had consulted my Collins French dictionary app before setting foot in the small pharmacie, next door to the Intermarché supermarket in St. Pée-sur-Nivelle. But perhaps I sounded tentative when I asked for *gaze*. The rotund man in a white jacket standing behind the counter looked at me quizzically from over the top of his reading glasses. Apparently my pronunciation of *gaze*, which means gauze, sounded a bit too much like *gaz*, something associated with gastrointestinal distress. As a pharmacist, he was probably more accustomed to having people ask him about how to *eliminate* gas – rather than *acquire* it. Eventually we established that what I needed were *les compresses de gaze*, or gauze compresses.

Fortunately our health issues in France didn't get much more complicated than that, but one always worries. In many years of foreign travel, there has been only one occasion when we came close to needing medical attention, but it was extremely frightening. That happened in 2010, during a two-week vacation to Tibet.

The day after we arrived, by plane, in Lhasa, where the elevation is nearly 12,000 feet, we were in our hotel room when I heard a thud. It was the sound of Ken landing on the bathroom floor as he fainted. It was not the first time he had been at altitude. When he was in his early 30s, he had climbed to the top of the Popocatépetl volcano in Mexico, at 17,802. And he had been fine when we had climbed to the summit of Mt. Kinabalu together.

About 20 minutes after that first thud in Lhasa, there was another one, as Ken fainted again – this time on the side of our bed. After he came to, I fired off an e-mail to his cardiologist in New York, not sure when he might receive it, since it was the cusp of the July Fourth weekend.

As Ken alternately slept and awoke, appearing confused, I waited for the doctor to write back, wondering if he was starting his holiday weekend or if we would need to evacuate to Singapore. Within two hours I received a reassuring reply advising me how to adjust the medications that Ken was taking – to lower his blood pressure and combat altitude sickness. There was no need to evacuate to Singapore or to break open the canister of oxygen in the hotel minibar (which I had also mentioned in my e-mail). But we did follow his further instructions to drink plenty of fluids and take it easy.

Ever since then, even when going to less adventurous destinations, we have bought insurance that would cover medical expenses overseas and evacuation, if necessary. Except in an emergency, our health insurance, like many plans (including Medicare), does not pay for medical care abroad. To shop for coverage in this changing industry, I rely on Squaremouth.com, a consumer-friendly website, which makes it easy to compare policies. Cost is based on age and the length of a trip. When I most recently priced it for a three-month journey, we could get $1 million worth of emergency medical evacuation insurance and cover up to $50,000 of medical expenses, per person (subject to a $250 deductible, with the plan paying 80 percent of expenses after that), for as little as $400. I consider that a small price to pay for peace of mind. As with all insurance, the proof of the pudding is how accommodating a particular company is in processing claims. So far we have fortunately had no experience with that in this context.

Still, being far from home does tend to magnify the slightest physical symptoms as well as the anxiety that goes along with them. Over a period of several weeks, while we were living in France, I developed a series of mysterious welts, which I postulated might be, in roughly the following order: bedbugs, body lice or other insect bites; a newly developed food allergy; or (heaven forbid) shingles. Based on digital photos that I sent my primary care physician in New York, along with a somewhat frantic e-mail, he said all evidence pointed to insect bites but did not specify what kind. I never found out what caused the welts, but eventually they went away.

Before that happened, I got some additional practice with pharmacie French. My first foray into one of those establishments, with the green neon cross out front, was in Le Puy-Notre-Dame. Between looking up every other word on my dictionary app and pantomiming all the others, I managed to explain my mysterious bumps. The very kindly woman who worked in the store handed me a small box, with what I assume was the French equivalent of Benadryl, and another box with a topical gel to apply two or three times per day. They didn't work.

Subsequently, in Bayonne, I went to a pharmacie in search of baking soda. My doctor had suggested I combine it with water and apply it as a paste to my welts. This didn't work, either, and the paste made a big mess. However, the good news is that my transaction in the pharmacie went very smoothly. I checked my dictionary, asked for *bicarbonate de soude*, and the woman behind the counter handed me the right stuff. Just like that.

Taking (or perhaps mistaking) this one small victory for a sign of my growing aptitude with pharmacie French, I got really ambitious. On a subsequent trip to Bayonne, I went into a different pharmacie to satisfy my curiosity about something that had been on my mind. *"Est-ce que vous avez de l'Actonel?"* I asked. (Do you sell Actonel?)

Before leaving New York, I had laid in enough of this medicine, which slows bone loss, to last for the 89 days that we would be in France. That required me to present a photocopy of my airline confirmation to my friendly neighborhood pharmacist in Brooklyn so that he could help me get what's called a "vacation override" from my health insurance company: permission to be dispensed three months' worth of medicine, which I take weekly, instead of buying it just one month at a time.

But this drug is expensive in the U.S. It would have cost $231.48 for each box of four pills, were it not for the fact that, as a result of Ken's surgery two months before our departure for France, our family had not only met our annual deductible of $3,600 but also hit the maximum out-of-pocket expenditures for the year of $5,600. In

France, on the other hand, I could buy a one-month supply of Actonel for $27 – not the generic, which I cannot take because it upsets my stomach, but the name brand.

Suddenly I realized what the ultimate souvenir from French Basque Country would be. It was not the tablecloth and napkins that I had already bought, or the espadrilles that I had decided not to buy, or the Moroccan-made market bag with leather handles that I regretted not buying in the previous week's Saturday market in Bayonne. For me, that souvenir came from a pharmacie – the place where I had the least facility with the French language but stood to save the most money. I saw the opportunity to bring home enough Actonel to last until my next trip to France, at a cost saving that could finance the trip. I could feel my pulse go up.

And standing in front of me were two female pharmacists who would be very pleased to make that happen. One, who was about my age, spoke no English and seemed to be in charge, told me that she would prefer to have *une ordonnance* (a prescription) from my doctor. The other, who was just a few years older than my son, Jack, spoke enough English to help get me on the pharmacy Wi-Fi so I could send an e-mail to my doctor in New York, asking for a prescription.

By the time I woke up the next morning, her assistant had sent an e-mail with an ordonnance attached for a 15-month supply of Actonel. I was absolutely thrilled. This was also one of those occasions when I felt extremely fortunate to have doctors who enjoy technology as much as I do. If any of them mind my occasional offbeat queries from over-seas, they have never said so.

In any event, it took me about an hour, French dictionary in hand, to compose an e-mail forwarding l'ordonnance to the Bayonne pharmacie. When I did not receive an instantaneous reply, I called to confirm that it had arrived safely. This was a high-stakes deal. I wasn't leaving anything to chance.

Two days later I stopped at the pharmacie en route to the Saturday market. They had the five boxes of pills waiting for me, in a little basket, and greeted me like an old friend. The weather was unseasonably cold, and everyone was wearing scarves, but they assured me that it would warm up later in the day. *"Quatre saisons en un jour"* (four seasons in a day), I said, showing off the expression I had learned to describe the weather in Basque Country and relieved to be speaking something other than pharmacie French with these two lovely ladies.

The total tab, at what was then the conversion rate, came to $402.50. By stocking up in France, I had saved about $3,000. The pharmacist in charge packed the five boxes of pills into a plastic bag, along with a copy of l'ordonnance that she had printed out – just in case, she said, I needed it for U.S. Customs.

To celebrate, I crossed the bridge over the Nive to the Saturday market and bought the French market bag that I had coveted on previous shopping trips. The straw tote bag with leather handles, made in Morocco, cost €20. My initial hesitation stemmed from uncertainty about whether it would fit in our suitcase. This time I was so euphoric about my pharmacie souvenir that I tossed all practicality aside.

29

AUTUMN ROSES

"How long does it take to know a place? ... The visual quality of an environment is quickly tallied if one has the artist's eye. But the 'feel' of a place takes longer to acquire. It is made up of experiences, mostly fleeting and undramatic, repeated day after day and over the span of years."
–Yi-Fu Tuan, *Space and Place: The Perspective of Experience*

WITH LESS THAN A WEEK left in Sare, our lives felt as jittery as film shot with a handheld camera. We continued a ritual that we had begun in Le Puy-Notre-Dame, of traveling along roads not yet taken, and making lists of places we still wanted to visit.

Fall had arrived. Roses still bloomed, though in the company of fiery foliage and bright-orange bittersweet berries. Crews were at work pruning all the branches off the plane trees, leaving nothing but nubs atop their exfoliating trunks. Piles of firewood appeared on the farms.

Day and night were of about equal length, but it didn't get light until nearly 8:30. We needed to turn on the heat to ward off the damp morning chill. By noon the fog had lifted, on most days the sun was shining, and we could no longer bear to stay inside. Autumn tends to be rainy in Basque Country, but it had been unusually dry during our visit. Laurence kept telling us, *"Vous avez de la chance avec le temps."* (You are having good luck with the weather.)

On one such day we drove two hours north and west to the coastal village of Zarautz, Spain, making separate stops along the way to gaze at the waves and inhale the scent of the eucalyptus forest. We arrived at Asador Izeta, a traditional Basque grill high on a hill above the town, in time for lunch. The place was mobbed. At one long table was a family celebrating Grandpa's birthday. At another, a group of 12 businessmen were having a leisurely lunch, each with his own bottle of wine or cider. We followed their example and ordered a *chuleta* – a thick-cut T-bone steak that is the house specialty.

Charcoal grilled and then sprinkled with coarse salt, it was the best steak we had ever eaten – ambiance aside. Perhaps the reason that we ate so well in Basque Country was that the animals do, too. The sheep, whose milk went into all the *fromage brebis* that I had consumed, graze on fresh grass in the mountain air. Cow feed includes discarded apples.

In St. Jean-de-Luz we lunched on fresh fish, then shopped for souvenirs with a vengeance, as if this were a way of taking a piece of Basque Country home with us. I finally went into Laffargue, a leather-goods store I had admired many times because of the brilliantly colored cowhide accessories displayed in its window.

Founded in 1890 by Joseph Daniel Laffargue, a saddlemaker's son, it is still family-owned and has only this one shop; the atelier is in the back of the store. Their specialty is handbags, belts and leather accessories with studded patterns, adapted from old harness designs. I bought a wide, contoured black belt and returned several days later for a narrow one, in red. Though they weren't cheap, everything was handmade, the quality was incomparable and they were a much better value than what we could buy for the same money in the U.S.

We could wear our belts on the plane going home, but our suitcases would be bulging with the other Basque souvenirs we had acquired, especially linens purchased in St. Jean-de-Luz, Biarritz and San Sebastián. There was a tablecloth in a traditional pattern – seven dark red stripes (each representing one of the Basque provinces) against a white background; six napkins to match; dish towels; and a pastel-striped apron. And, of course, I was toting the made-in-Morocco French market bag that the vendor had assured me could eventually be packed. (I had yet to figure out how.)

On one of the few rainy days, we felt cozy in our Basque house, looking out over the undulating green hills. When the showers stopped, at about 5 p.m., we walked into the village and, on the way back, stopped to admire two rainbows. Cars whizzed by without seeming to notice the sky but perhaps wondering why we had come to a halt.

Our household in Sare had become what the French might call *un mélange* of autumn traditions. Ken subscribed to a version of NFL Game Pass available only outside of the U.S. that enabled him to watch any NFL football game, on his iPad or on my computer, in real time. Depending on where the game was played, this could be a sleep-altering event, as he would slip out of bed for a 2 a.m. kickoff. The games were accompanied by three-way text messaging with Jack and our nephew Howard in Florida, all of them fans of the Philadelphia Eagles.

On the last Sunday in October, we found ourselves hiking, from our parked car, more than a mile into Espelette, a village that a few weeks earlier we had pronounced a tourist trap. The occasion was the much anticipated *Fête du Piment*, marking the chile pepper harvest – yet another celebration of a single Basque food.

The second day of the festival, when we visited, Espelette was so choked with visitors, many of whom seemed like out-of-towners, that it was necessary to park on the side of the road, far out of town. This would have broken the rules back home but was perfectly normal on festival days in Basque Country. And the walk into the village helped us work up an appetite for everything we ate once we got there.

I started with *talo* – a flatbread made with cornmeal that is reminiscent of the Mexican tortilla. Wrapped around a filling, it is peasant food, traditionally brought by farmers, miners and factory workers to eat on the go. Those sold at festivals are generally filled with a thick slice of *ventrèche* (pork belly). They're tasty but tend to sit low in the stomach.

That still left room for a light, fluffy *macaron* – this one red-tinged and filled with ganache caramel and Espelette pepper, bought at the stand outside Boulangerie Patisserie Berterreix. Produced only from May until late October, these ethereal cookies cost €.90 apiece, and dissolve in the mouth in a sweet and spicy blend of chocolate, caramel and pepper.

Next came a parade down the main street of children dressed in traditional Basque costumes, with espadrilles (these shoes are a Basque invention, though most are now made in China) and crinoline-lined dirndl skirts. Also in the parade were representatives of various trade guilds for local products, in cleverly designed costumes – brown velvet for mushrooms, gold for wine and red for peppers, for example.

We returned a few days later, hoping to buy more of those sugar-and-spice macarons, but found a sign outside the boulangerie that said *Fermé*. It was closed for a two-week vacation. Euzkadi, the restaurant that had been bustling with locals during our Saturday lunch there in early October, was closed for a month longer than that – and not just the restaurant but also the hotel under the same management. Menus for Christmas and New Year's were posted in the window.

This was *Les Vacances de la Toussaint*: the week or two that schools are closed for vacation around All Saints' Day, which is November 1. That day is called *La Toussaint*, which is a contraction of *Tous les Saints* (All the Saints). It was the second holiday period that we had bumped up against during our three months in France. Although the sun was shining and the temperature was approaching 70, we had crossed a chronological dividing line: the official end of the autumn season for visiting southwestern France.

La Toussaint happened to mark the first anniversary of my departure from The Content Mill. Travel had transported me not just physically, but also mentally, from that awful work environment. I was engrossed in a challenging new project that applied my skills in exciting ways.

France was also an escape from the ageism and youth culture we experienced back home. In France I saw women in their 50s and 60s – women like Laurence, with whom I could identify – looking confident, comfortable and beautiful in their own skin. Strangers everywhere treated us with dignity and respect. In the many markets we visited, we observed others, our own age and much older, handled with equal kindness. I worried that our return to New York would feel like a setback.

At what would be our last Saturday market in Bayonne, we split up, as usual, to make our purchases. Despite the summery weather, the market was autumnal. The mushroom vendor had posted a sign indicating that this would be the last day for cèpes. My favorite vegetable vendor performed his usual shtick, doing the math in his head as he weighed, and then tallied, the items. The total for my purchases, of pumpkin, zucchini, red peppers, pearl potatoes and onions, came to €5.50.

While I wondered whether he had neglected to count something, he apparently thought I might have forgotten a necessary ingredient. *"Vous ne prenez pas de persil?"* he asked, after I handed him the exact change. (Don't you want to take some parsley?)

I shook my head. He reached into a plastic crate and, with two hands, presented me with a bunch of parsley, as if it were a bouquet of flowers.

In her 2011 book *La Seduction: How the French Play the Game of Life*, Elaine Sciolino, former Paris bureau chief of *The New York Times*, describes the seduction scene that she has observed at the market in St. Denis, a heavily Arabic suburb of Paris. She writes: "Here the merchants and their clientele – no matter what their color, religion, age, ethnicity, or country of origin – seduce each other. They share a common purpose: buying and selling food products, of course, but also anticipation of the shared pleasure that comes with cooking and eating." Though we knew few people in this part of the world, the Bayonne market had begun to feel like our community.

On that last visit, Ken met me in front of George & Co – the oyster bar that I frequented. I had perched on a stool outside and ordered one last No. 4 – six oysters and a glass of white Bordeaux. Ken, too, had acquired a bunch of parsley; his was courtesy of the fishmonger. Parsley is such an important ingredient in Basque cooking that it is customary to offer it gratis.

The George Clooney look-alike waiter was standing in front of the storefront, shucking each oyster with a quick flip of the wrist, then dipping it, on the half shell, in a bucket of water to rinse out the sand.

A waitress quickly brought my wine, but I had to wait my turn for the rest, since several tables of four people had apparently placed similar orders, and there were just two servers working the crowd.

Three young couples and a little girl, who looked about eight, arrived at the table adjacent to mine. She climbed up on a stool as the grown-ups stood beside the table, which didn't have enough seating for all of them. Their bottle of wine arrived in a plastic tote bag filled with ice. For the girl, the waitress brought a large glass of what looked like water tinted with red wine.

Several of the grown-ups lit cigarettes. Excluded from their conversation, the girl squirmed, shaking her shoulder-length brown hair. She was dressed in a pink denim miniskirt, white tights and pink floral Mary Janes and was wearing an oversized pair of white sunglasses, also printed with pink flowers. The handsome waiter, standing beside her shucking oysters, tried to engage her in conversation. She was too young to appreciate the gesture or to flirt back.

"There are three things you need to learn how to say," he told her in French, perhaps feeling rebuffed. *"Bonjour, s'il vous plaît et merci."*

I noticed that the word bonjour was first on the list. Every daytime conversation in France starts with this courtesy, whether one is asking directions, ordering food, browsing in a shop or just passing a stranger in the village on the way to buy bread.

"How are we going to go back to Brooklyn?" Ken and I asked each other. People will think we are crazy if we start acting this friendly. "What will we eat?" We had not only gotten spoiled by all the fresh produce in the market, at prices that were less than we paid back home, but also the bread, which was freshly baked several times a day.

As we neared the end of our French adventure, I felt renewed, but still unsettled about the life transition I was going through. While overseas, I had been contacted by junior-level staff from two different websites trolling for people to produce "content" (there was that word again). One was looking for someone to write about estate planning on a continuing basis and would pay me based on the web traffic my articles generated. The other didn't specify what they wanted me to write about but offered compensation as a percentage (he wouldn't say how much) of the ad revenues associated with whatever I produced.

This was the business model that had taken over my industry, in various degrees, during the past several years. I had resigned from a staff job because, despite my decent salary and excellent benefits package, I felt stuck in a hamster wheel. But I still loved reporting and writing.

"So now what?" I asked Ken one morning, referring to the uncertain future of my career. It happened to be La Toussaint, which, in addition to being part of a vacation period in France, is a day for remembering loved ones who have died. For the past week chrysanthemums had been for sale everywhere. It's customary for people to bring them to cemeteries, as Laurence had done; both sets of parents and grandparents were buried nearby.

Another reminder that life is short.

"We worked all our lives to get to this point. We're doing what we wanted to do. So enjoy it," Ken said, replying to my existentialist query. "And, besides," he added, motioning to the scenery that had been our backdrop for six weeks, "this isn't going to last forever." Though he hadn't directly answered my question, I realized that he was right.

30

THE LAST SUPPER

⌒

O N THE EVENING of November 1, I received an e-mail from
Laurence with the subject line *Au Revoir*. I opened it expec-
tantly. We knew that she had a trip to Paris scheduled and would be
leaving Sare before we did. I wasn't sure how we would say good-bye,
and I was dreading it.

For all our initial hesitation about our *maison mitoyenne*, the arrangement had worked out extremely well. Our primary concern, about
whether we would have enough privacy, turned out to be unfounded.
Although our living spaces were attached on all three floors, the only en-
try that Laurence and Emmanuel used was the basement one and, except
for the evening when the village lights went out and Laurence suddenly emerged from the other side of the house with two battery-operated
lamps, they always checked with us before coming over.

Though our garden was right outside their front door, no one disturbed me when I sat there reading or writing. Their garden, which we

did not have access to, was at right angles to ours, on the other side of the house, behind a gate that was closed when we arrived. As we all got comfortable with one another, I noticed that it was left open, but we never crossed the line into their space. Nor did I ever ask for a tour of their side of the house, curious as I was, after our dinner there, to see the upstairs. The respect for privacy was reciprocal.

At the same time, with our landlords on the premises, we had all the benefits of living in a historic home with none of the burdens. When the microwave conked out, Laurence brought over an extra, which belonged to one of her daughters, until she could exchange ours for a new one. She was the one who made the phone calls to *Le Plombier* and the refrigerator technician, and stayed home to await their arrival. It was Laurence raking the leaves or supervising the gardener who came to prune the plane trees and the hedges. We generally did our own housekeeping but accepted an offer from Laurence, about midway through our six-week stay, to send her cleaning lady over to vacuum and clean the bathroom.

On occasions when repairs required access, Laurence scheduled them at our convenience or, if we would not be around, asked for permission to enter what she began to call *chez vous* (your house).

In all our conversations, we continued to address each other with the formal pronoun *vous*. In this respect, her e-mail, about her impending departure, was as unpresumptuous as our prior communications. *"Je pars mardi à Paris voir mes filles et je ne rentrerai pas avant votre départ! Emmanuel, lui, reste là! Pourrai-je venir vous voir demain en fin de journée pour vous dire au revoir? Dites-moi, à quelle heure est-ce possible?"* (I'm leaving for Paris on Tuesday to see my daughters and will not return before you depart! Emmanuel will stay here! Could I come see you tomorrow at the end of the day to say good-bye? Tell me at what time that would be possible.)

When her message landed, I was making soup, half hoping we might all have dinner together one more time, and replied with an invitation for them to be guests *chez nous* (at our house) the following evening.

"C'est très, très gentil! Avec plaisir," she replied 35 minutes later. *"À quelle heure?"* (That's very, very kind. With pleasure. What time?)

I was doctoring the soup when they arrived, having taken too many liberties with the recipe for butternut squash and apple soup that I usually make for Thanksgiving. Most of my tweaks had worked well: Instead of butternut squash, I substituted pumpkin from the Bayonne market; used farm-fresh unpasteurized apple juice instead of cider; and, in lieu of mace, cardamom powder and curry powder, I used a few teaspoons of Colombo.

But having ignored the advice in my two-pound Basque cookbook, "Don't serve it to your friends until you've tried it yourself at least once," I was now paying the price. My addition of two sliced Espelette peppers gave the soup such a kick, that when I tasted it a couple of hours before their arrival, I began to worry that it might be too spicy.

In a frenzy, I tried to correct that, first by stirring in a container of *mamia*, another Bayonne market acquisition. It did nothing to tone down the soup but curdled at the top, making the lumpy mixture look like vomit.

Yikes! I put the whole thing through a strainer to remove the curds, and out with it came at least some of the chopped chiles. But by then the soup was infused with heat from them, so it didn't help much. As a counterbalance, I added more apple juice, a teaspoon of salt and a few lumps of sugar, and started it on a slow simmer. It was still bubbling when they arrived. I couldn't help noticing that the silk shirt Laurence was wearing was the same deep orange color as the soup.

As an aperitif, I served the last bottle of the Carrefour-brand Bourgueil 2014 that I had brought with us from the Loire Valley. When they complimented our choice, we told them about our secret source. They weren't the slightest bit surprised. And they laughed approvingly at my rendition of *pintxos* to go with it: thin baguette slices spread with a tongue-tingling sundried tomato tapenade that I had bought from a Moroccan vendor at the Espelette festival.

They were a great audience, but how would they react to the soup? When it had reduced by about one-third of its original volume, I took it off the heat, stirred in the last container of the coconut milk that Barbara and Ray had brought when they visited us in the Loire Valley, and announced, *"La soupe est prête,"* assuming, apparently correctly, that was the French equivalent of, "Soup's on!"

They both had seconds, no doubt ruining their appetite for the Thai lemongrass chicken that Ken prepared as a main course. For dessert we served a *Gâteau Basque* from Maison Pereuil, the bakery we liked in St. Pée-sur-Nivelle.

Our conversation was easier this time, though not because our French had gotten much better. It was our last chance – at least for a while – to spend time together. And, having all taken certain risks with the sharing economy, we could celebrate the success of that experience. As my friend Deborah, who has also lived abroad, observed: "When language is somewhat of a barrier, what is left comes straight from the soul."

I asked the question that had occurred to me during the previous six weeks, during which we had been observing Basque pride, and the rather insular Basque culture: What was it like for someone without Basque blood to move into this community?

"Nous sommes étrangers," Emmanuel quickly replied, and then translated, "We are strangers." Though Basque Country is part of their family tradition and many relatives are buried there, it is not in their DNA. Laurence interjected, in French, that having school-aged children helped them make the transition to living in Sare because there were opportunities to interact with other mothers.

I began to notice that, when Emmanuel spoke with us in English, she seemed to understand – more than she took credit for. At one point that evening I noted, a bit playfully, that Laurence understood English but was bashful about *speaking* because she liked to be perfect at everything. She subscribed to my philosophy, that it was more important to understand each other than to be perfect, as long as it was *I*, making a fool of myself in bumbling French, not *she*, struggling to speak English.

She smiled coyly, as her husband laughed uproariously. His reaction confirmed my hunch. This woman, who was so talented in her work, was reluctant to dabble in something if she could not excel at it.

Laurence was proud of the fact that she is an architect – she had mentioned it on various occasions – having studied for five years to become one. And yet, she was modest about the ways she had applied her skills to the renovating and decorating of our apartment, simply saying they were done *"avec plaisir"* (with pleasure). Only if asked, would she tell the story behind specific items.

And so I asked.

The fine Basque linens, including the napkins we had on the table that evening, had belonged to her mother, as had the 18th-century dining room chairs we had been sitting on for the past six weeks.

The heavy, elaborately carved oak door, which separated the living area from the bedroom corridor, had a history. They had found it in a dump in St. Tropez many years before and, after restoration, installed it in each house they lived in after that.

The biggest revelation was that the family still uses the space. When they are together for vacation – for a month in the summer, two weeks in the winter and on various weekends – the eldest daughter, along with her husband and children, occupy the apartment. During the winter Laurence and Emmanuel move in there themselves to cut down on the heating bills. *"C'est cosy"* (It's cozy), Laurence noted. They laughed when I observed that they have a summer home and a winter home under the same roof.

I was touched at how many items, precious to her, she was willing to share with people who started out as total strangers. As a relative new-comer to the sharing economy, she had done everything in her power to offer her guests a perfect stay.

She was eager for me to post a comment saying so on the Airbnb page for the house. Recommendations were vital to her future business, and she wasn't shy about asking for one.

I was waiting for this, or some other segue to disclose something that I hadn't revealed earlier: that I was working on a book about our experiences. I hadn't told them sooner because I didn't want any special treatment. At dinner, I tried to explain, as best I could in French, that I preferred not to post comments on home-sharing websites lest it com-promise my journalistic independence.

I wasn't sure whether they understood my ethical concerns, but they didn't seem surprised that I had a book project under way; by then I had produced e-mails totaling about 70,000 words and organized them into a rough table of contents. We knew that they observed our comings and goings. On many days we didn't leave the house until almost noon, because I spent the morning writing. Occasionally, when we ran into Laurence after not moving our car for a full 24 hours, she would ask, "Did you go anywhere yesterday?" To which we would reply (and it was true), "Yes, we walked to the boulangerie."

In this sense, our farewell dinner provided some closure. Without having to ask, "Why on earth did you spend six weeks here?" they had satisfied their curiosity.

I, on the other hand, still had more questions. Who had done all the cross-stitch embroidery? Laurence. How about the curtains and matching throw pillows? Laurence. She had not only upholstered all the furniture herself but had also made the beautiful white slipcovers that could be washed between tenants. Though the sharing economy is wide open to amateurs, this was no amateur production.

I wanted to take her home to make a few upgrades to our house in Brooklyn.

"Quel talent!" (Such talent!) I exclaimed. To which she replied, *"Je ne parle pas d'autre langue, et je n'écris pas de livres."* (I don't speak other languages and write books.) I was taken aback. *"Chacune a ... "* I began the sentence, and we finished it in unison, laughing, *"ses talents."* (Each one has her talents.)

We said au revoir to Laurence that evening, and to Emmanuel five days later, when we set out for Paris. Though reluctant to leave the tranquillity of Sare, we looked forward to visiting this magical city, where we had been before. Compared to everything we had done the previous three months, Paris would be the least adventurous and most predictable leg of our journey. Or so we thought.

PART FOUR

PARIS PAST, PRESENT, PERFECT

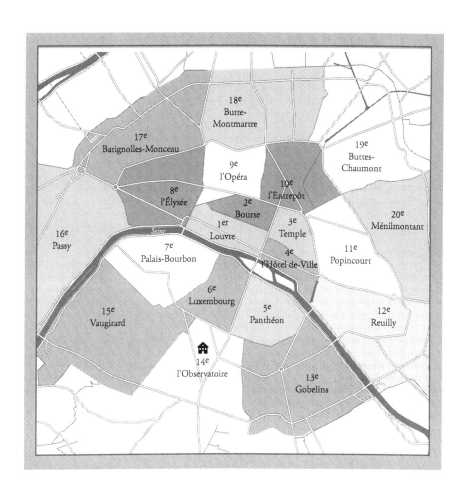

31

COUNTRYSIDE
in the CITY

HAVING LIVED at the foot of the Pyrenees for six weeks, we
found Paris both energizing and an assault to the senses. The
Airbnb headline for the apartment we had booked read "Countryside
In Paris!" We were more than a little skeptical.

Other elements of the listing, for a three-room flat in the Denfert-Rochereau neighborhood in southwestern Paris, seemed to meet
our needs. The words "quiet, within a big private park," certainly got
our attention. I had learned to avoid places described as "charming" or
"cozy" (translation: small), as well as those situated in a "lively" (a code
word for noisy) part of town. A *charming* flat that we rented during the
summer of 2012, on rue Buci in the *lively* St. Germain-des-Prés neighborhood, was within walking distance of the Louvre Museum, but we
dragged our feet there, having been awakened each night during our

one-week visit by drunken revelers leaving the nearby bars. This time, consistent with our goal of experiencing local life, we wanted to rent in a more residential neighborhood.

Oddly, finding a space for our car was just as important as where we slept. Drastic changes to our itinerary had left us stuck in Paris with a car we had initially reserved until the date of our departure. That was more of a liability than an asset. Rather than forfeit the last two weeks of the sale-buyback plan, we figured we could use the car for day trips and for the final haul to the airport with our much-expanded luggage. Otherwise, we would rely on public transit. But we were in a quandary about where to put the car during our stay in the city.

The response from several potential landlords whom we queried about this was discouraging. Most said we should ditch our car or pay €20 to €30 per day for parking. At "Countryside In Paris," parking was included with the rental.

The owner – call her Rebecca – divided her time between Paris and Tel Aviv, and rented out what she described as this "typically Parisian flat" when she wasn't there. About a dozen recent reviews on Airbnb described it as well located, spacious and just as depicted in the photos.

Through nail-biting Paris traffic, our GPS directed us to an enormous wrought-iron gate facing Avenue du Général Leclerc, a busy thoroughfare. I hopped out of the car and, referring to instructions from Rebecca, entered a code in the box attached to the gate. It swung open, revealing an enclosed garden surrounded by plane trees and a courtyard where we could leave our car. Around the garden were 21 low-rise apartment buildings and freestanding houses collectively called Villa Adrienne. Our search for traditional accommodations with free parking had led us to one of the treasures of Paris.

In French the word *villa* is used to describe a mansion, but in this context it meant something else: garden homes or enclaves within the city, situated along a narrow alley or behind a gate. I would later come across mentions of about 20 others, many of them identified in *Quiet Corners of Paris*, a highly informative little 2006 book by Jean-Christophe Napias, a Paris-based journalist and author. Napias, who organizes his survey around the 20 municipal districts known as *arrondissements*, notes that some villas, such as six of them in the 13th arrondissement and a considerably larger collective in the 20th, originated as affordable housing. Others, including villas in the 16th and 18th, were designed for the bourgeois. He calls Villa Adrienne "one of the stars" of the 14th arrondissement.

Even the houses in Villa Adrienne had highbrow names, in homage to poets, artists and philosophers. Ours was *La Fontaine*, after Jean de La Fontaine, the 17th-century poet and fabulist. Typical of those around the rectangular-shaped garden, it was a four-story yellow-brick walk-up with an Art Nouveau glass awning on its front. Adjacent to it was a two-story limestone structure with shutters and a dormer that seemed to date to an earlier period, with an attached extension that looked like it might once have been a stable. On the villa map posted outside the concierge office, it was labeled *La Petite Chocolatière* (the little chocolate factory). Today it houses a branch of Jacadi, an upscale children's clothing store that fronts on the boulevard.

A row of private homes extending back from La Petite Chocolatière was marked with the names of their current owners and, in some cases, their provenance. One federal-style house, for example, built in 1948, had a plaque on the side, indicating that Carl Walter Liner, the Swiss painter who died in 1997, lived there during the final years of his life.

Our apartment, one of two on what in France is called the first floor but which we would call the second, was a bright, airy railroad flat. Along its corridor were eight doors that in some cases closed off rooms and in others divided the apartment into sections. From the vestibule, one stepped immediately into a bedroom just big enough to hold a queen-size bed and two tall, skinny dressers. Sliding shoji screens separated it from a foyer and the garden-facing windows that provided the only source of light and ventilation to these sleeping quarters.

The next door led to a hallway off of which there was another garden-facing bedroom that I wound up using as my office. This room, with a trundle bed, was considerably larger than the one we slept in, with two casement windows that opened onto a French balcony (a fancy name for nothing but a railing).

Another door, to the left of that room, separated the back of the apartment from the front. Off the hallway, on the other side of the door, was a walk-in closet on one side, and a bathroom and WC on the other. The front room, consisting of a small living room area with a sectional sofa and a much larger kitchen, faced west onto Avenue du Général Leclerc. As at least one review on Airbnb indicated, with the windows closed, one could hear only a faint din of traffic from the street, and with all the hallway doors closed at night, it was not audible at all.

No one had mentioned the grungy bedding or the musk-scented oil sticks in each room. (Another reminder of how uninformative website reviews can be.) Guests weren't supposed to smoke, but was the owner – or her boyfriend – a smoker? They had been in the apartment a couple of days before we arrived. Perhaps they had set up the oil sticks to mask the smell of smoke. Or was there some even more odious odor in the building that Rebecca was trying to hide? Either way, the intrusive smell delivered an olfactory wallop each time we entered the apartment and clung to most of our clothing after we departed. When we got back to New York, we put everything in the wash.

With every move during our French adventure, including this one, it took us several days to adapt to our new living environment and learn our way around. Whereas hotels offered a built-in support system, with our latest mode of travel we needed to be more independent.

In Paris, we got a brief orientation from Sonia, who was Rebecca's cleaning lady and had her own apartment in Villa Adrienne. From the living room window, she pointed us in the direction of two different boulangeries and motioned across the street to the Mouton-Duvernet Métro station, with its original Art Nouveau ironwork. Voilà! As she prepared to leave us to our adventures, Sonia, apparently as instructed, asked for a €300 security deposit, in cash.

Not another legal issue! We refused, said this was against the Airbnb policy and told her that we would take it up with Rebecca. Sonia hesitated, as if this was a situation she hadn't yet come across.

In an e-mail to Rebecca, I sent a link to the Airbnb rules and summarized them. No money is allowed to change hands directly between guest and host. At the time of booking, the listing must indicate that there is a security deposit and say for how much. Then, if there is a claim, the host must file it within 14 days of checkout or before a new guest checks in, whichever is earlier. Only Airbnb can disburse the funds.

Rebecca promptly wrote back, pleading ignorance and apologized profusely. She also said taking a cash security deposit was common in France. (Not in our experience.) That note, plus a follow-up phone call from her the following day, left no doubt in my mind that she didn't intend to break the rules. But again, this was a situation in which a host – and apparently many guests, too – had transacted business on a platform, unaware of the terms and conditions of using it.

Still, the apartment was ideally situated. With a little practice, we discovered that by using one transportation system or another, we could get almost anywhere in the city in half an hour or less. From the Denfert-Rochereau station of the RER, a five-minute walk from our apartment, we could catch the B train that took us to the cathedral of Notre Dame in ten minutes. During off-hours, when there was no concern about traffic, we could travel aboveground, taking the No. 68 bus, from in front of Villa Adrienne, to the Louvre, the Musée d'Orsay or Marché Raspail, one of the well-known *marchés volants* of Paris. For €130 per night, including parking, it was an excellent value.

Our choice of location, though driven – as it were – by the car, turned out to be fortuitous. In her 2014 book *The Paris Vacation Apartment Guide*, Robyn Webb recommends choosing a less expensive arrondissement that is contiguous to one that is more upscale. Though this wasn't our game plan, it happened to work out that way, since the 14th abuts the more chic 6th. We were just a few Métro stops from popular destinations there, including the Luxembourg Gardens and three legendary Montparnasse cafés that Ernest Hemingway used to frequent – La Closerie des Lilas, La Rotonde and Le Dôme.

Within a five-minute walk, down rue Mouton-Duvernet or rue Brézin, we had our pick of boulangeries and restaurants, a couple of butcher shops, a fish store, a *fromagerie* (cheese shop) and a branch of Picard, the gourmet frozen-food store. Just a few minutes' walk west of there, toward Avenue Denfert-Rochereau, was a pedestrian mall on rue Daguerre, with an assortment of specialty food stores and restaurants. For supermarket-shopping, there were two different branches of

Monoprix within just a five-minute walk, in opposite directions, along Avenue du Général Leclerc. On Tuesdays and Fridays there was also a market at Place Jacques Demy, where local residents, including many pensioners, seemed to shop.

One thing I needed badly after three months in rural France was a *cordonnerie*, or shoe repair. I discovered one a few blocks from our apartment and learned a new word when a cobbler observed that there wasn't much left of my *talons* (heels). For €14 he fixed that and made me very well heeled.

Other residents of Villa Adrienne ranged from families with young children to elderly folks who may have lived at this address for many decades. If they minded transients like us, they certainly didn't show it. As we approached the locked iron gate on Avenue du Général Leclerc, we occasionally found ourselves behind them. Everyone smiled and said *bonjour*, and motioned for the other person to enter first. Sometimes there were so many exchanges of *après vous* (after you) that the gate, which worked on an automatic mechanism, started to slowly swing shut. Villa Adrienne was a very pleasant place to live.

As for the Airbnb headline "Countryside In Paris," it was once used in a less glamorous context. *Campagne à Paris*, Napias notes, was a low-cost co-op housing association that about a century ago bought up large land tracts that, initially, no one wanted. When Paris had been rebuilt in the late 19th century, under the stewardship of Georges-Eugène Haussmann, Emperor Napoléon III's head of public works, the debris had to go somewhere. As Haussmann masterminded grand boulevards and stately apartment buildings, construction rubble got dumped into quarries in the 20th arrondissement. Starting in 1926, along three streets, about 90 simple brick houses with stone or stucco facing were erected. The project had been named Campagne à Paris.

32

FROM TERROIR to TERREUR

U NTIL FRIDAY, NOVEMBER 13, 2015, we connected with the French people through the ordinary experiences of daily life. Then suddenly we found ourselves sharing the sorrow of an aberrant and historic event.

We had eaten seafood for dinner, purchased at a neighborhood fishmonger – tuna for Ken and a dozen oysters for me – and were having a quiet evening in our apartment when we heard more than the usual number of sirens outside.

Ken checked the headlines. "There's been a shooting in Paris!" he exclaimed. The story got worse as the evening progressed, with reports of coordinated attacks at five locations around the city: shootouts at several restaurants; a suicide bombing near the Stade de France sports stadium during a soccer match between the German and French national teams; and the taking of 100 hostages at the Bataclan music hall during a concert by the American band Eagles of Death Metal. By the end of the evening 129 people were dead.

As an American tourist in Paris, I felt the same numbness I had experienced 14 years earlier, on 9/11, living in Park Slope, Brooklyn, about five miles from Ground Zero. Our first impulse was to touch base with the people who might worry. Rebecca, our landlady, sent an e-mail from Tel Aviv, "Please let me know you are safe, and stay home for now." We tried to preempt similar inquiries from friends and family by letting them know, via e-mail, text messages and Facebook posts, that we were shocked but otherwise unharmed. Later that evening Facebook activated its Safety Check for Paris, providing a way for us, with just a few clicks, to mark ourselves safe.

Saturday morning, just as we did after 9/11, we looked for signs of life in the terrorized city. Though Paris was on lockdown, from the front window of our apartment, facing Avenue du Général Leclerc, I saw buses and plenty of cars. A woman had a cabbie wait while she went to the cash machine. There were people coming from the boulangerie with baguettes under their arms.

We flashed back to how carefree life seemed before crisis hit – how Paris perfect. On our first Sunday there, we had gone to the enormous outdoor market at the Bastille. At a fruit stand, a vendor was handing out samples of persimmons. The shopper next to me was going on about how they were not ready to eat that day but would be fine the following one.

How French. Eating fruits and vegetables at peak ripeness is such a priority that standard-issue brown paper produce bags in France have a box to check, indicating which day of the week the contents are expected to reach the right level of maturity. Reasonable minds can – and do – differ, of course. Hence the stranger's monologue.

After tasting the persimmon, I nodded in agreement to her that these were tomorrow's fruit and not today's. With the first French words out of my mouth, though, my cover was blown. This Parisian stranger, who had mistaken me for a local, was embarrassed. She apologized, in English. But why?

I assured her that no apology was necessary. Actually, I was thrilled. For three months I had been trying to blend in. Finally, I had succeeded. The vendor, who seemed amused by our exchange, threw an extra persimmon into my bag, gratis, and said *à la prochaine* (see you next time).

Even the weather was ideal that day, with an absolutely clear sky and temperatures in the high 60s – unseasonably warm for November. That evening, wanting to see the City of Light from the Seine, we headed to the pier near the Pont de l'Alma, where the Bateaux Mouches dock. Ordinarily we would have skipped these sightseeing boats, which have plied the Seine since the mid-19th century. (They were originally operated by steam.) But Laurence, the *parisienne*, had insisted that this was not to be missed, suggesting that to fully appreciate Paris from the river, we should take the cruise both in the daytime and at night.

As in other matters involving aesthetics, Laurence turned out to be correct. The view of Notre Dame, in particular, flooded in light, was spectacular. From the water we got a much better appreciation of the medieval ramparts of the Île de la Cité. Cruising by the Louvre Museum reminded me of how vast that building is. The Musée d'Orsay was also especially dramatic; from this vantage point, it was easy to see that it was housed in a former train station.

"We couldn't have planned this if we planned it," I said to Ken, admiring the illuminated Eiffel Tower. This "Yogi-ism," as he called it, referred to the wonderful good fortune we were enjoying after a bumpy start to our French adventure.

Then came more bumps. Not just a little turbulence, but a tragic terrorist event that shook the world. And we were in the middle of it. Again.

What happened next was reminiscent of 9/11. As we digested the horror of what had happened and waited for further news, we comforted ourselves with daily routines.

"Il faut continuer, mais ce n'est pas fini," a store clerk told me the day after the Friday night massacre in Paris. (It's necessary to continue, but it's not over.) Her comment turned out to be prophetic. In the months following our return from France, there would be more attacks – in Brussels, Istanbul and Nice.

After the Paris attacks, several friends asked, via e-mail and social media, whether we would take the first possible flight out of the city. My answer was an emphatic, "No."

For the second time in my life, I was living through the aftermath of an attack on a city that I loved. And the best way I could show my support to the French people was to stay, though, for the first couple of days after the massacre, we could not do most of the things that tourists generally do in Paris. Lucky we took that Bateaux Mouches ride when we did.

Saturday morning I wrote to Laurence. Our e-mails crossed in cyberspace. Hers to me, titled "News," began *"Rassurez-moi!"* (Reassure me!). Mine to her had the subject line, *"Tout va bien?"* (Is everything okay?). I was concerned about their daughter Justine, who lives in Paris. Fortunately, we were all safe.

There was train service from the Métro station outside our apartment, so we traveled a few stops to the tony 6th arrondissement, gaping at the headlines on display at newsstands there, just as in our own neighborhood. One on the cover of *Le Figaro* put it bluntly: *"La guerre en plein Paris"* (the war right in Paris).

A stroll through the Luxembourg Gardens might be soothing, we thought, but they were closed – patrolled by police who were visible through the locked gate. A van full of soldiers about Jack's age drove by. The cafés along rue du Montparnasse were open but not busy, and no one was sitting outside. Chocolate shops were bustling, but the sweetness was fleeting. We were all swallowing hard.

For the previous week in Paris, we had barely heard our neighbors. Saturday afternoon, just as it was starting to get dark, their activities became very audible. In the safety of Villa Adrienne's private garden, children were frolicking in the leaves as grown-ups watched. I heard their squeals from our window and went outside.

As I descended the stairs from our apartment, I recognized a Strauss waltz blasting from the apartment immediately above ours. From the garden, I could see our upstairs neighbor, smoking a cigarette as he hung over the French balcony. He, too, was watching the children play. I waved and said *bonjour* to this stranger, who smiled and waved back.

We awoke Monday morning, three days after the attack, to the cacophony of arborists pruning the plane trees in the garden – the autumn ritual that we observed all over Basque Country. As Paris went back to work, schools and municipal offices were open. So were parks, open-air markets and museums. It was not a return to normalcy, but we were all doing our best.

So, no, we did not go home until our previously scheduled date. We went to France for three months because we wanted to experience French life. And, for that moment, this was life in Paris.

33

MOURNING,
PUBLIC and PRIVATE

⁓

I USED TO THINK that mourning was a very private process. So there's something extremely unsettling about the public rituals that have developed in reaction to the increasingly frequent acts of terrorism. By the time of the November 13 Paris attacks, the routine had become hackneyed: choose a logo; schedule a moment of silence; and create a public shrine. In Paris the logo was the Eiffel Tower, contained in a peace symbol. TV reports to the contrary, we saw no sign of the moment of silence being observed. And the shrine was established at the Place de la République.

This square, which borders the 3rd, 10th and 11th arrondissements, is one of the largest in Paris. At its center is a 31-foot bronze statue of Marianne, who symbolizes freedom and personifies the French Republic. As Elaine Sciolino, former Paris bureau chief of *The New York*

Times, writes in her 2011 book *La Seduction: How the French Play the Game of Life*, "Marianne is the closest thing France has to Uncle Sam, if Uncle Sam had breasts."

The rendition of Marianne at the Place de la République was a 19th-century creation by the sculptor Léopold Morice and his brother Charles, an architect. Their version of Marianne was chosen in an 1879 contest, sponsored by the Paris City Council. By that time Napoléon III had dismissed his prefect of the Seine, Georges-Eugène Haussmann, who oversaw the rebuilding of Paris, but Haussmann's initiatives to modernize the city continued. At what became the Place de la République, the goal was to create a monument for the 90th anniversary of the French Revolution.

In her raised right hand, Marianne holds an olive branch; in her left is a tablet engraved with Les Droits de l'Homme, the declaration of human rights adopted in 1793. She sits on a 75-foot pedestal on which are positioned three smaller statues that represent liberty, equality and fraternity.

Around this pedestal, after the November 13 attacks, mourners placed candles and flowers, as the Place de la République turned into a media circus. When we visited, three days after that unspeakable evening, it was a melting pot of languages, as reporters did their stand-ups and other visitors took selfies. In the crush of the crowds we could feel no emotion except the urge to retreat.

On the opposite bank of the Seine, we found a quiet spot for reflection at the northwest tip of Île St.-Louis, the smaller of the two islands that are part of Paris. There, on a deserted sliver of green space at the edge of the river, was a sign containing this piece of prose by Louis Aragon, a French poet, novelist and journalist:

Connaissez-vous l'île
Au cœur de la ville
Où tout est tranquille éternellement

(Get to know the island at the heart of the city where everything is eternally tranquil.)

Based on what they saw on TV, friends in the U.S. got the impression that Paris was on lockdown. Though that hadn't been true since the night of the attacks, the atmosphere for the first several days after it was tentative and tense. For example, though morning news reports had indicated that the Eiffel Tower was open, we arrived one day to find it closed, reportedly due to staff concerns about their safety. Most of the souvenir stands at its base were closed, too, though selfie-stick vendors continued to circulate, apparently thinking there were still enough narcissists to sustain their business.

Museums were closed, but only for a day. We saw soldiers with machine guns standing next to the I.M. Pei glass pyramid at the Louvre Museum – a strange juxtaposition. Three heavily armed gendarmes (police) were just an arm's length away as we rode home on the Métro. French President François Hollande announced that he would ask Parliament to extend the national state of emergency for three months.

Within a five-minute walk of our apartment, we found another way to pay our respects – with a visit to the Paris Catacombs.

Going to the Catacombs wasn't originally on our to-do list. Compared with other tourist attractions, they draw relatively few visitors – about 300,000 per year, compared with the Louvre, for example, which is the most visited museum in the world and in 2015 had 8.6 million entrants. But with the end of our Paris sojourn approaching, we noticed the Catacombs entrance one day on our way to buy groceries.

And we figured that since we were living nearby, we shouldn't miss it. When the Catacombs opened on the Tuesday after the terrorist attacks (they are always closed on Mondays), we made a beeline there.

We would later learn that people sometimes have to queue up for several hours to enter – only 200 people at a time are allowed in. But we walked right in, and during the two hours that we spent there, had it completely to ourselves. Especially under the circumstances, that gave special meaning to our visit.

Many centuries newer than its counterpart in Rome, the Paris Catacombs were developed in the late 18th century to address an urban-planning challenge. The macabre concept was to close many of the city's overcrowded and overflowing cemeteries, which had become a public health threat. Their contents would be exhumed and deposited into abandoned quarries where limestone building materials had been excavated from the subsoil in what were then the Paris suburbs.

The process began in 1786 with the Cimetière des Saints-Innocents, which had been a site of mass graves since the Middle Ages. Through a series of exhumations over a period of 15 months, the remains of 2 million Parisians were removed from that cemetery alone. The process continued as 16 more cemeteries, many adjacent to churches, were eliminated between 1792 and 1814. The Catacombs were enlarged from 1859 to 1860, to make room for the contents of additional cemeteries unearthed during the rebuilding of Paris, overseen by Baron von Haussmann. By then the Catacombs held 6 million human remains, most of them moved from other burial grounds. Only in several cases of mass carnage, all during the French Revolution, were people directly buried in the Catacombs.

The Paris Catacombs were not initially a matter of common knowledge. It was Louis-Étienne Héricart de Thury, then Inspector

General of quarries, who turned them into a public monument in 1810, during the Romantic period. Quarry inspectors offered tours, initially to VIPs, and later to the general public. During World War II parts of the Catacombs were used as a shelter. For many years they could be viewed only by candlelight, or later flashlight. Electricity was not installed until 1974.

Not for the physically infirm or claustrophobic, a Catacombs tour requires visitors to descend 131 steps at the entrance, climb 83 steps back up to the exit, and in between walk 1.4 miles along a circuitous route between two Métro stops.

Situated up to 82 feet underground, this is an eerie place, where water drips from the ceiling, as rows of skulls, interspersed in stacks of shinbones, stare out at visitors. But this oddly poetic subterranean museum also offers a fascinating piece of Paris history.

Today one enters through an unassuming façade, painted green, to the left of one of two identical buildings on either side of Avenue du Colonel Henri Rol-Tanguy. Though called the Barrière d'Enfer (Gate of Hell), these 18th-century buildings are unrelated to the Catacombs. They were once tollhouses used to deter tax evaders. The Denfert-Rochereau Métro station is across the street.

An excellent audio tour is included with the €5 admission ticket. For those who crave more detail, the 2014 book *The Catacombs of Paris*, by Gilles Thomas, is for sale at a gift shop across the street from the exit. I wished that I had been able to read it before our visit.

Even with all this background, the décor is hard to stomach: stacks of bones and skulls, mostly arranged symmetrically, and in one spot skulls positioned in the shape of a heart. A sign over the ossuary vestibule quotes a passage from the 18th-century French poet Jacques Delille, *"Arrête: C'est ici l'empire de la Mort."* (Stop. Here is the empire of death.) Delille, as it happens, is not buried in the Catacombs but in Père Lachaise Cemetery, in the society of such other dead talent as the Polish composer Frédéric Chopin; the American singer, songwriter and poet Jim Morrison; and the French cabaret singer Édith Piaf.

But for all the dignity and respect the Catacombs exude – stacks of bones are labeled by cemetery and year they were exhumed – there is something terribly ghoulish about art constructed with human remains. Threading through room after room of it is both creepy and humbling. Eventually this is where life leads all of us, some sooner rather than later. In the wake of the terrorist attacks, especially, we needed no reminder of how ephemeral our existence may be. As we mourn for others, we also grieve for ourselves.

Beneath the bustling streets of 21st-century Paris were all these remnants of life in generations past. There were the old street names inscribed as directional signals at various junctures; evidence of quarrying techniques, which created supporting pillars and stone walls to avoid structural collapse; and initials of various quarry inspectors on the walls.

For me, one of the most moving sections of the Catacombs had nothing to do with its original purpose but with one man's creative impulse: an elaborate sculpture of the Port-Mahon citadel carved into the Catacombs' limestone walls. This was the handiwork of an 18th-century quarryman known officially only by his last name, Décure. As a member of Louis XV's armies, he is believed to have been imprisoned by the British on Minorca, one of Spain's Balearic Islands. Later, as a quarryman in Paris, his co-workers nicknamed him *"Beauséjour"* (beautiful sojourn), as they observed him craft this detailed sculpture from what he apparently recalled as paradise. From a distance, it looks like a giant sand castle, but up close one can see individual buildings in the town and black flint stone tiles that represent the sea. After working on this labor of love from 1777 to 1782, Décure was constructing a staircase to access it, when he was killed by the collapse of a quarry roof.

What a cruel irony! In today's litigious society, the fact that Décure was pursuing a hobby when he was killed, rather than tending to official business, would likely have disqualified his family from any recompense. But perhaps those were kinder, gentler times. Gilles Thomas notes: "Despite the fact that this deadly accident had occurred while he was performing non-commissioned work, the Quarry Inspection Unit granted his widow an allowance for life."

Elsewhere in the Catacombs' dark and gloomy depths, I paused to read the poetry or brief quotations posted next to many bone stacks. Not surprisingly, most dealt with the frailty or brevity of life. Some like *"Croyez que chaque jour est pour vous le dernier"* (believe that each day is your last), attributed to Horace, the ancient Roman lyric poet, were cliché. In a similar vein, but more chilling in light of the recent massacre, was the unattributed turn of phrase, *"Pensez le matin que vous n'irez peut-être pas jusqu'au soir et au soir que vous n'irez peut-être pas jusqu'au matin."* Think in the morning that you will not exist until the night and in the night that you will not exist until the morning.

34

ACTS of DEFIANCE

A CLOUD HUNG OVER the pleasure capital during the remainder of our visit. On the morning of November 18, we were reluctant to leave our Paris apartment – not because we felt afraid to go out, but because it meant breaking ourselves away from the TV news. There had been an early morning raid on a terrorist hideout in the suburb of St. Denis. Ultimately, reports confirmed that police had killed Abdelhamid Abaaoud, the 28-year-old organizer of the attacks five days earlier.

But the worldwide threat of terrorism wasn't over. Not by a long shot. The day before, two Air France jets bound for Paris – one coming from Los Angeles and the other from Washington, D.C. – had been diverted because of telephone bomb threats; it turned out to be a false alarm. Friends back home, who worried about our safety in Paris, reported that there were soldiers with automatic weapons at entrances to the New York City subways.

Paris felt cold and dark as the shortest day of the year approached. During our last week there, the sun didn't rise until after 8 a.m. and it set at about 5 p.m. And then it began to rain. Not just a drizzle, or a shower here and there, but the kind of relentless, driving rain that beats against the windowpanes and wakes one before daylight. We fished out the raincoats that we had packed in a suitcase with our souvenirs, over-optimistically thinking that we wouldn't need them for the rest of the trip.

Between the rain, the news and the impending end of our French adventure, I began to feel like a character out of a painting from Picasso's Blue Period. During this stage, after the suicide of his friend Carlos Casagemas, in 1901, at L'Hippodrome Café in Paris, Picasso's paintings depicted the agony of life in sickly yellow and blue tones.

We knew from our experience with 9/11 that a crisis forces us to rank our priorities. But it tends to be temporary. As time passes, we return to the obsessions and minutiae that occupied us before. That's what happened in Paris. The media circus petered out as fewer people showed up at the Place de la République. Holiday windows at Printemps, conceived long before the terrorist attacks, featured high-end brands. One, sponsored by Burberry, was filled with mechanical dolls dressed in Burberry trench coats lifting their Burberry scarves. In another, for Christian Louboutin, the French luxury footwear company, chorus-girl dolls did the can-can, revealing the patented red Louboutin soles each time they kicked up their heels.

Across the street, at the Galeries Lafayette department store, some of the doors were locked, and all bags were being inspected as people entered the premises. Did someone say Chanel? A line of Asian tourists queued up outside the designer's first-floor boutique, where there seemed to be a run on the company's signature quilted handbags with chain-link straps. If anyone thought there was a sale on them, they were misinformed.

On Day 4 after the terrorist attacks, the French flag flew at half-mast beside the upscale Tuesday market on a slender median that divides Boulevard Raspail, where it meets rue de Rennes. But most of the conversations I overheard there were about food, not the latest terrorism. At a stand selling *brocante* (bric-a-brac), a shopper expressed enthusiasm for a new gadget she had just purchased, which looked like a bizarre cross between handcuffs and a nutcracker. When I asked what it was, she explained that it was to open bottles of Champagne: Using the tool's spring action, you grip the top and twist.

"But why not use your hand?" I attempted to ask in French, making a turning motion with my own hand as I posed the question.

"Because this does it so well," she replied.

Little by little, the cafés started filling up again. By Saturday, November 20, we had to wait for a table at La Rotonde in Montparnasse, where I savored six Fine de Claire oysters from my spot on a red-velvet banquette. At Café Bonaparte, in St. Germain-des-Prés, we watched one customer after another burst in on an especially raw afternoon, shake their umbrella and complain about the weather, though it was normal for the season. Inside the café, with its mosaic-tile floors and standard-issue wooden chairs, all seemed right with the world. The couple to our left both ordered hamburgers and proceeded to eat them with a knife and fork. At the table on our right, two women gossiped over glasses of Champagne.

That week the illustrated cover of the satirical weekly *Charlie Hebdo*, whose offices had been attacked by terrorists the previous January, showed a man with a bottle of Champagne in one hand, his head tilted back as he held up a glass in the other, pouring a fluid into his mouth. His body was riddled with what looked like bullet holes, but instead of blood gushing out of them, he was bleeding a yellow liquid. The caption, against the cover's red background, read, *"Ils ont les armes. On les emmerde, on a le Champagne!"* The New York Times may have cleaned up the language a bit with its translation: "They have weapons. Screw them, we have Champagne!"

A Moveable Feast, Ernest Hemingway's memoir of his experiences in Paris during the 1920s, turned into a symbol of French defiance, as protesters left copies of it, along with flowers and candles, at memorials for victims of the recent attacks. Its title in French, *Paris est une fête*, means Paris is a celebration. No editor could have put it better in any language. Published posthumously in 1964, this memoir was enjoying a sudden revival.

Though *A Moveable Feast* was reportedly sold out at Paris bookstores, it was available in English on Amazon in both print and digital versions. I read it on my Kindle, and then listened to the audiobook, narrated by the actor John Bedford Lloyd. "We ate well and cheaply and drank well and cheaply and slept well and warm together and loved each other," Hemingway had written, with all the romanticism one might expect of an old man looking back on life.

I enjoyed the mentions of familiar street names and cafés that still exist, including some that we had visited, but another aspect of the book was far more compelling and, in some ways, inspiring: Hemingway's lengthy descriptions of his struggles as a writer. He had arrived in Paris in December 1921 as a newlywed, having quit a newspaper job to try his hand at fiction. In the space of five years he transformed himself from a virtual unknown to a bestselling author, but ruining his marriage and multiple friendships along the way.

Curious to know more about this complicated man and his creative process, in the months after our return from France, I would dig into biographical material about this stage of Hemingway's life. I didn't share his interest in macho sports like bullfighting, horse racing, fishing or boxing. I was considerably older than Hemingway was when he lived in Paris. In fact, I was nearly the same age as he was when he wrote his memoir. I came to disrespect him for the way he backstabbed friends and colleagues, and especially for his treatment of women. My sympathies lay with Hadley, the first of his four wives, whom Hemingway portrays as a passive victim of his infidelities.

Yet I was fascinated by the various accounts of his early career. Hemingway had defied literary norms, among other things, ignoring some advice he received from Frazier Hunt, a literary talent scout for Hearst Magazines. In a 1922 letter Hunt had written: "What they can't buy in the States at this time is enough nice love stories with youth and beauty and spring and all that stuff – and humor stories. ... if you do some more stories and if you can just as easily do a bright and 'sweet' yarn as you can a tragic one, you will find your market will be 50 percent easier to make." Hemingway was not so inclined.

I thought of my own acts of defiance, leaving The Content Mill and now writing a book on spec.

No wonder I admired Hemingway's perseverance. He kept honing his craft, despite rejections from New York publishers who were put off by his use of profane language and descriptions of sex. He shared this affliction with James Joyce, whose book *Ulysses* was banned under the U.S. Comstock Law, an 1873 federal statute that made it illegal to circulate so-called obscene literature through the mail. *Ulysses* was originally published in 1922 by Sylvia Beach, the American owner of Shakespeare and Company, a Paris bookshop that Hemingway frequented.

Those who think of self-publishing as a 21st-century phenomenon and a product of the internet overlook many pages of history. On the Left Bank of Paris during the Jazz Age, American writers who defied the norms in their own country could find a home with small presses, or self-publish their work, as Hemingway's mentor Gertrude Stein did. Hemingway's first book, *Three Stories and Ten Poems*, was published in 1923 by Contact Publishing Company, a small and short-lived Paris enterprise founded by Robert McAlmon. It had an initial press run of 300 copies. Some of those short stories have become classics, published and republished in various Hemingway collections.

Three years later Hemingway hit pay dirt when an eminent New York publisher, Charles Scribner's Sons, published his first novel, *The Sun Also Rises*. It not only broke ranks with Victorian literary tradition but became a bestseller. As his divorce settlement with Hadley, Hemingway gave her all the royalties to the book, written while they lived together in Paris. She didn't need to worry about money for the rest of her life.

At the Musée d'Orsay, situated in a former Paris train station, I admired the work of other artists who had defied popular trends. Paul Signac was ridiculed by Paul Gauguin for his pioneering use of "decomposition" – small, separated dots of color – in his paintings. Reacting to Signac's 1892 painting *Women at the Well*, Gauguin called it "nothing but confetti." Signac, together with Georges Seurat, who also was known for this technique, would become founders of Neo-Impressionism.

Several decades earlier Édouard Manet's painting *Olympia*, a modern rendition of the female nude, had been poorly received when it was displayed in 1865 at the Paris Salon. What a difference a century and a half makes. When I saw *Olympia* at the d'Orsay, it was featured in a temporary exhibit on prostitution as a theme in French art. Scarves that riffed on the painting were for sale in the museum gift shop.

Yet another reminder that change may not come easily.

35

MINOTAUR MOVING HIS HOUSE

B Y THE TIME we got to Paris, we couldn't even *pretend* to be traveling light. I was ashamed to be the person who, while still employed at The Content Mill, had written a heavily trafficked blog post titled "How To Travel Anywhere With Nothing But A Carry-On Bag." In it, I described my method for packing like a minimalist, by mixing and matching outfits to create multiple looks, and taking very few toiletries. "To pack light, you must be willing to live with less," I had written. "Remember, it's only temporary; consider it a vacation from your possessions."

If I succeeded in letting go of the place we called home, I didn't do nearly as well taking a vacation from possessions. Perhaps, in a deep psychological sense, the two were related – that in this long absence from home I had unconsciously clung to transitional objects. (Freudians could have a field day.) Might this explain the fact that I packed belongings that I rarely use at home – like eye shadow? I have no idea why I thought that I would need eye shadow in France, but as it turned out, I didn't. Ken and I also packed household items that we have never before taken on a trip: an apron, a vegetable peeler, an external iPhone speaker and a travel pillow. Though we did use all of these things during our French adventure, we certainly could have done just as well without them.

Meanwhile, at a kitchenware shop in Amboise, I acquired another possession that I don't normally bring but needed: a slender 12-ounce French press. I bought this coffee-brewing device (known as a *cafetière*, or *cafetière à piston*) because neither of the coffeemakers at the winemaker's cottage worked. I used it in Le Puy-Notre-Dame and in Paris as well, since the small electric coffeemakers in both those places were also broken.

And then there were the books. These have always been my passion and my weakness. My argument, which I think is extremely persuasive, is that I am a writer and need a traveling library. Anecdotally, I like to mention that Somerset Maugham, in his chronicles of years spent in Malaysia, describes traveling with a duffel bag full of books. But Maugham had a servant to tote that duffel, and no Kindle.

E-books ought to have lightened our load. We owned plenty of those. But that did not deter us from bringing hard copies of books that were not available in digital format. There was the book on French cheeses, and two others by the same publisher – a Paris guidebook and another, on wines. They were compact and didn't take up much space, but each added more than a pound to our luggage. To help us study French, we brought the textbook from Ken's course at Baruch – a large loose-leaf.

I threw in a slender brochure with quotations from René Magritte. This was a freebie from the Musée Magritte in Brussels, which we had visited three years earlier. It weighed only two ounces. I thought reading it would be a fun way to improve my language skill. Given that I could barely converse in a French market, and was linguistically challenged in a *pharmacie*, one might consider this a lofty goal. Suffice it to say that the brochure made the round-trip across the Atlantic without my opening it.

The reason for our initial lack of restraint was that we expected to be in one place for three months. When our French adventure turned out to be more adventurous than we ever imagined, it seemed easy enough to just put everything in the car.

But our traveling library, which for these reasons started out bulky, quickly got out of hand. In the Loire Valley Barbara and Ray brought us a lovely Vietnamese cookbook when they visited. In Basque Country I just had to buy the previously mentioned two-pound red-and-green cookbook. Then I purchased a couple more reference books – about Basque architecture. On various visits, to make repairs in our apartment, Laurence and Emmanuel must have noticed that we liked books. When they came to our side of the *maison mitoyenne* for dinner, wouldn't you know, they brought us a very thoughtful gift: a beautiful souvenir book with photographs of many of the nearby villages that we had visited. We added it to our traveling library.

The day before the Paris terrorist attacks, we went to a blockbuster exhibit at the Grand Palais called "Picasso Mania!" It covered both the influences on the artist's work as well as how he influenced others, including David Hockney, Roy Lichtenstein, Willem de Kooning, Andy Warhol and Jasper Johns. To resist the temptation to buy another book, I stayed out of the museum shop. But there was one work of art in that exhibit that just spoke to me. It was Picasso's 1936 painting *Minotaur Moving his House*.

The exhibit audio guide explained that Picasso painted this picture at a time of turmoil in his life: He had recently left Olga Khokhlova (his first wife), and his mistress, the much younger Marie-Thérèse Walter, had given birth to his child. The minotaur – a mythical character that appears elsewhere in Picasso's work – represents the artist. In the painting, he is laboring to pull a cart filled with his most valuable possessions, including a painting. Meanwhile, in the cart, an upside-down mare is giving birth. The minotaur is moving his house and changing his life.

As we prepared to move back to the U.S., after three months living in France, I couldn't get that picture out of my mind. While struggling to reinvent my life, I was also giving birth – but to a book – lugging my laptop and my traveling library as I went. And Picasso's art would continue to be an inspiration.

Most immediately, it inspired me to unload some of the possessions that I was carting around, much like the minotaur. A few doors down from our apartment was a large post office. And on the off chance that a society as literary as the French might have a special shipping rate for books, we stopped in there to inquire. Sure enough, for about $30, plus about another $3 for a couple of sturdy, self-sealing cartons sold at *La Poste*, we could ship home most of our traveling library, which weighed about 24 pounds on the post office scale. It seemed like a small price to pay.

The clerk, who spoke no English, repeated the word *bateau* several times, to be sure we understood that the books would go by boat. We got the drift. He said the voyage would take six weeks.

He was wrong. But this time the wind was at our backs. The smaller of the two boxes, weighing about ten pounds, arrived in Brooklyn just three days after we did, taking only ten days in transit. The second one showed up the following day. Since the accompanying paperwork was stamped "documents," there was no issue with U.S. Customs.

After dropping off our books at La Poste, we were in good shape with our packing – for about a day. Then we visited the cookware stores in the Les Halles area looking for a quiche pan with a removable bottom. It wasn't the quiche pan, bought at Mora, that was a problem but what came after it. On the way out of Simon, another shop nearby where we bought several lovely olive-wood spoons, I spotted something we had searched high and low for back home: a heavy metal griddle with handles on both sides.

We had owned such a pan, sometimes described as a pancake griddle or pizza pan, for at least 18 years. It was falling apart, and we had so far been unable to replace it. This griddle – the last one left in the shop – was a find! We suddenly became €100 poorer and had gotten ourselves right back into a tight spot packing-wise.

I packed and repacked until I had no more wiggle room. Into one 22-inch rollaboard went the 15-inch griddle, swathed in clothing to protect it from aggressive luggage handlers. Into another 22-inch rollaboard went the straw Bayonne market bag, slightly compressed, since at its widest point it was one inch wider than the suitcase. This meant that most of the other suitcase contents had to go in or around the market bag.

With checkout time in our Paris apartment rapidly approaching, we were under duress. We made an executive decision to leave behind a half-bottle of Woolite, an unopened jar of axoa, a bag of pasta, what remained of the Belgian Ketjep and all our Asian spices. We offered them to Sonia, the cleaning lady, when she arrived to retrieve the keys. She did not seem thrilled.

While we were putting the finishing touches on our packing, Sonia was taking the first steps to spruce up the apartment for the next guests, who were scheduled to arrive a few hours later. The first thing she did was remove the cover from the duvet and, apparently not the slightest bit discomfited by the prominent stains we had noticed on it, hung it out the garden-facing window, in plain view, to air. We averted our eyes and went back to our packing.

Whatever else didn't fit into the suitcases, we loaded into the Aerobed bags and took with us to the Charles de Gaulle Airport Sheraton, where we were spending the night before our very early morning flight the following day. With not much to do there, we figured we would have the evening to sort it all out.

We arrived in the late afternoon to find the hotel on lockdown. (By then we were at Day 9 after the terrorist attacks.) Our hand luggage was searched on the way in, and there were soldiers with machine guns pacing the lobby. Since our Aerobed bags had been rifled, we assumed everyone knew our dinner plans, to consume the last items we had brought from our apartment (salad and dressing, orange juice and milk, half a jar of axoa), along with the fresh baguette that I had carried into the hotel under my arm. After this final picnic of our three-month journey, we slept in luxury on the hotel's silky-smooth white sheets. I did not peek inside the duvet cover.

The next morning we tried to download the remaining contents of the Aerobed bags into our suitcases. By that point there wasn't room for anything more than one-eighth-of-an-inch thick. We left behind a bottle of baby powder, half a tube of toothpaste, three apples and a jar containing several tablespoons of black cherry jam from Itxassou. We wore our bulkiest clothing: Ken was dressed in hiking boots, a blazer and a down jacket; I sported the black leather contour belt I had bought at Laffargue in St. Jean-de-Luz.

Even after checking our three rollaboard suitcases, I still felt like the minotaur, but without a wheeled conveyance. My capacious shoulder bag (the manufacturer called it a weekender) seemed to get heavier by the minute. In addition to my computer and other things I needed for the plane, I had stuffed it with items that were too bulky to fit in my suitcase – like the travel pillow that I hadn't used much and the French press (€10 on sale), which by then had paid for itself many times over.

Before the pain of these exertions wore off, I charted a return to minimalism. On the nine-hour flight back to the U.S., I revised our packing list for the next trip, whenever it might be. We swore to never again deviate from what, until this journey, had been our mantra as we limited ourselves to two rollaboards, plus hand luggage: If it doesn't fit, it doesn't go.

PART FIVE

REENTRY and REINVENTION

36

"SEMI-COLON" and EXCLAMATION POINT

MORE SURPRISES AWAITED US in New York. We came home to find our own house spotless but needing repairs. Our tenants said the broken front-door lock, dresser handle and dimmer switch, all of which worked fine when we left, had suffered "normal wear and tear." We gave them the benefit of the doubt about everything except the chips and cracks caused by their baby gates, deducting from their security deposit charges for one day of our painter's time. Afterward, we discovered crayon marks on our walls and leather couch, and a tear in the kitchen screen.

In the scheme of things, this was all pretty minor. But I did flash back to Ward's reaction when he brought his children to visit and his son had jumped on Jack's bed. "It's not our house yet," he had told his preschooler. While we were away, it became their house.

It took a couple of weeks to make it our house again and get reacclimated to our Brooklyn lifestyle. As I put back in place belongings that we had stored, I sometimes had trouble finding things – like the squirrel that has forgotten where she buried her acorns. Having grown accustomed to a limited selection of outfits, I had too many choices about what to wear. I found myself turning the wrong knobs for our stove burners and having to think twice as I pressed the appropriate buttons to operate the washing machine. After working for three months on a laptop, I had the sensation of being at the movies as I sat in front of the two computer monitors in my home office.

The weather had been unseasonably warm in New York, and some of the perennials in my garden were still blooming. But our light-hearted autumn reentry quickly turned to darkest winter.

In anticipation of our homecoming, Ken and I had each scheduled various year-end doctor's appointments. For me they included a routine colonoscopy, since colon cancer runs in my family. I had been having these odious exams ever since my father died of intestinal cancer when I was 40 and had been "clean" every time. So I assumed my upcoming exam would be another case of wash, rinse, repeat. Then I got a very somber phone call from my gastroenterologist.

I was walking in a chilly rain, late for a dentist appointment, when my cell phone rang. As I hurried along Central Park South, where I had exited the subway, my doctor, who had diagnosed cancer in both my parents, explained that my recent exam had revealed a large polyp with a high level of precancerous cells. Because of its shape and location, it could not be totally excised during the procedure. Without doing that, there would be no way to know whether or not I had colon cancer. I needed to have part of my colon removed. I was stunned.

Five days after getting this news, I was on the operating table. The urgency was more financial than medical: Because of Ken's spine surgery, we had not only met the deductible for our health insurance but also hit the $5,600 maximum out-of-pocket for the year. By having my surgery before year-end, I wouldn't have to pay a dime, whereas, if I waited a few weeks, our family would be out another $5,600 all over again.

The day of the operation the surgeon came to see me in the hospital's pre-op area. Already stripped of my dignity, I was wearing a hospital gown, and my hair was held back with what looked like a paper shower cap. "I may look like an old lady, but I still wear bikinis, and I would like to keep it that way," I told him. I wanted to have the smallest possible scar on my abdomen.

At that particular moment, I couldn't have looked less sexy. He would have been within his rights to say, "Lady, you should be hoping you don't have cancer, not worrying about the size of your scar." Instead, he kept a straight face, promised to do his best within the limits of what was medically necessary and hurried off to his next case. If my request was the subject of operating room banter, at least I was under anesthesia by then and do not recall it.

My next memory was of a recovery room nurse, named Ophelia, who took care of me for about six hours until a bed became available. She asked me to rank my pain on a scale of 1 to 10. "'I'm more of a words person than a numbers person,'" Ken recalls me saying in a state of twilight consciousness and true to form. "'It feels like I just did about 500 tummy crunches.'" I hadn't been in the hospital since giving birth to my son 18 years earlier and wasn't ready for everything that went with it.

Nor was I prepared for one of the many routine questions a nurse asked when I was moved to my room: "Are you employed, unemployed or retired?" This was the first time in my life anyone had asked whether I was retired. I figured that I must not be looking so good and decided not to mention the bikini.

Things got better from there. After the first gruesome night, with a noisy roommate who seemed to have an endless stream of visitors, I had the semi-private room to myself. It happened to be the Christmas holiday, which is a bad time to be in a hospital if you have postoperative complications, but a great time if all you need is nursing care. I was in the latter category, and with fewer patients on the floor, for the next five days the staff went out of their way to make me comfortable. Still, the four walls of the institution were a sad contrast to the green hills of Basque Country or the bridges over the Seine.

Back home, I traded the foods of France for a transitional diet of previously unappealing substances: farina for breakfast instead of a crusty baguette from the boulangerie in Sare; Smart Balance in lieu of sheep's milk cheese from the Bayonne market or buttery *Gâteau Basque* from the bakery in St. Pée-sur-Nivelle; and steamed carrots in place of fresh vegetables from the *marchés volants* of Paris. Meanwhile, I digested the recent bizarre turn of events.

Having dodged the bullet in Paris, I had managed to dodge the next one – my family medical history. Five days after my discharge from the hospital, my surgeon called to say that the pathology report showed no cancer cells. The surgery, done laparoscopically, had left three small incisions. If I really wanted to, I could still wear a bikini.

I had told practically no one about the operation in advance, not wanting to spoil the holidays or cause undue concern. Plus, I was determined to spend all my energy healing, not communicating with well-wishers by phone, e-mail or, God forbid, social media. If I had cancer, I wanted total privacy about it so that I could try to continue leading a normal life.

If, on the other hand, my news was good, I had planned to share it. So in New Year's greetings, I declared myself a poster "child" for routine screenings. I was extremely lucky that doctors had found my polyp – a variety that is difficult to see – and luckier still, given my family history. I was also really glad that we hadn't postponed that trip to France.

I had lost about five inches of my colon, but more than four feet of it remained. Once I felt better physically and got back to work, I could not resist a play on words: Exclaiming great joy about the happy ending to my story, I proudly announced that I was a writer with a "semi-colon"!

37

HOW MUCH to SHARE – AND WITH WHOM?

D URING THE MANY WEEKS that I spent recovering from surgery, I felt alternately happy to be in my own house and itchy to go overseas again. We loved our new way of life. But renting our house was a prerequisite for future sojourns.

Living on the sharing economy had put us in the real estate business and given us plenty to do back in Brooklyn. Among other things, we had additional capital improvements planned to make the place even more comfortable for future renters.

In the dead of winter we had ductless heating/cooling units installed on our first floor. For nearly 18 years we had survived sweltering summers with nothing more than ceiling fans and cross ventilation to cool this level of our house. Almost immediately, we enjoyed the winter benefit of this upgrade, as the supplemental heat source took the edge off some very cold spots. "Why did we wait so long?" we asked each other. Until now, in so many contexts, we had delayed gratification. Ironically, we were treating our tenants better than we had treated ourselves.

At times we felt on edge waiting for them to materialize. Excited about each inquiry, we would tally up how much income it would provide, check our calendars and discuss possible itineraries. "Paris could be beautiful in April!" we exclaimed after receiving several requests for spring bookings. But as these possibilities and others fizzled, we tried to curb our enthusiasm. Prospective tenants were exploring various options, just as we did when we looked for overseas rentals. And though we kept reminding ourselves that, "it takes only one," we had far more nibbles than viable deals.

In the space of about three months, we heard from four neighborhood families who were in transition and needed temporary housing between April and June while their children finished the school year. One, with two children in private school, were relocating to an affluent community in northern Westchester. Having already sold their house in our neighborhood, they were renting it back from the new owners at what the wife described as "an exorbitant price."

She hoped that we would offer a discount – she didn't say how much – since the family planned to spend weekends in Westchester, and this would reduce the wear and tear on our house. Creative, but she wasn't exactly hard up. By clicking through her Airbnb profile, I discovered that she owned a three-bedroom house in a Vermont ski resort that rented for $800 per night – about three times the cost of our Brooklyn townhouse!

Another local resident got my attention when he wrote, "As our current landlord will attest, we are quiet, responsible tenants." He and his family needed a place to live for ten weeks while their new co-op apartment was being renovated. When I asked him, in a phone call, what they were currently spending on rent, the number he cited was less than half our price. At least he had been honest when he said, at the outset, that he couldn't afford it. (I suppose he thought it was worth a try.)

Such candor was refreshing compared with what happened on Valentine's Day. It started when the doorbell rang in the early afternoon on the coldest day of the year, with temperatures hovering around zero degrees. Through the glass door I saw two men, who looked like members of the Orthodox Jewish community, standing there with their coats open. Since I didn't recognize them, and this was New York City, I waved them away without opening the door.

Later, when I checked my e-mail, there was a message via Airbnb saying, "I'm looking for a short-term stay in Park Slope to get the feel of the area before I make a purchase or a long-term rental. I will be there with three roommates. We work together." He wanted to move in a week later and stay for five weeks.

I had already declined his request, since we were not interested in renting our home as a share house, when I received an e-mail from Terry Baum about someone else who happened to need the house just as urgently. The story was slightly different. This man, who mentioned that he had also seen the house on Airbnb, wanted to rent it for one of his female employees for about six months.

With a little online sleuthing, I found photos of the man who contacted Terry and the one who messaged me through Airbnb. They were the same guys who had rung our doorbell together. My Google search also gave the citation to a federal lawsuit. I signed on to PACER, a website for retrieving electronic court records, and downloaded the key documents. They revealed that the men who wanted to rent our house had been codefendants in a federal fraud case, settled a year earlier. In it, they were accused of embezzling funds from a business with which they had once been associated.

How did they come to ring our doorbell? As best we could connect the dots, these two jokers had seen our listing on the website StreetEasy, where Terry had posted it with our consent. That site includes addresses, and thinking they could avoid her broker's fee, they had come right to our door. When I wouldn't let them in, one of them contacted me through Airbnb, while the other dealt with Terry. Apparently they weren't crafty enough – or were in too much of a hurry – to keep their stories straight.

That evening I asked Terry to take down the listing from StreetEasy. We also removed photos of the front of the house from sharing economy websites where we had posted the listing ourselves. The maps on these sites made it possible to identify the street on which the house is situated, and with that information it was too easy to use the photo to chart a path to our door. Though we didn't feel in any particular danger in this case, it was a frightening experience and an inexpensive lesson.

Meanwhile, the activity on Airbnb improved our status on the site's search engine algorithm – the criteria used to bump us up in the rankings as people looked for housing in our geographic area. Within a couple of weeks we had a new inquiry – unfortunately from yet another bottom-fisher. This one was the wife of a Hollywood movie producer who was looking for a place for the two of them to stay for seven weeks during the spring – presumably because they were working on a shoot. Over the course of several hours she was relentless about asking us to lower our price.

We knew, from being on the other side of the sharing economy, that some owners offer discounts of up to 10 percent for weekly or monthly stays. Just as often, hosts politely declined when we inquired about a discount, saying, "The price is what you see on Airbnb."

We liked this wording enough that we got in the habit of using it ourselves with hagglers, but it was not enough to turn back the Hollywood Producer's Wife. She agreed that, based on comparable properties, we had priced our house fairly. "It's a steal and beautiful!" she conceded in the first volley of messages. But an hour later she was back with this: "I'm assuming you'll say no, but we're working our numbers to the limit and figured it was worth one more try." She went on to offer us 25 percent less than our posted rate.

Besides being competitive, the rent had to cover both our monthly carrying costs and what we would need to spend to live someplace else when we vacated our house for our tenants. Otherwise, our financial model of living on the sharing economy wouldn't work. That's the difference between renting a primary residence and a vacation home that would otherwise be empty. (But again, more than 90 percent of the listings on HomeAway, for example, fall into the second category.)

Another Hollywood producer, who wanted to rent our house for five months, didn't quibble about the price. "Your place looks perfect," wrote the producer, who contacted us via VRBO. He described himself and the other two potential residents as "mature adults whose wives will visit occasionally." During the busiest part of their production schedule, as he outlined it, there would also be up to seven other people working in our house.

Once again, I considered the wear and tear on our hundred-year-old parquet floors; potential plumbing backups; and the possible disturbance to our neighbors of staff parties, or people coming and going at odd hours. Without raising any of these issues, I wrote back, "It looks like our son, who is a college freshman, will be home for the summer, so the house is not available." It was the truth, but only part of the story.

And then there was The Chinese Housewife. (That's how she described herself in her Airbnb profile.) "My family just arrived in NYC today, and we're trying to find the right house for us," she wrote. "On the airplane I saw a movie named BROOKLYN. . . . Now I want to feel Brooklyn myself, with my family and friends."

I didn't understand the movie reference, so I watched *Brooklyn* on Amazon Video. It's a sweet love story set in the 1950s, about an Irish immigrant who falls in love with a second-generation Italian. Some of the scenes are shot in brownstone Brooklyn. Other than that, I had no idea what it had to do with renting our house.

I did know this, though: The Chinese Housewife and her family, and some close friends, who she said "might drop in and live with us for some days," were in a hurry. They wanted to come the very next day to see the house, and move in two days after that, for three months.

She didn't say what brought them to the United States or why, with two children under the age of five accompanying them, they were making living arrangements at the last minute. Since we couldn't move out on two days' notice, and since Jack was coming home for the summer, we declined. So we never had a chance to satisfy our curiosity.

If there was one benefit to the flurry of inquiries, it was all the practice it gave us vetting potential tenants. This is something homeowners should always do, but it's especially important with long-term rentals, both because there's more time for damage to the house and, because under the law in some states, you could get stuck having to evict tenants who stay longer than the lease permits and, in the process, acquire squatters' rights.

The internet, which makes it easier to trace a person's digital footprints, also enables fraudsters to create – and hide behind – false identities. Nor may their motives be entirely clear.

After we left Basque Country, a couple inquired, via a HomeAway listing, about renting the home of our landlords, the Chambons, for two weeks. At first they were delighted. But it turned out the potential tenants wanted to pay them $7,000 more than the two-week rent and have the Chambons wire the excess to their son. Thinking it sounded like a money-laundering scheme, the Chambons declined, and never heard from them again.

The Airbnb site has a "profile verification" feature. To trigger it, users can connect an account to their identity on Google, Facebook or LinkedIn, for example. Those who complete the process receive a "Verified ID badge" that appears on their profile page. Hosts can require guests to take this step, but what good is it? Text on Airbnb warns that "it's not an endorsement or guarantee of someone's identity." Sharing websites don't want to be blamed – or sued – as a result of your bad experiences, so disclaim liability, even for the efficacy of what look like consumer-friendly tools.

In fact, the Valentine's Day huckster who contacted me had an Airbnb Verified ID. Only by downloading the court papers in the fraud case that involved him did I discover he also had an alias. And though he indicated, when he contacted me, that he wanted to stay in my house because he was contemplating a purchase in the area, that seemed unlikely, since my Google search also revealed that he lived just a few neighborhoods away. I shudder to think what his real motives might have been and who – or what – he planned to shelter in our home. Fortunately, I am adept at online research.

Perhaps inadvertently, online platforms discourage this kind of careful vetting, since they are designed to close the deal quickly. Airbnb hosts are reminded that if they decline "many or most booking inquiries," that could negatively impact the future placement of their listing. It also has an "Instant Book" feature that hosts are encouraged to activate. This enables guests who meet certain requirements (for example, with recommendations by past hosts) to book automatically, without prior approval by the host. A lightning bolt icon identifies these listings, and Airbnb's promotional materials tell hosts that it will help them earn more. (HomeAway also has an Instant Book option.)

Even without Instant Book, a built-in urgency to finalize the transaction runs at cross-purposes with hosts' need to vet guests. Independent vetting is made more difficult on Airbnb by the fact that guests can identify themselves only by first name when making the initial contact. In contrast, with HomeAway, both first and last names are displayed when a potential tenant contacts a homeowner.

When Airbnb users click the "Contact Host" link on a listing, they are prompted to share a little about themselves, say what brings them to the area, who will be living with them and what they like about the listing. That's a good start, but for long-term rentals of a primary residence (rather than a vacation home or a property maintained solely as a rental), one needs to know more: their reasons for renting; what kind of home they own or rent; whether they have pets; and what they do for a living. Ideally, we would want to chat by phone with prospective tenants or, if possible, meet them in person.

Still, try as one might to vet tenants, with credit checks, references, Google searches, phone calls and in-person meetings, you can't control what happens in your absence. Someone who looks good on paper "might have cocaine-fueled parties" in your house, said Michael Klein, of Onefinestay, the high-end vacation-rental company.

I flashed back to his comment a year later, when we rented our house again, this time via Airbnb. Having thoroughly vetted our tenants, we felt confident that they would take great care of our home. During the next three months, while we returned to France, they sent glowing reports of how happy they were living there, and assured us that they were treating it as their own. In what I took as a demonstration of house pride – albeit a vicarious one – they even attached to one e-mail message a photograph of a late-blooming rose in our front garden.

After our return we learned, from our cleaning lady, that they had blatantly violated a provision in our lease (meant to minimize wear and tear) prohibiting them from moving furniture into our house without permission. As she described it, while living in our house, they had filled every available space with their own belongings, turning it into a big storage locker. We had been deceived.

While the grown-ups violated our trust, their children violated our property. The string of seven water marks on a nightstand was careless – hadn't anyone noticed the glass that seemed to have been placed there night after night? Other furniture damage seemed malicious: There was an "X" mark etched into the surface of a cherry desk that Bill Streett had built for my office. In Jack's room, there was a similar mark, an asterisk, on one of the solid oak built-in bookcases. And the striped fabric of an upholstered chair had been colored with what looked like Magic Marker.

At least there were no cocaine-fueled parties – as far as we know.

38

IN GUESTS WE TRUST

ON THE TWO OCCASIONS, so far, when we have rented our home – each time for three months – we wound up charging our tenants' security deposit for about $400 worth of property damage. In each case we also absorbed the cost of several hundred more dollars' worth of repairs when we weren't totally certain that breakage (for example, of locks, door mechanisms and drawer pulls) was their fault.

There were moments when we questioned whether it was all worth it. Then we reminded ourselves that our house had created a significant income stream that made it possible to divide our time between Brooklyn and France. Letting go of our precious home was the price for that.

All we could hope for was to get our house back roughly the way we left it and be able to remedy anything that had gone wrong. As we summoned various workmen to do that, they told us that almost everything could be returned to its previous state. (The one exception was the chair, which was permanently stained with Magic Marker.)

Time and energy spent on these efforts was the cost of doing business. Just as when we first embarked on our plan to live on the sharing economy, we needed to put aside our emotional attachment to the house and see things purely from a practical perspective.

Here are other lessons for homeowners based on our experiences.

Give them space. Declutter, remove personal items and create shelf, drawer and hanging areas for tenants' belongings. Store your valuables in locked closets or off the premises. Then thoroughly clean your home and make the bed with fresh, high-quality linens – preferably white, which can be bleached. Each time we rent our house these steps, which include emptying food from the refrigerator and kitchen cabinets, take us about a week. (Therefore, we would never book tenants for less than a month, and we would rather rent for longer than that.)

Protect furniture. Double up on mattress pads. If buying a new sofa, choose something durable – like leather – or consider slipcovers that can be laundered between rentals. These items are especially susceptible to stains and spills, which can be costly, if not impossible, to remove.

Leave coasters on wooden tabletops and consider covering those that are heavily used. A piece of Plexiglas cut to fit our nightstands would have avoided all those water marks. Laurence put an unattractive piece of oilcloth over the beautiful dining room table in our apartment in Basque Country. Though we didn't like the way it looked, we understood her reasons and left it in place during our six-week stay.

Have boots on the ground. This might be a cleaning lady who comes weekly (at your tenant's expense), or a handyman whom you pay to handle maintenance and repairs in your absence. You or that person should do an initial walk-through with your renters and show them how everything works. A walk-through can also reduce calls from guests and avert damage.

Whether you hand over the keys yourself or have your representative do it, insist that the tenant lock and unlock each door before leaving them on their own. Do this no matter how much they insist it's silly or unnecessary and no matter how many doors they have opened in their lives. In an ounce of prevention in my own house, I also spray all the locks with WD-40 lubricant shortly before tenants arrive. This makes the bolts turn more easily and decreases the likelihood that newcomers will yank – and potentially break – the hardware before they get accustomed to the mechanism.

Send redundant messages. A lengthy house manual will get less attention than a single page with the Wi-Fi code and other key information. Put Post-it notes in spots that require special care – for instance, a reminder like the one Laurence hung near the shower, not to leave wet bath mats on the wood floor. In a couple of locations, I left picture frames in which I had placed more detailed precautions, such as not to flush diapers, baby wipes, paper towels or feminine hygiene products down any of our toilets. Don't worry that guests might think you have gone overboard: You can't take their vigilance for granted, and there is no harm emphasizing the care you expect them to take.

Cover contingencies. Notify your homeowner's insurance company that your house will be rented, Laura Clark, senior underwriting manager at the Chubb Group of Insurance Cos., told me in an interview after our first rental. Chubb charges 25 percent more in premiums for homes that are rented, rather than owner-occupied, she said, partly because "renters don't take as good care of your stuff as you do." I know from firsthand experience that this harsh reality can be difficult for homeowners to accept.

Most insurers will continue covering the dwelling and your personal liability – say, if my tenant's child fell down the basement stairs and was injured, Clark says. But some exclude your possessions while the house is rented, and they typically won't cover your tenants' belongings. (Make this clear in a lease.) Ask your tenants for the declarations page of their homeowner's or renter's policy, and make sure their liability limit is at least $500,000, Clark advises.

Homeowners who rent through Airbnb automatically get supplemental property insurance through the company's Host Guarantee, and in a growing list of countries, including the U.S., personal liability coverage under its Host Protection Insurance.

Require a security deposit. With extended stays, it makes sense to charge about half the weekly rent, Jon Gray, chief revenue officer at HomeAway, told me; others recommend 10 percent of the total tab. Hold it long enough after your tenant leaves to discover any damaged or missing items – one month is acceptable, says Terry Baum.

Here, Airbnb gives you less discretion. As I reminded our Paris host after her cleaning lady asked us for €300 in cash the day we arrived, this platform doesn't allow you to collect a security deposit upfront. Airbnb authorizes the guest's credit card up to the amount of the security deposit. And, if you have a claim, you must submit it through Airbnb, which disburses the funds.

Hosts must file any claims within 14 days of the checkout date or before the next guest checks in, whichever is earlier. By contacting Airbnb Customer Service, you can get the deadline for notification extended if you can't physically inspect the property during that time frame (for example, if you are out of the country) and, meanwhile, another guest isn't scheduled to check in.

If you and your guest can't agree on a settlement, you can submit your dispute to the Airbnb Resolution Center, which has the last word.

No matter which platform you use for your bookings, a desire to protect their security deposit could cause tenants to hide things or fudge the facts in their favor. To document your claim, take photographs and get estimates for repair or replacement. No matter how angry you feel, stick to the facts. Since conversations and e-mails about the damage tend to escalate, keep them to a minimum. If your rental was through Airbnb, do all your communication through their platform. That way, case managers can see the thread if you wind up needing them to resolve the claim.

Be aware that Airbnb policy prohibits mentioning the dispute in online reviews. If a guest does this or retaliates with a negative review, the host can ask Airbnb's dispute resolution team to remove it, says Nick Shapiro, the company's global head of crisis communications and issues management.

Compare rental platforms. You'll cast a broader net by listing on more than one site. Their rules vary in key respects.

One important distinction, especially if you are booking far in advance, is that with HomeAway you can require full payment upfront, whereas, with Airbnb, you won't get a dime until 24 hours after guests check in, even though their credit card is charged the entire sum when they make the reservation. Meanwhile, you don't have the use of the money – Airbnb does.

Another significant difference between these two sites is the ease with which you can communicate with potential renters. Airbnb wants you to do everything through their messaging system, which blocks phone numbers (even if you spell them out in words) and URLs until you have made the booking. Shapiro says these procedures are set up to protect hosts and guests. But this can also make it difficult to vet renters.

When I wanted to talk with one prospective tenant, I had to devise a work-around: I asked him the name of his employer and the e-mail convention of the company, then sent him an e-mail with my cell phone number. After a cordial chat, we arranged for him to come see our house, which he and his family wound up renting.

After that, though, I initiated all communication through the Airbnb message system. This electronic trail gave me some comfort when they initially balked at paying for the furniture damage. (Ultimately they backed down from the argument that they had paid so much for rent that these additional charges involved "haggling" on our part.)

With the sharing economy evolving, platforms are periodically updated. Each time you land a rental, it's worth brushing up on what's new. Do the same if problems arise.

Treat your rental as a business. I have a new job: property manager. On the front end, it involves advertising our house, responding to inquiries from prospective renters and stashing our belongings. On the back end, I must arrange for the repair of any damage and keep our house in the best possible condition for the next tenant.

39

TURNING the PAGE

"You must be prepared to work always without applause. When you are excited about something is when the first draft is done."
–By-Line Ernest Hemingway: Selected Articles and Dispatches of
Four Decades

W HEN I LEFT The Content Mill, I envisioned writing a book about the forces that cause baby boomers to burn out at work. While living in France, I was going to focus on that project. In retrospect, it was a ridiculous idea. Not the part about boomer burnout, which is a serious problem, but the notion that France would put me in the right frame of mind to tackle it. As my own symptoms subsided, I no longer wanted to write about the effects of ageism. Transported to a world far beyond The Content Mill, endless possibilities replaced what had previously seemed like insurmountable constraints.

The roughly 60 e-mails that I sent into cyberspace during our three months abroad were just a very rough chronicle of my life-altering journey. Using the table of contents that I had sketched out by the end of the trip, I began to expand, cut and then shape that material into the narrative thread of this book.

In the process, I changed the order of chapters, moved text between chapters, shifted chapters between parts, cut tens of thousands of words and wrote at least as many more. Though the book tells the story chronologically, and by region, I skipped around as I wrote. Often I worked on several chapters together that touched upon a particular theme, like parenting, the sharing economy and my evolution as a writer. At one stage or another, every chapter went through multiple revisions. More than one writer before me has reached for a metaphor most often attributed to the sportswriter Red Smith: "Writing is easy. You just open a vein and bleed."

Back in New York, Picasso was as much the talk of the town as he had been in Paris. While the blockbuster exposition there had been at the Grand Palais, in New York the hot ticket was an exhibit of his sculpture at the Museum of Modern Art, or MoMA. Many of the works on display came from the Musée national Picasso-Paris, where a number of galleries were closed when we visited, because so many objects were on loan to MoMA.

Most important, from my perspective, was the career message that emerged from the chronological survey at MoMA. Picasso, who lived to be 91, had never stopped challenging and reinventing himself. After World War II, when he was in his 60s, he had learned how to do pottery. The fact that he had no training as a sculptor never deterred him from pursuing this art form sporadically throughout his career. While living in Cannes, on the French Riviera, during his 70s, he reportedly scavenged dumpsters there for objects to incorporate in his sculptures. These works are "characterized, first and foremost, by the sheer pleasure of invention and experimentation," the handout for the MoMA exhibit notes. As writing in France had been for me.

After that exhibit closed, I returned to MoMA for a close look at Picasso's 1907 masterpiece *Les Demoiselles d'Avignon*, done early in his career. What interested me most was how the painting, of five prostitutes, evolved and drew from diverse sources. On display at the Grand Palais, in Paris, when we visited, was a sculpture fragment from New Guinea that was part of Picasso's vast collection of fetishes. Two of the figures in *Les Demoiselles d'Avignon*, presumably suffering from syphilis, have similar mask-like faces. In another exhibit, at the Musée d'Orsay, was a pastel study of the upper torso of a woman, with one arm held over her head. And there she was in the finished painting at MoMA.

No analogy to Picasso intended here, but in this painting, sometimes heralded as the start of Cubism or the birth of modern art, we can see Picasso making drastic choices – the kind we all have to make at various junctures. With low stakes, he experimented on a small scale before painting on a larger canvas, as I had done with my e-mails from France. Picasso, too, had devoted months to revising his work. The figure in the far left of *Les Demoiselles d'Avignon* holds back a curtain while inserting a large foot into the room. Art historians have postulated that the foot is a remnant of a doctor, or perhaps a male patron, entering the brothel. Picasso painted over him to create a female prostitute. The artist had changed his mind. He held all the power.

Not so with most of us baby boomers. In the dead of winter, after our return from France, with upcoming layoffs rumored at *The New*

York Times, a contemporary of mine, who feared he was a target, vented on Facebook. Trying to be supportive, I posted a comment that said, "Have faith in your human capital. It's good currency wherever life takes you." I also sent a private message suggesting we meet for coffee.

Minutes later, he fired back, "Human capital comes with an expiration date." Ouch! That stung.

Within the hour he had apparently thought better of such brusqueness and edited his comment to read: "Well, human capital comes with an expiration date in the job market. But I appreciate the reminder. Thanks!" He did not reply to my private message, and we did not get together for coffee.

The exchange saddened me on more than one level. Decades earlier, when we worked together in a different newsroom, he would have stopped by my desk to vent, and by the end of the conversation, we would have both found something to laugh about – friends can be a wonderful source of comic relief. Now we rely on social media, because, after all, who has the time? It reaches a broader audience but, in contexts like this, may be far less satisfying.

What distressed me more, though, was to see this very capable professional thrown off balance by forces that now dominate the American workplace. From an employer's standpoint, mature workers are expensive and expendable. We get the message, and it bruises our souls. Articles about the occasional enlightened companies that accommodate older employees – with sabbaticals, part-time or flexible work arrangements – are newsworthy because these companies are the exception rather than the norm. Many of us, in a wide variety of fields, work in places like The Content Mill.

By the time my friend's Facebook post landed, I was immersed in a new job, of my own making, using all the human capital that I had accumulated during three decades of work. So my perspective was very different from his. At a key crossroads in my life, I traveled thousands of miles and took one risk after another, confident that it would somehow work out, but without knowing how. Though we could chart a course, there was a limit to how much we could plan. Once the extreme disappointment subsided, or the crisis passed, that was a good thing. If the job at The Content Mill had been more satisfying, or the winemaker's cottage had lived up to expectations, I would have missed everything that followed.

I was just finishing this book when I ran into one of what Ken calls my "swim buddies." These are the locker room friends that I have developed at the gym, through serendipitous meetings over the years. Susan, as I will call her, is two years younger than I and has always seemed among the most resilient of them. A high-level executive in the health care field – another industry undergoing cataclysmic changes – she advanced confidently within organizations and between jobs. On more than one occasion, she has been my sounding board, with great suggestions about navigating office politics.

For scheduling reasons, we hadn't seen each other since my return from France, and I immediately noticed the strain in her eyes. She glanced over one shoulder before spilling the news: She had a new boss, was miserable at work and had been coping for months with some scary health issues involving her husband.

With the help of a longtime colleague, she had gotten her foot in the door at another institution and gone through three rounds of interviews. Then came radio silence. As a manager, she understood that a younger person would be "more trainable" and adaptable, she said, but quickly added: "I would like to think I have something to contribute. But I don't want to beg."

A bit awkwardly, we parted ways – she, to apply the makeup that was her work face, and I, to swim. Afterward, as I walked home, replaying our conversation, I realized what a distance I had traveled.

FURTHER READING

I recommend the following books for additional detail about some of the places, people and themes mentioned in this one.

Basque History, Language, Culture and Cuisine

Barrenechea, Teresa with Mary Goodbody, *The Basque Table: Passionate Home Cooking from Spain's Most Celebrated Cuisine*, The Harvard Common Press, 1998.

Esteban, Mixel, *Les Maisons Basques*, CPE Éditions, 2009.

Hochschild, Adam, *Spain in Our Hearts: Americans in the Spanish Civil War, 1936–1939*, Houghton Mifflin Harcourt, 2016.

Kurlansky, Mark, *The Basque History of the World: The Story of a Nation*, Penguin Books, 1999.

Raij, Alex with Eder Montero and Rebecca Flint Marx, *The Basque Book: A Love Letter In Recipes from the Kitchen of Txikito*, Ten Speed Press, 2016.

Confronting Mortality

Albom, Mitch, *Tuesdays with Morrie: An Old Man, a Young Man, and Life's Greatest Lesson*, Broadway Books, 2002.

Ephron, Nora, *I Feel Bad About My Neck*, Alfred A. Knopf, 2006.

Gawande, Atul, *Being Mortal: Medicine and What Matters in the End*, Metropolitan Books, 2014.

Kalanithi, Paul, *When Breath Becomes Air*, Random House, 2016.

Kinsley, Michael, *Old Age: A Beginner's Guide*, Tim Duggan Books, 2016.

Pausch, Randy with Jeffrey Zaslow, *The Last Lecture*, Hyperion Books, 2008.

Quindlen, Anna, *Lots of Candles, Plenty of Cake*, Random House, 2012.

Fiction Set in Places We Visited

Balzac, Honoré de, *Eugénie Grandet*, translated by Katherine Prescott Wormeley, Digireads.com Publishing, 2011. (Saumur)

Belfoure, Charles, *The Paris Architect*, Sourcebooks Landmark, 2013. (Paris)

Hannah, Kristin, *The Nightingale: A Novel*, St. Martin's Press, 2015. (Loire Valley, Basque Country, Paris)

Hemingway, Ernest, *The Sun Also Rises*, Charles Scribner's Sons, 1926. (Basque Country, Paris)

French Language and Culture

Barlow, Julie and Jean-Benoît Nadeau, *The Bonjour Effect: The Secret Codes of French Conversation Revealed*, St. Martin's Press, 2016.

Child, Julia with Alex Prud'homme, *My Life in France*, Alfred A. Knopf, 2006.

Mayle, Peter, *A Year in Provence*, Alfred A. Knopf, 1989.

Sciolino, Elaine, *La Seduction: How the French Play the Game of Life*, Times Books, 2011.

Home and the Sharing Economy

Gallagher, Leigh, *The Airbnb Story: How Three Ordinary Guys Disrupted an Industry, Made Billions . . . and Created Plenty of Controversy*, Houghton Mifflin Harcourt, 2017.

Tuan, Yi-Fu, *Space and Place: The Perspective of Experience*, University of Minnesota Press, 1977.

Paris

Gopnik, Adam, *Paris to the Moon*, Random House, 2000.

Hemingway, Ernest, *A Moveable Feast*, Charles Scribner's Sons, 1964.

Lebovitz, David, *The Sweet Life in Paris: Delicious Adventures in the World's Most Glorious - and Perplexing – City*, Broadway Books, 2009.

McCullough, David, *The Greater Journey: Americans in Paris*, Simon & Schuster, 2011.

Sebba, Anne, *Les Parisiennes: How the Women of Paris Lived, Loved, and Died Under Nazi Occupation*, St. Martin's Press, 2016.

Wells, Patricia, *The Food Lover's Guide to Paris: The Best Restaurants, Bistros, Cafés, Markets, Bakeries, and More* (5th Edition), Workman Publishing, 2014.

Writers and Writing

Dillard, Annie, *The Writing Life: Writers on How They Think and Work*, HarperCollins, 1989.

Karr, Mary, *The Art of Memoir*, HarperCollins, 2015.

King, Stephen, *On Writing: A Memoir of the Craft*, Scribner, 2000.

Phillips, Larry W., editor, *Ernest Hemingway on Writing*, Touchstone, 1999.

Pinker, Steven, *The Sense of Style: The Thinking Person's Guide to Writing in the 21st Century!*, Penguin Books, 2014.

INDEX

ABOUT the AUTHOR

 **Deborah L. Jacobs** is a lawyer, entrepreneur and award-winning journalist who has covered everything from travel to taxes. A former senior editor at *Forbes*, she has written for many national publications, including *The New York Times, Bloomberg Wealth Manager* and *Businessweek*. She is the author of **Estate Planning Smarts**, a bestselling guide for consumers, and **Small Business Legal Smarts**, geared to company owners. A graduate of Barnard and Columbia's Law School and Graduate School of Journalism, Jacobs now divides her time between New York and France.

For updates on her travels, writing and speaking engagements, you can follow her Facebook author's page: https://www.facebook.com/djworking. To see what she's reading, look for her on Goodreads. Jacobs also posts on Twitter about travel, taxes and transitions: https://twitter.com/djworking.

52109053R00170

Made in the USA
Middletown, DE
16 November 2017